T0065402

The Search for Bridey Murphy

The Search for Bridey Murphy

BY MOREY BERNSTEIN

DOUBLEDAY & COMPANY, INC., GARDEN CITY, NEW YORK, 1956

Library of Congress Catalog Card Number 55–10504

146087801

PREFACE

Tonight I will attempt an experiment in hypnosis that I have never before undertaken. The subject will be Ruth Simmons. This is November 29, 1952.

I entered the note above into my personal record, and then I sat back and gave some thought to the technique I would use that night. It was late Saturday afternoon; I would be starting the experiment within a few hours.

I decided that I would use an ordinary hypnotic age regression to take my subject back to the age of one year. And then I would suggest that her memory could go even farther back. It seemed rather simple, but maybe it would do the job.

The term "age regression" refers merely to the directing of the memory of a person, under hypnosis, to recall or relive detailed episodes of the past, even such incidents as may have occurred when that person was an infant.

It was one night after a club dance that I had discovered Ruth Simmons' ability to enter an uncommonly deep trance while under hypnosis. After the dance a group, about a dozen couples, had gathered together at the home of one of the club members. Several of the group were insisting that I give a demonstration in hypnosis. I explained as courteously as I could that I did not favor hypnotic "shows" but that I would consent to guide them in an exercise in progressive relaxation which might at least show them how a trance begins.

During the little experiment which followed, I spotted several among the group who were apparently good hypnotic subjects. But there was clearly one standout: it was Ruth Simmons. Weeks later I had still another opportunity to prove that my observation was correct; she was, indeed, a remarkable subject. She had the capacity, that is, for entering immediately into a deep trance.

So it was no accident that she would be here tonight. For this particular purpose, I knew, I must have a splendid subject.

This would be old stuff for Ruth Simmons; with me as hypnotist she had done the same thing twice before. On one occasion

7

she had shown conclusively that she could, while hypnotized, recall events which had taken place when she was only one year old. But tonight I was going to attempt something more than an ordinary age regression.

This time I would learn just how far back her memory could be taken.

I remember how long it seemed waiting for our guests. Finally Rex and Ruth Simmons arrived. Rex looks and talks, my wife keeps reminding me, like Tyrone Power. He's an insurance salesman; one of the best. Ruth is a vivacious brownette on the smallish side; she's trim, attractive, and one of the most sought-after partners at every dance. The two were an understandably popular couple, and it was getting more and more difficult to get them over to the house. Besides, they were not particularly interested in hypnosis.

I managed to sit through the conventional preliminaries of discussing everything from our new President-Elect to the fact that it was mighty cold outside. Rex explained that business was not quite what it used to be but he agreed with my sobering reminder that none of us had a right to expect it to continue at its past breakneck pace.

After what I considered a polite interval of conversation I turned to Ruth and asked whether she was ready to be hypnotized. With a shrug of her shoulders, she indicated that she was ready if I was. So I told her that tonight I would prefer that she would, instead of remaining in her chair, stretch out on the couch. I would get her a pillow and blanket to make her more comfortable. She thought that would be fine.

As soon as she had adjusted the pillow, pulled up the blanket, and become comfortable on the couch, I asked her to take seven deep breaths, just as deep as she possibly could. Because she was stretched out on the couch, I decided to use an old technique, the candle-flame method, to hypnotize her.

When she had finished with her deep breathing, I lit a candle and held it at about a 45-degree angle from her head and about eighteen inches from her eyes. I asked that she gaze intently into the candle flame while she listened to my voice.

It took only a few minutes to hypnotize her. No question about it, this girl was a rare subject; she slipped into a deep trance in a hurry.

8

As soon as I was satisfied that the trance was sufficiently deep I turned on the tape recorder and began speaking quietly.

". . . Now we are going to turn back. We are going to turn back through time and space, just like turning back in the pages of a book . . . And when I next talk to you, you will be seven years old, and you will be able to answer my questions . . ."

I waited for a few moments. Rex and my wife, Hazel, and I sat watching silently as Ruth seemingly slept deeply.

Finally I asked, "Do you go to school?"

Her voice came, clear and small, as she answered my questions. Later I asked, "Who sits in front of you?"

"Jacqueline."

"And who sits behind you?"

"Verna Mae."

In the same way Ruth was returned to her kindergarten days, when she was five years old. Asked who sat in front of her, she answered, "No one." Then she explained that she sat at a long table; nobody, therefore, would have been sitting in front of her. But she gave us the names of those sitting on each side of her at the time. She told us, moreover, that her favorite game was hopscotch, that her doll's name was Bubbles; and she described in considerable detail her black velvet dress with "little tiny" bows on the pockets.

Then Ruth at the age of three! She gave an elaborate description of her colored doll, and remembered her dog, Buster.

Farther and farther we went into memories stored deep, past the reach of the conscious mind, until Ruth remembered when she was only one year old. At the age of one year she had expressed her desire for water by saying, "Wa." But when she was asked to tell us how she had asked for a glass of milk, she replied, ". . . can't say that."

And now—now at last I was in a position to try something I had never before attempted. I was ready, that is, to take her "over the hump." In short, I was going to make an effort to determine whether human memory can be taken back to a period even before birth.

Only a few months before, such an idea had never even occurred to me. I had directed other subjects to recall or relive episodes of the forgotten past in age-regression experiments. I had even regressed some subjects to the scenes of their births, but who would have supposed that one need not stop there? Logically that had seemed the end of the road.

But several books and a couple of authorities changed my outlook. I had read the report, for instance, of a famous English psychiatrist and scientist who had over a long period of years performed pre-birth memory experiments with more than one thousand subjects! I had learned, furthermore, that there were many doctors, engineers, ministers, and others who were actively engaging in the same type of research.

Now it was my turn.

I instructed the entranced Mrs. Simmons, who was now breathing very deeply, that she should try to go still farther back in her memory . . . "back, back, back, and back . . . until, oddly enough, you find yourself in some other scene, in some other place, in some other time, and when I talk to you again, you will tell me about it." I finished, and then waited anxiously for a few long moments.

I returned to the couch and brought the microphone close to her mouth. This was the time, the important moment.

"Now you're going to tell me, now you're going to tell me what scenes came to your mind," I said. "What did you see? What did you see?"

". . . scratched the paint off all my bed!"

I didn't understand. I hesitated, and then asked the only question logical under the circumstances. "Why did you do that?"

Then we listened to that small, relaxed voice, so remote and so close, telling the logical, touching story of a little girl who'd been spanked and who had taken her revenge against a grown-up world by picking the paint off her metal bed. She explained that they had just "painted it and made it pretty."

This little girl seemed part of another place, another time. And when I asked her name, the answer came from my subject:

"Friday . . . Friday Murphy."

CONTENTS

PART ONE

Hypnosis, the First Step on the Long Bridge

CHAPTER 1

When the phone rang, it was night—a stormy night, at that
—and I was at the office, in the middle of picking a winner in our
slogan contest. I probably never would have answered the call
had I known that it would send me spinning into a whirlwind
investigation of hypnosis, telepathy, and clairvoyance; that it
would have me experiencing electric shock treatment and truth
serum drugs; and that it would start me, finally, probing the mystery of death.

At the moment I was measuring the huckster power of two slogans that had reached the finals. I was trying to keep in mind
that the winner must be one which would help merchandise everything from toilets to tractors. Then the phone rang again, so I
gave up and answered.

"Hello."

"Hello. I'm trying to find Morey Bernstein."

"This is Morey."

"I didn't mean to bother you. But I took off in my plane from
the Denver airport about an hour ago, and because of this sudden storm I've been grounded at Pueblo. So I called the hotels in
town, but it seems that Pueblo is a Colorado boom town. No
rooms anywhere. Then I remembered that my cousin, George Taylor, had told me to call Morey Bernstein if I ever got stuck in
Pueblo. So I'm stuck; so I'm calling. Can you help me?"

When he mentioned the name George Taylor, I knew that the
slogan contest was all over for that night. Taylor was a rancher,
a big operator, and one of our best customers. Slogans were out;
Taylor's relative was in. So I assured Taylor's relative that I would
pick him up right away if he would only tell me where he was.
And just before I put the phone down I remembered to ask his
name. It was Jerry Thomas.

Thomas turned out to be about twenty-five, pleasant, and per-
sonable. As soon as I took him out to my house and stowed his stuff
in the guest room I suggested that we join a party that was already
in progress at a friend's house.

Although the storm forced us to drive slowly, we were soon at the house of my friend. I observed that this boy Thomas was a real charmer. It was thoughtful of our customer to have such a pleasant cousin, even if he had messed up my progress in the slogan contest.

At first the chatter was of the usual cocktail-party variety. I can't remember how the conversation finally drifted to the subject of hobbies. But I do remember—I'll never forget—the burst of laughter when it came Thomas' turn to speak up. His hobby, he asserted, was hypnotism. We assumed, of course, that he was kidding.

He was not kidding. Indeed, he patently resented the laughter and rebounded with a challenge: "If you don't believe me, I ask only that one of you be my subject, and I will prove it!"

While I was trying to decide whether he could possibly be serious, a tall, attractive blond girl spoke up and offered to be his subject. She had always wondered about hypnosis, she admitted, since the time one of her teachers had discussed the matter many years ago.

This, then, was to be my first close-up of hypnosis. I had heard about it, read about it, seen it on the stage. But I did not believe in it.

During my college days, for instance, I remember walking out on a stage demonstration of hypnosis; I wanted to make sure that my college chums understood that this silly business was beneath my intelligence. If they were willing to waste their time on such foolishness, fine and well, but it was not for me.

Now, however, I couldn't walk out. Thomas was my guest. Besides, I was curious to learn just how he was going to pull himself out of this hole. So I sat back and watched.

The volunteer was told by Thomas to stretch out on the couch and make herself comfortable. He then removed a ring from his finger and asked her to stare at it. He explained that she must focus her attention upon the ring and continue to stare at it until it became hazy and obscure. He merely held the ring above her eyes and waited. We all waited.

Eventually we became restless, almost bored. Nothing was happening. The girl looked at the ring. Thomas looked at the girl, and we continued looking at Thomas. As the uneasiness mounted, some of the group stopped watching and began to whisper among

16

themselves. Others drifted out into the kitchen. It looked as though our hypnotist had drawn a blank.

Then suddenly he was talking softly to his subject. Her eyes were closed and she seemed to be going to sleep. He continued talking, but I was not close enough to hear the words. In a few minutes he turned around and walked into the kitchen, where the majority of the group were evincing more interest in food than in hypnosis.

Thomas confidently proclaimed to the gourmets in the kitchen that they would soon have evidence of his hypnotic ability.

He urged all of us to sit down at the large kitchen table and go to work on the food. He assured us that his subject was sleeping comfortably, but that he would soon awaken her. After she awakened, he promised, she would be perfectly natural. Natural, that is, with one exception.

"After she has taken two bites of her food," Thomas said, "she will suddenly reach down and remove her left shoe and stocking."

This I wanted to see.

I had not long to wait, for Thomas went back to the girl, and after more soft words he finally awakened her. Immediately upon getting up she went into the kitchen and took the place that had been left to her. As she started to eat she told us how much she had enjoyed her little nap. "Wonderful relaxation," she testified. "I'm ready for that any time."

After her second mouthful of food she abruptly dropped her fork and removed her left shoe and her left stocking. There wasn't a sound in the room; everybody was staring at her.

As a result of the staring and the sudden silence she soon grew self-conscious and looked around, asking what was wrong. There she was with her shoe and her stocking, just removed, clutched in her hand, and she wanted to know why everyone was so quiet and staring at her. What had she done?

Finally her escort spoke up. "What about your shoe and stocking? You're sitting at the table eating. Why did you take off your shoe and stocking?"

For the first time she looked down at her leg and then at the shoe and nylon hose in her hand. I shall always remember her blank, incredulous expression because I have seen it on others, perhaps a thousand times, since then. She was completely bewildered. For a minute she said nothing, then she looked up and slowly shook her head. She just didn't know; she couldn't explain why her shoe and stocking were in her hand. She didn't even try to explain.

Thomas, clearly pleased with the performance, glanced at me. He seemed to be remembering that it was I who had laughed the loudest at his assertion that he was a hypnotist. Now he was silently suggesting that I swallow some crow as gracefully as possible. Actually, he said nothing. But I answered him anyway.

"I don't believe it!"

Thomas looked puzzled; he really didn't understand what I was talking about. "What don't you believe?"

"I don't believe that she was hypnotized."

Now Thomas was really puzzled. He simply didn't understand my skepticism. He got up and walked back and forth in front of the table, wondering how to handle my challenge. Then he turned to me and asked whether there was anything he could do to convince me that his subject could actually be placed in a hypnotic trance.

"Put her back under, if that's what you call it," I said. "After all, we aren't sure that there was no collusion between you and her. We didn't hear everything you said. You may have suggested to her that you could both have some fun if she went along with the gag. So put her back under, and we'll think of some tests."

He promptly obliged. This time he did the job quickly. He merely counted to three, snapped his fingers three times, and the girl apparently "went out." As I learned later, the speed of this second induction was made possible by what are known as post-hypnotic suggestions. In other words, before Thomas had awakened her the first time, his soft whispering had included the suggestion that in the future she would slip immediately into the trance state when he counted to three and then snapped his fingers three times.

So here it was again; our "test case" was ready. Thomas repeated his earlier question: "Now what do you want me to do to prove that she is really hypnotized?"

Then the girl's fiancé spoke up. "Let me try something. I know her well enough to be sure that I can make her burst out laughing if she's just faking."

So our hypnotist instructed his attractive subject that she would not laugh under any circumstances, that she would maintain a poker face, that she would show no emotion whatsoever. Furthermore, he had her open her eyes while he kept her in the trance state.

Then the boy went to work. He commenced by kissing her, in a rather silly fashion intended to evoke laughter. But when she did not so much as blink an eye, he launched into a series of wild antics.

But the girl might as well have been far away.

Before we conceded, however, I asked for still more proof. I wanted, for instance, to see how she would react to tests concerned with pain. So the unfortunate subject was forced through another series of tests which included having a needle passed through the skin on the upper portion of her hand. But, regardless of the nature of the test, it was clear that she was in a state that I had never before thought possible.

I was beginning to realize that I was licked. I had always thought that the subjects of hypnotists were stooges—shills—or that the minds of the subjects were so simple that they could be shoved around at the will of the so-called hypnotist. But this girl was neither a fake nor a fool. On the contrary, she filled all the specifications for the intelligent, normal, healthy, wholesome female.

"O.K., Thomas, you win; you can wake her up." I sank into a chair, totally defeated. But there was more than defeat; there was an overwhelming sense of amazement, of wonder, almost of shock.

Having finally learned that hypnosis is a reality, I machine-gunned a round of questions at our victorious hypnotist. If this thing is true, if this is a fact, then why is it not more widely used? . . . If the mind can be so detached, then aren't the possibilities infinite? . . . If suggestion is so powerful in this state, then is this not a powerful weapon for good? . . . If the human mind can be so directed, so molded, so impressed, then why does not every doctor understand the fundamentals of hypnosis? Why is it not a "must" for every psychiatrist? . . . Why, at least, is it not a requisite for every student of psychology? . . . What is the reason that science does not show more interest? . . . Why do people like me have to become acquainted with hypnosis only through stage performances or as a result of accidents like this? . . . And what about practical applications in the fields of education, law, business, dramatics, advertising, and almost everything else under the sun? Why hasn't more been done about it?

I got my answer. It was the same answer I was to receive over and over again during the next ten years. It was a shrug of the shoulders.

Driving slowly home through a storm that was now subsiding, Thomas explained how he had learned about hypnosis in the first place. A relative had been ill and he had sought a way to relieve her pain. He had, consequently, enrolled in a psychology course at a university; it was one of the few courses available which dealt with hypnosis to any extent. And even this course, he admitted, only briefly explored the subject. It had been expanded beyond the confines actually set by the textbook only because of the instructor's personal interest in hypnotism.

When we reached home we promptly retired, and I could hear Thomas snoring before a quarter of an hour had passed. As for me, there was no sleep that night. I was thinking about this stranger I had just met, hypnosis.

Although I didn't know it then, I had just stepped onto a long bridge, a bridge that was to span two continents, two eras in time. And at the far end of the bridge was a woman I was to know as Bridey Murphy.

CHAPTER 2

The next morning I was back at my office. Legally and commercially, it is known as Bernstein Brothers Equipment Company (in Pueblo, Colorado), but we in the family refer to it as Ulcers, Incorporated.

My grandfather had started the place more than sixty years ago, which means that three generations have wrestled with it. I'm the third generation.

When Granddad opened shop in 1890, it was nothing more than a junk yard. Grandfather would wreck practically anything just to salvage the scrap material. He admitted that his ancestors had not come over on the *Mayflower* but he was convinced that his forebears must have scrapped the big ship.

With the second generation, my father and uncle, the company expanded vigorously. The accent shifted to buying and selling merchandise, anything from concrete mixers to diesel tractors, from bathtubs to oil tanks. Franchises for nationally advertised industrial and agricultural products were acquired, and both wholesale and retail outlets were opened. What had once been a scrap yard was now a merchandising power, a sort of industrial department store distributing more than one thousand items. "From the bottom of a pile of scrap iron to the top of Dun and Bradstreet," a local reporter had written.

By the time I was ready for college, our company was well known throughout the West. So it had never even occurred to me that I might do anything other than take my place in the family business. Accordingly, I chose a school that specializes in turning out executives, the University of Pennsylvania's Wharton School of Finance. There, for four years, I polished up on everything from business law to stock-market analysis. After that I returned to Colorado to put the theory into practice.

I had been trained for my job, and I liked it. For several years I added new products and departments and intensified our advertising. I enjoyed every phase—choosing new products, buying trips, sales promotion, merchandising. So I should have been pleased, that morning after hypnosis had flown into my life, to get back to the slogan contest just where I had left off the previous night. But somehow I had rough going that day. My mind wouldn't fix itself on the job at hand; it kept wandering back to the episode of the night before. Soon I was calling a bookstore to order a half dozen books dealing with hypnosis.

When the books came, I stopped reading novels. Even magazines and trade journals were neglected to some extent. I just couldn't tear myself away from the hypnotism books; I was utterly enchanted. Whether the book was concerned with the history of hypnosis, the technique of trance induction, medical hypnosis, the treatment of undesirable habits—whatever the topic—I gobbled it up. I was still overwhelmed by a single question: Why hasn't science done more with this near miracle? In the years to come I was to learn why science was restrained in this field, and I was also to discover more proof that this phenomenon was, indeed, a near miracle.

I read, studied, wondered, and then read some more. But still I had not hypnotized anyone. I had to find a subject, a guinea pig. Who would be willing to submit to an amateur hypnotist? I took

21

the problem to my wife; perhaps she would have a suggestion. She did.

"Why don't you try this hypnosis stuff on me?" Hazel asked. "I've got another splitting headache; maybe you can do something about it. I'll try anything!"

Every doctor who had examined her, every clinic she had gone through (including the Mayo) assured her that her headaches had no organic basis—no tumor, no kidney disease, no high blood pressure. Strictly psychological, they all insisted; and her last physical check-up had been taken only a few days previously. So what was I waiting for?

"Give me some time to make an outline," I told her, "and I'll tackle that headache." Then I went into another room with a stack of textbooks and started my outline. When I had finished I went back to Hazel.

But it was too easy! I didn't believe it.

Hazel responded just as the texts had assured one and all that a good subject should respond. And when I awakened her, she insisted that her headache, much to her amazement, had somehow faded away.

But even though her astonishment seemed genuine enough, I felt that my good wife was reacting in the same way that I sometimes feel obliged to do with one of her new recipes—just swallowing hard and forcing a big smile. I had to find out.

So I hypnotized her again and this time I had her extend her right arm straight out from her body, telling her that the arm would become rigid, "just like a steel rod welded to her body." I assured her, furthermore, that the "steel rod" could remain in that position indefinitely, that it would feel surprisingly pleasant, that it would not bring her any discomfort at any time.

I sat down opposite her and just watched for several minutes. Then, noticing that there was a *Reader's Digest* near my chair, I picked it up and thumbed through it. Later I glanced over at Hazel. Holy Mahoney! This girl wasn't bluffing. Her arm was still stiffly extended in the same position.

After giving her a post-hypnotic suggestion in order to check further the reality of the trance, I awakened her. There seemed to be practically no doubt about it: my first subject, my own wife, had been hypnotized.

Soon thereafter the most potent of all advertising agencies, the grapevine, went to work. Friends and neighbors began to bring their problems. And what was most surprising to me was that this hypnosis business really helped them.

A case in point, for instance, developed one day after an old friend had telephoned me. He was worried about his nephew, and he went on to add up his nephew's good points: The boy was captain of his basketball team; he had made the all-state high school team; he was being scouted by several college coaches; he was husky, handsome, intelligent, and a nice person.

"Then what in the world are you worried about?" I asked.

Finally he told me. "I have reason to believe that he might have been considering suicide. You see, he stutters. Bad."

The uncle made it plain that if the matter had not become genuinely serious he would not be calling me. (This was a sort of backhanded compliment to which I soon became accustomed; hypnosis was always the last resort.) He was not exaggerating the case, he insisted, and he wanted me to promise that I would see his nephew as soon as possible. So I suggested that we all get together the following Thursday evening.

When I met the boy, it was soon evident that his uncle had accurately stated the facts. The lad was, indeed, a fine, handsome specimen. But his stuttering had him coming apart at the seams. He couldn't remember a time when he had been free from this affliction; apparently he had never in all his life known normal speech.

He said that looking forward to each new day was a terrifying prospect. He dreaded going to classes for fear of being called upon for a recitation; as captain of the basketball team, he would be called upon for a speech, and the very thought was paralyzing. And as far as girls were concerned, he was sure that even when they asked him to parties they really only wanted to laugh at his efforts to answer.

What is more, he had recently met a fifty-year-old man who stuttered; the man had told him that he had talked that way all his life. The lad admitted that if he too should be forced to stutter through all those years he would rather not go on. Obviously he had reason to be in bad shape.

Nevertheless, after we had had only four one-hour sessions together, he telephoned—using a telephone in the past would have been quite a stunt for him—to tell me that he wouldn't need me any longer. In a clear, smooth voice he unhesitatingly assured me that he no longer stuttered; he thanked me and told me that his new life was a thrilling one.

Apparently he had been cured. More than a year later I checked with his uncle. At first he almost forgot that his nephew had ever stuttered, then he assured me that the boy had never experienced any difficulty after our sessions together.

But all this was not quite so simple as it might sound. Even though each session with the subject lasted only one hour or less, there were many hours devoted to advance research, preparation, outlining, and rehearsing. For one forty-five-minute session with a hysterical paralysis victim I spent several hours in preparation. Everything from my entrance into the room with the subject to the final words of departure was outlined and rehearsed in advance.[1]

There followed a number of gratifying experiences with disturbed cases, including some concerned with migraine, insomnia, excessive smoking, and bad habits. And then a really significant opportunity presented itself. A well-known local doctor who knew of my interest in hypnosis told me of a current problem with a polio victim. The woman, he explained, had real polio involvement in both legs, but the case had been complicated by the development of hysterical paralysis in the right arm. (Hysterical paralysis is the result of a neurosis rather than an organic cause.)

The doctor did not have to ask me twice for assistance. The chance to do some good on a real hospital case was too alluring. Besides, all the books assured me that this type of paralysis—that is, the symptom itself—was routine work for a competent hypnotist.

The woman, about thirty-five, had lost a ten-year-old daughter with polio at the same time that she herself contracted the disease. This, together with still other grave difficulties, understandably left the woman in serious condition, both emotionally and physically. It was no wonder she had developed the hysterical contracture.

I had agreed to tackle the case before I had even seen the condition of the patient. But when I walked into the hospital room and saw the woman's horribly knotted arm, my first impulse was to turn around and make for the door. How, I asked myself, had

[1] See Appendix A.

I ever talked myself into this? That arm was something to behold! It was like a chunk of gnarled, petrified wood with twigs, which used to be fingers, jutting out at the end.

I was stuck. I had promised the doctor that I would try. But had he known how scared I was at that moment, I'm sure that he would not only have excused me, he would even have helped me out of the room. As it was, though, he showed me the arm in a manner which clearly indicated that this was old stuff to him. So I pretended that it was old stuff to me too.

The doctor explained that her arm had been in this condition for more than four months and that nothing seemed to help. It did not respond to any sort of therapy, and of course there is no medicine for that sort of thing. "Well, now let's see what you can do," he told me.

Shakily I went to work. A trance was induced rather easily, and then, after eliciting ordinary hypnotic phenomena, I finally suggested that she could move her fingers in rhythm with my slow counting. She could. Nobody was more surprised than the hypnotist. I repeated this exercise several times, left some post-hypnotic suggestions, awakened the subject, and called it a day.

In three subsequent weekly sessions I repeated the same general technique, each time getting more of the arm to move until, during the fourth session, the entire arm was freed from paralysis. After that she once more began to use the arm, and within a short time it appeared to be completely normal. My fourth session with her was the last one necessary.

The post-hypnotic suggestions given to the subject were concerned primarily with instruction in the use of autosuggestion: the intimation that the hospital therapy would prove surprisingly more effective in the future; that she would be capable of responding more fully to the directions given by the physiotherapist; that she would now employ to a greater extent her native gifts of cheerfulness and a sense of humor; that she could optimistically look forward to total recovery.

The efficacy of autosuggestion in these cases proves once again how much we can all do with our own minds by simply utilizing the power of suggestion. With all of my subjects I have advised the application of self-suggestion at night just before retiring, in the morning upon awakening, and sometimes during the middle of the day, perhaps just before lunch. During these specified times the stutterer, for instance, repeated his key sentence, "When I speak slowly I speak perfectly." He also imagined himself making speeches to large groups, or as a lawyer making dramatic appearances before a jury. The paralysis victim was told that she would at these fixed times repeat certain simple exercises performed during the trance; also that she would imagine that she was once again using her arm in a normal manner. All these subjects, in short, were taught to combine autosuggestion with the creation of vivid mental pictures. The persistent use of these mental images is astonishingly effective.

As my studies continued, I began to experiment with one of the most fascinating phenomena in the field of hypnosis—the marvel of age regression. This refers, as we have already seen, to the ability of the subject, while under hypnosis, to relive or recall detailed incidents of the past even though such incidents may have taken place during infancy. There are two general types of age regression. In one the subject recalls a particular experience as though remembering or witnessing it.

The other is called true or total regression, and is one in which the subject appears to be actually reliving some past episode. The subject, while under hypnosis, is usually told that his mind will turn back through time and space and actually relive a certain scene; that he will speak in the very same voice as he did then; that he will experience the same sensations, the same emotions, the same reactions, the same total experience as he did upon, let us say, his third birthday.

I have kept tape recordings of experiments with both types of regression, and I am continuously confronted with gasps of astonishment from audiences listening to the recordings. Many, I am sure, simply do not believe what they hear. Remembering my own amazement during my earlier experiments, I am not surprised that listeners are dumfounded by simple age regressions which hundreds of hypnotists, psychologists, and doctors are performing every day.

Let us admit that it is a stunning spectacle to watch a grown man return to the scene of his third birthday, recalling the events of the day in minute detail and perhaps even speaking in the voice of a three-year-old. Indeed, he might accurately describe every present he had received on that day. The wealth of remembered detail is awesome.

26

It is interesting to note, furthermore, that changes in handwriting, behavior, vision, and reflexes all take place during hypnotic age regression. For instance, the signature of one of my subjects, told that he is eight years old, will be substantially different from that of the same person when he is told that he is only six years old. When the five-year-old level is reached, perhaps the subject can print his name; and at an earlier suggested age he will be capable neither of printing nor writing his name. Handwriting experts will usually confirm that these samples of writing, when compared with specimens which were actually produced during the childhood of the subject, are practically identical.

I also learned that intelligence tests and reading tests given at various levels during an age regression confirm its reality. Moreover, a person who stuttered at, say, the age of seven, will likely do so once again when regressed to that level; and then the defect will disappear as earlier periods are suggested. Regressed subjects will also re-experience traumatic events, illnesses, and earlier episodes of almost every nature.

An especially convincing proof of the verity of hypnotic age regression has been demonstrated in experiments concerning the stroking (tickling) of the sole of the foot. If the bottom of the foot of a normal adult is stroked, the big toe tends to turn downward; this is known as flexion. However, in infants up to about seven months of age the toes will turn upward (dorsiflexion) in response to this same stimulation.

With these facts in mind two experimenters, working with three adult subjects, proved that the response changed from flexion to dorsiflexion when the subjects were regressed to the age of five or six months. Then, going the other way, it was found that the reflex altered again to the adult form as age progression was suggested. These findings, furthermore, were confirmed by experiments of Leslie Le Cron, one of the most effective researchers in modern hypnosis.

As interested as I was in this technique, I still had no clue as to just how far back the mind of man can be regressed. Nor did I have any idea that this tool of hypnotic regression was being employed by a few scientists to unveil some of the mysteries of man. Such revelations came much later.

Much later, too, came the discovery that this technique of regression provided the path that would ultimately lead to Bridey Murphy.

CHAPTER 3

Meanwhile the number of my experiments kept piling up and I began to learn the answers to questions which are fired at every hypnotist. The first query is the most easily disposed of. Indeed, one must dispose of it because as yet nobody seems to know the answer. The question "What is a trance?" remains essentially unanswered. In other words, we do not know what hypnotism is nor just how much it can actually accomplish. During the next twenty-five years, perhaps, science will turn its spotlight toward hypnosis; then the secrets will be exposed.

Fortunately, however, there are some issues which have been settled. Such problems as the following, for example, have already been answered: Is there any danger of remaining permanently in the trance? Must the hypnotist possess any extraordinary powers? Can a person be hypnotized against his will? Can a hypnotized person be forced to commit a crime or an immoral act? Is it dangerous? Why is it not more widely used? Can anybody be hypnotized?

There is virtually no danger, I learned, of remaining indefinitely in the trance. Even if the hypnotist should place the subject in deep hypnosis and then leave the room, the subject would eventually drift into ordinary sleep and awaken in his own good time. Most hypnotists would state positively, without reservation, that there is no danger on this score. I understand that there have been extremely rare cases which involved difficulty in awakening the subject, but these cases are so infrequent as to be scarcely worthy of mention.

I found out that anybody can learn to hypnotize; there are no mysterious forces involved. Just as anyone can learn to dance—and to become a very proficient dancer if he combines a degree of natural talent with practice and training—so it is with hypnotism. Anyone can learn to induce the trance, but he who conscientiously applies himself to the study of the science and has a gift for the practice, or art, will obviously make the most satisfactory hypnotist.

In both dancing and hypnosis there are many performers; a few are outstanding.

The hypnotist, then, is a guide. And while some guides are far more accomplished than others, the fact remains that no weird, Svengali-like attributes are involved. Everybody can hypnotize someone.

The question of whether a person can be hypnotized against his will really has two answers—a general answer, and its rare exceptions. In general, I find it impossible to put anyone into a trance against his will. If a subject refuses to co-operate or merely decides that he will not be hypnotized, that usually determines the issue right there. However, there are a few cases on record which indicate that certain subjects, despite all efforts to resist, will drift into a trance. The British *Journal of Medical Hypnotism*,[1] for instance, relates the case of a nurse, an especially good subject, who was purposely instructed to resist the efforts of a doctor to hypnotize her. Nevertheless, within a few minutes—and in spite of general noisemaking, including her own talking and shouting—she gave up to the persistent voice of the doctor, who had continued to talk steadily all through the clamor. Such rare subjects are the exceptions that prove the rule.

And there is another query with a two-pronged answer: Will a hypnotized subject commit a crime or an immoral act? The definite consensus, I learned, is that nobody will do anything under hypnosis that is fundamentally against his or her principles. On the other hand, it might be possible, over a period of time, to engineer the suggestion so that the final result is an act contrary to the basic principles of the subject. Thus again we have a "No" in general and a very rare "Yes." A wife, for instance, would not react to the hypnotic suggestion that she poison her husband. She might even awaken the moment the suggestion was made. But the same wife, repeatedly told under hypnosis that her husband was slowly poisoning her children, might conceivably be convinced that the only way to save her children would be to poison her husband.

However, this whole question is purely academic. Obviously no serious operator would even be concerned with the matter. As psychologist Leslie Le Cron wrote, "There is about as much danger

[1] Summer 1951.

29

for one to become involved in hypnotically inspired antisocial actions as there is to being struck by a flying saucer."[2]

An example is provided by one of my good subjects, then twenty-one years old, with whom I was working on an age regression. When he had been regressed to the age of eight, I asked for the name of the person who sat behind him in school; he promptly replied with a boy's name. Then I asked, quite innocently, whether he liked this boy. "No!" he said emphatically.

"Why don't you like him?" I asked.

Bang! That simple question was apparently loaded! He awakened with a start. Ordinarily, when this lad is in a hypnotic trance, a bugle blast in his ear would not stir him. But this naïve question somehow agitated him immediately; he jumped to his feet.

I reviewed the session for him, explaining that he had suddenly burst out of the trance when I asked why he didn't like the boy—and I used the name he had given me—who sat behind him in the third grade.

"Oh," he said, "I can understand that!" And that was all. Tact required that I press the question no further.

Why he avoided answering this question under hypnosis I'll never know. But here was another affirmation that a subject will not ordinarily even discuss a matter which goes against his principles. After all, most subjects know what is taking place throughout the trance, and they can exercise a degree of judgment and censorship at all times.

Now to the big bugaboo: Is hypnotism dangerous? More nonsense has probably been written on this matter than any other. The truth is, and I believe all authorities will agree, that hypnosis in itself is entirely harmless. No bad effects, mental or physical, have ever been incurred by anyone as a result of his merely being hypnotized.

Like any good tool, it might conceivably be detrimental in the wrong hands; every effective instrument may be misused. Electricity is our most dynamic servant; uncontrolled, it results in death and destruction. Water keeps us alive, but we can also drown in it. As Shakespeare put it, nothing is good or bad, but thinking makes it so.[3]

[2] Leslie Le Cron (ed.), *Experimental Hypnosis* (New York: Macmillan, 1952).
[3] See additional material in Appendix C.

It is also important to note that the trance state in no way weakens the mind or the body; the subject, furthermore, will not remain under the influence of, or dependent upon, the hypnotist. In no sense is the possibility of addiction involved. In this connection another personal experience is in order.

I had just finished my second session with a case which I had undertaken at a doctor's request. The subject's husband, who had been a witness at all times, drew me aside. I presumed that he wanted to thank me because his wife was showing very marked improvement.

His first words, therefore, threw me completely off balance: "The hypnotism must stop!"

As soon as I caught my breath I asked, bewildered, "But why? Your wife is making remarkable progress!"

"Yes, so I see. But what good is it when she will have to go right on seeing you for the rest of her life?"

I slumped into a chair. When I recovered from the surprise blow I asked him where he had picked up that idea. He admitted that his authority was an elderly woman who, having read stories on the subject, warned him that his wife would now be subject to a lifelong addiction!

So I started from scratch, outlining for him the history of hypnosis, debunking the nonsense, and reviewing modern accomplishments. Then I gave him some books and medical journals to look over.

While this fellow had been a victim of misinformation, he was far from a fool. He diligently read all the literature I had given him and then visited the library to dig out more. And he didn't stop there. He personally interviewed two persons who had considerable experience as hypnotic subjects, quizzing them in detail particularly about the matter of addiction, will power, and general aftereffects.

When he was fully satisfied he returned to me, apologized profusely, and urged that I continue the work with his wife. He is now one of hypnotherapy's most enthusiastic advocates.[4]

When I encountered the question as to whether just anyone can be hypnotized I ran smack into a major drawback of hypnosis. The answer as of today is an emphatic "No." Having just admitted

4 See Appendix C.

that the hypnotist possesses no supernatural abilities, let me now go a step farther and acknowledge that it is the *subject*, and his reaction to the operator, that is the most important single factor in the business of hypnosis.

At this point then let us consider the subject himself. What qualities or personality characteristics combine to make a good hypnotic subject? First it must be admitted that this is a question which has never been adequately answered, for it is, after all, necessarily related to the fundamental problem: "What is a trance?" Even so, experience has contributed a certain amount of pertinent data, and at least some facts have emerged. It seems clear, for instance, that ordinary normal, healthy people are the best subjects. Intelligence and concentration, moreover, are decidedly favorable factors. The higher the intelligence and the steadier the concentration, the better a subject is likely to be.

But there is something more than this. And defining that "certain something" is a job calling for intensive scientific research. Some subjects simply have it; others do not. "It" is the inexplicable something which, with the guidance of the hypnotist, enables the subject to pass into the trance state. True, a good operator can accelerate the process of induction, or he might be successful with certain refractory subjects with whom less skillful hypnotists have failed. Nevertheless, there are still some people who just won't be hypnotized.

Since I happen to be one of these people—for what reason I do not know—I offer a personal report on this matter. Few will understand the lengths to which I have gone in an effort to become a good hypnotic subject. I have submitted myself to some of the finest and best-known hypnotists in the United States. Failing there, I have tried successively an electric shock treatment, a carbon dioxide treatment, narcosynthesis (hypnosis under drugs), and finally an equalizing pressure chamber which actually permits the cessation of breathing. I'm still a complete failure as a subject.

Why all the fuss to become a good hypnotic subject myself? For two reasons. First a serious obstacle to the progress of hypnosis, as we have seen, is its apparent inapplicability to all people. If, therefore, a process could be developed which would enable anyone to enter readily into the trance state, then hypnosis will have taken a tremendous forward stride. Consequently I have incessantly sought some universal key which could be utilized by everyone.

Second, having seen the mind control demonstrated by good subjects, even when they had been self-hypnotized, I was eager to attain the same ability. A good subject can sharpen his concentration, wondrously accelerate his mental activities, transcend his normal mental capacity, anesthetize any portion of his body, control pain, relax completely under almost any circumstance. In short, he can become master of his mind. Is this not, then, a goal worth seeking?

That is where electric shock and other treatments came in. I had an idea that if I could smooth out some of the kinks in my nervous system I could then relax and be hypnotized. Consequently I started my search for the universal key. To a friend, a psychiatrist, I pointed out the possibility that if shock treatment could convert a psychoneurotic to normality the same treatment given to a supposedly normal person might eliminate some of his nervous habit patterns—might, in other words, calm him down, make him more easygoing.

The doctor agreed that this was a possibility; he laughingly proposed that I find out for myself. I startled him by immediately agreeing to do just that.

I am sure that the doctor had doubts as to whether I was serious about this shock business until one afternoon when I showed up at his hospital and reminded him of his offer. For a time he attempted to discourage the plan, pointing out that shock treatment was not exactly comparable to sticking your finger in a light socket. Besides, he admitted, this idea of somebody's just walking in and asking for a shock treatment wasn't in the book.

Finally, however, curiosity overtook him too. After some preliminaries, including a careful physical examination, he led me down the corridor and into the electric therapy room. I was surprised to learn that the contraption which is responsible for the whole show is not much bigger than a cigar box and quite simple. I have operated more complicated electrical apparatus myself.

I had read and heard a great deal about these treatments, and none of it, except the results, was pleasant. I knew, for instance, that the patient must remove his shoes, otherwise his violent thrashing might cause some damage. Likewise, he must wear a mouthpiece similar to that used by boxers to prevent the teeth from being rattled out of his head.

I knew, too, that the patient is instantly knocked unconscious, after which he sucks in air with a desperate reflex action. The body goes completely rigid, followed by hideous convulsions somewhat similar to those of an ordinary epileptic fit. During this time the patient must be held down by attendants to prevent injury from the violence of the contractions. Even so, there are records of fractured spines, jaws, arms, and hips.

Well, I would soon have firsthand knowledge of the whole thing —the first jolt, whether there is any memory of the convulsions, and the sensations afterward.

The doctor called in four attendants, two male and two female. I looked them over carefully, wondering whether they would be stout enough to hold me down when my limbs started to flap all over the place. I noticed that they regarded me with complete indifference; this was just another distasteful, routine job to them. I only hoped that they would not continue to ignore me once the electricity went on.

I was asked to lie on a flat, narrow table; then the doctor placed a pillow, not under my head but under the small of my back. He asked an attendant to remove my shoes, and then he smeared some paste over my temples to insure the electrical contact, after which he strapped a belt-like gadget around my head. This, I knew, held the electrodes against the temples.

The rubber mouthpiece was jammed into place. I braced myself and waited for the impact of the first jolt.

BUT IT NEVER CAME. The next thing I recall was looking at two attendants, who were still just as bored and disinterested as regulations permit. I looked at the woman, then at the man. I'm not sure that I knew, at that first moment, who I was. I still wish that someone had quizzed me at that point so that there could have been a check on just how much of my memory had temporarily lapsed.

Again I looked at the woman, then at the man. By now they were the only two left in the room besides myself. The doctor had just left. They watched me get off the table; as soon as they saw me in action they walked out too. But the woman turned at the door as though she had forgotten something and shouted back, "Do you know where you are?"

Since I was aware of the table and the shock apparatus and the general hospital accouterments, I somehow managed a stumbling bit of deduction: "Yeah, I'm taking a shock treatment."

Even though she wore the same cold expression, that answer must have satisfied her; she wheeled around and went down the corridor, leaving me all alone. Believe me, I was confused. I knew who I was as soon as I had answered her question concerning where I was. But that was just about the sum total of my knowledge.

I reached into my pocket, looking for anything that might serve to fill in the blanks for me. I pulled out a letter. From its date I oriented myself to some degree; and from the contents of the letter, which concerned a current business project, I learned more about myself. Enough, at any rate, to venture forth into the hall.

I bumped smack into the busy doctor, who had apparently forgotten all about me by this time. "Oh, hello," he said. "How do you feel?"

"Fine. This is Saturday, June twenty-first. The time is 3:15 P.M., and I just took a shock treatment for experimental purposes." The time had come from the clock in the therapy room, and the remainder of the dope had been wrung from the letter.

I expected the doctor to break out in applause at this fine performance. But he merely nodded his head and rushed on.

Wandering out on the hospital grounds, I kept piecing together the balance of the puzzle. When I finally remembered how I'd got to the hospital I found my car and drove home.

Within three or four hours my memory was back to normal. But I must admit that during these hours some of the questions I put to my wife, who did not at that time know about the treatment, had her watching me out of the corner of her eye. When I asked, for instance, whether my father was in town and what college my brother attended, she began to grow a little concerned. But she became downright alarmed when she found me trying to recall what she had served me for lunch only a few hours before. So I finally told her about the shock experiment.

It should be emphasized, however, that the shock treatment was not painful in any manner whatsoever. I felt nothing; I had no stiffness, no bruises, no damaging aftereffects of any kind. Even the temporary loss of certain memories was only silly, not frightening. Referring to the doctor's earlier comment that this was not comparable to sticking a finger in the electric light receptacle, my own conclusion was that the sensation from a light socket is somewhat more unpleasant.

Afterward I really did feel calm, relaxed, somewhat more at ease than usual. And remember that the whole purpose of this experience was to achieve a relaxed state in order to determine whether in such a condition I was readily hypnotizable. But I am afraid that the effort was wasted; my hypnotist friend, Bill Moery,[5] could not work on me—I learned at the last minute—that night. Days later, when Bill ultimately got to me, I was back in the old groove at my office; those post-shock moments of tranquility were all gone.

But if the shock treatment had been surprisingly pleasant, my next venture, the carbon dioxide treatment, provided retribution with interest. It was unexpectedly harrowing. Believe me, never again will I walk into a treatment room and ask to have a carbon dioxide mask clamped on my face. What a trial of feverish panic that was!

I had learned about this relatively new treatment from a young psychiatrist. The two of us had been brought together through our mutual interest in hypnotism. Unfortunately the doctor had been unable to evoke any real interest in hypnotic therapy at his institution. Although he himself was using it to a limited extent, the frowns of his associates made it clear that efforts in this direction were not entirely welcome. I suppose, therefore, that we first came together to deplore the general neglect of this mighty scientific tool.

However, the interests of this young doctor were certainly not confined to hypnosis. He intensively researched into practically every aspect of the psychiatric field, especially seeking out any new developments. There were stacks of medical journals in his apartment, and he really read them. One day he read that a type of carbon dioxide treatment was being used with some success on an imposing number of mental cases.

Off he went, racing to the nearest hospital where he could learn more about this relatively new application. He studied the apparatus in detail, finally promoted its installation in his own hospital, and then he took the first treatment himself.

[5] Moery was kind enough to give me permission to use his real name in this book.

Here I want to doff my hat to our many, many doctors who, like this young medic, are striving incessantly to find better ways to help the sick. Few of us can realize how sincerely and strenuously these weary men are grinding away at the stumbling blocks in the way to better health.

After my medical friend took his carbon dioxide (CO_2) treatment he told me about it. "It gives you a wondrously relaxed feeling," he said.

There was my signal again!

I was soon maneuvering to get myself one of these CO_2 treatments. If this was so "wondrously" relaxing it might be that key I was seeking to prepare me for hypnosis.

To my surprise, no stratagems were necessary. Before I could even jockey into position, he sensed what I was up to and asked whether I would like to take one of these treatments.

So the next day I was once again stretching out on a white table in a psychopathic hospital, this time getting instructions for the administration of a combination of 80 per cent oxygen and 20 per cent carbon dioxide.

The doctor explained that the whole point was to inhale this gaseous mixture until passing into a coma, as it was this state of stupor which somehow always seems to result in a blissfully relaxed state afterward.

Then I was shown the mask, which looks harmless enough; also the bottles of oxygen and carbon dioxide, the controls, and the small-diameter hoses leading from the bottles to the mask. Nothing there to worry a fellow; it was rather like the old-fashioned dental gas equipment. I presumed that I would start inhaling normally and that, little by little, my breathing would become deeper until I drifted off to sleep.

But the doctor's next words straightened me out—stiffened me, in fact. "This may become a little unpleasant," he said. "You might experience an odd breathless sensation."

This comment, I was soon to learn, was a most flagrant understatement.

But before he finally fixed the mask over my nose and mouth he explained his technique: As I inhaled he would count out loud the consecutive number of each one of my inhalations, and at some point during the counting he would suddenly pull off my mask and ask me to repeat the last number that he had called out. This device would serve as a gauge to the progress of the treatment. My degree of confusion in attempting to answer him—or my complete failure to respond—would obviously provide him with the cues he needed.

He then called in a husky nurse, introduced me to her, and explained that she would hold my hands. I thought that he must be joking. What was the need for holding my hands?

But he meant exactly what he said. The hand-holding was necessary, he told me, because there might be a tendency on the part of the patient to pull off the mask. Tendency! Another understatement.

He asked me to lie back and give my hands to the nurse. He took the mask and I saw it coming down over my face. That very first instant I was gasping for life! I was sucking desperately, helplessly for air. I was certain that there had been a mistake; that something had gone wrong with the controls; that I was not intended to suffocate from the very first moment. I had expected that the sensations would compare to those experienced while running for some distance—at first you breathe perfectly naturally, and then as the concentration of carbon dioxide builds up respiration becomes gradually more labored. But no! This satanic machine would not even grant a period of adjustment; it was a fight for life, as far as I was concerned, from that very first instant.

In frenzied panic I instinctively moved to tear off the mask. But the nurse must surely have been a former female wrestling champ; my hands were locked. While I exhaustively strained for a breath of air I visualized the article—one I would never see—in tomorrow's paper: "Psychic research leads to accidental suffocation of local businessman."

Suddenly the mask was yanked off and the doctor was shouting into my puffing face, "What was the last number?"

"Ten," I panted. Boom! Down came the mask again before I could even gasp that I was strangling. Incredibly, this went on until the count of fifty, at which time the doctor stopped the whole thing.

He was shaking his head. "That's funny," he said.

My face was a blazing red; my lungs were pumping like bellows; I had narrowly escaped suffocation.

"Funny," he said again, but the look on his face indicated that what he really meant was that he was puzzled. "The average patient," he explained, "passes out somewhere between the counts of ten and thirty. Perhaps you were getting some outside air from leakage at the bottom of the mask. We'll try it again and I'll watch more closely this time."

I was faced with a decision. Which was worse: to admit that I was a coward and that I could not take any more; or to go through that ordeal all over again? While I was making up my mind, down came the mask and we were off again.

It turned out to be an almost exact repetition of the first round, so the doctor gave up—thank heaven!—concluding that there had definitely been a leakage.

Even so, I was very pleasantly relaxed during the remainder of the day. When I got back to my business that afternoon, for instance, my father noticed and commented on my relaxed, easy manner. "Well," I improvised, "I have just been taking some new exercises. An almost breathless experience!" Then I darted upstairs to my office to cut off any further probing. But when my hypnotizability was tested that night—and, after all, that was the whole idea of the treatment—there was no apparent change. I was still a poor subject.

Still there remained an ace in the hole. A group of doctors and psychologists had repeatedly insisted that an almost positive method of breaking down resistant subjects was readily available in a process known as narcosynthesis. This imposing term merely refers to hypnosis by means of drugs; and the drugs most commonly used for the purpose are sodium amytal and sodium pentothal; scopolamine and paraldehyde are sometimes employed too.

It may be recalled that narcosynthesis (sometimes alluded to as the truth serum treatment) was highly publicized during World War II, when there was a desperate necessity for developing accelerated methods of psychotherapy, principally to relieve battle fatigue. Since the war, however, the use of this valuable therapeutic tool has been ebbing.

The idea is simple and makes sense. Hypnosis is superimposed on one who has been rendered sleepy by one of these narcotics. Then, while the subject is in a deep state of relaxation—and possibly in deep hypnosis too—post-hypnotic suggestions, aimed at making him easily hypnotizable in the future, are drilled into his subconscious. In other words, if post-hypnotic suggestions are so powerful and if the subject will follow, after he awakens, almost any such directions given him, then why should he not also respond to the charge that he become a good hypnotic subject?[6]

To me this appeared entirely logical, and I had always recognized this possibility as a last resort. Now that I was so friendly with the young psychiatrist, here was my chance to take the final plunge. I discussed the subject with him and once more I found that he was as eager as I to investigate narcosynthesis and the possibility of becoming a good subject through this means.

But the doctor made it clear that he would not merely jab a needle in my arm and start pouring out suggestions that I would become hypnotizable. Instead he insisted upon at least a superficial degree of psychoanalysis before attempting the narcosynthesis. In short, he wanted to be in position to probe more intelligently the meanings of my "block" against hypnosis.

So I spent my evenings with the doctor while he probed my family background, my childhood, my disappointments and triumphs, likes and dislikes, habits, emotions, goals—what "made me tick." He admitted that this was far from a full-scale psychoanalysis, but it would serve as a guide when he ultimately administered the drugs.

Finally one Saturday night he told me that we were ready. Because it would be necessary for me to sleep off the effects of the drugs, he suggested that I undergo this treatment in my own bed. This was agreeable to me; I was wearying of my former experiences on hard surgery tables.

When the doctor came over he first gave me another physical examination, being especially heedful of my heart. I passed my examination and got into bed. Then came the needle. Ordinarily the patient drifts into unconsciousness within a relatively few seconds. But here again the usual pattern was altered; an unexpected incident delayed our progress, but it added a delightful little twist.

As soon as the doctor inserted the needle he told me to start counting backward from one hundred. When I had reached the mid-eighties I was already feeling pleasantly lightheaded. And then his needle jammed. He had to remove it and find the trouble.

Keep in mind that I already had been injected with a fair load

[6] See Appendix G for additional information on post-hypnotic suggestion.

of pentothal. Not enough to knock me out, but just enough to maintain me in that magical in-between land. So while he perspired over the needle I was dreamily floating in bed.

I lazily assured the doctor that he need be in no hurry to continue, that I could languish in this heavenly state forever. While I was sailing farther into this blissful sea I began to wonder whether this could be similar to any of the superconscious states of ecstasy described by the science of yoga. I babbled airily on and on about philosophy, stopping only briefly to describe my sensations to the doctor.

Strangely he was interested in neither the philosophy nor the sensations. He told me to shut up while he fixed the needle.

Soon he was resuming the treatment, and this time I didn't remain conscious very long. I remembered nothing more until I found myself opening my eyes and being vaguely aware that the doctor was still hurling questions at me.

Apparently part of his technique included quizzing the patient while he slowly awakened and was still in a sort of semiconscious state. Here was one more time when I didn't know for a few minutes where I was, who he was, or what day it was. He didn't ask me who I was. A good thing; that might have been very embarrassing.

But I was soon fully oriented. The doctor didn't seem overjoyed with whatever he had managed to pump from me, but he was confident that I would in the future be a good hypnotic subject; he assured me that he had repeatedly filled me with adequate post-hypnotic suggestions. He would come back the following evening and demonstrate the progress that had unquestionably been made. Now, he told me, go back to sleep. I did.

When he arrived the next night he first told me that he had been surprised that while I was under the influence of the narcotics I had told him practically nothing of value. Oddly enough, he observed, I had freely given him much more intimate, personal information during our discussions prior to the truth serum. He told me, for instance, that when he asked certain questions about various members of my family—questions which I had already answered for him without the persuasion of drugs—I had replied, "I'll have to get their permission before I answer that."

"But at least," he affirmed, "we'll now have better luck with the hypnosis."

41

I was convinced too. After all, I had witnessed the power of post-hypnotic suggestion frequently enough to know that my subconscious must now be ready to perform in a similar fashion; surely my mind was loaded and ready for the discharge.

The doctor went to work. Fortified by years of experience in hypnosis—and with the advantage of my narcosis of the previous night—he had good reason for confidence. Meticulously and smoothly he moved along the map that he had undoubtedly impressed upon my mind the night before.

Results: negative.

Either my "block" was insurmountable, or somehow hypnosis had not been superinduced on the narcotic state. This is a point about which there is considerable hubbub in medical circles. Some of the British psychiatrists, pioneers in narcosis, insist that almost all the failures with this method can be traced to the fact that hypnosis was not induced on top of the narcosis.

Next on my list of experiments came a most remarkable machine. From a reprint of a New York *Times* article I had learned that a New York doctor had conceived the idea for an equalizing pressure chamber which enables the patient to stop breathing!

Whereas the machine had been developed primarily as a local lung-rest therapy for tuberculosis victims, I had a different interest. We have all heard of the psychic effects of non-breathing exercises. The yogis have made such techniques famous. Their demonstrations of the rejuvenating effects, on mind and body, made possible through breath control are little short of fantastic. The yogi enters a trance-like state and remains motionless for long periods without any apparent restlessness of mind or body. In short, the yogi achieves the trance state through training in breath control. Perhaps, then, I could do the same thing by means of this yogi-like machine.

This pressure chamber, let me repeat, actually makes it possible for its occupant to stop breathing. Understand that it is not like an iron lung. The chest doesn't budge; the lungs make no movement; breathing actually stops. The chamber is designed so that an equal pressure is maintained on both sides of the chest, and also on the upper and lower surfaces of the diaphragm. Then, by manipulating the pressures within both the body and head compartments of the chamber, oxygen is brought into the lungs and carbon dioxide eliminated. The volume within the lungs is kept constant, but the density changes. All this without taking a single breath![7]

From the moment I read the article I could hardly wait to try that machine. Here, I thought, was the hypnosis machine for which I had been searching.

When company business next sent me to New York, I took advantage of my first free hour to rush to the office of the doctor who had created the pressure chamber. Here again I was to encounter another sample of the co-operation which I have found so prevalent within the ranks of the men of medicine during my pursuit of knowledge of hypnosis. Although the doctor expressed surprise that I was anxious to submit myself and my wife to the pressure chamber, he made all necessary arrangements immediately.

Within a few days, therefore, my wife and I were standing before a casket-like affair at a hospital in New York City. My wife, Hazel, had to be included in this experiment because somebody would have to be inside the chamber while I attempted to superimpose hypnosis on this state of non-breathing. Besides, Hazel by now had become accustomed to my perpetual experimentation and she was as interested as I.

With us were two doctors, researchers at the Columbia University division of the hospital and old hands with the pressure device. "Are you *sure* you want to enter the chamber?" one of the doctors asked.

This made the third time that I had been questioned, apparently with some degree of sympathy, as to whether I really knew what I was getting into.

"Why do you ask?" was my question. I was remembering the carbon dioxide experience. "Will this machine give me a rough time?"

[7] The doctor who originated this therapy is quoted as saying, "The effect of cessation on the central nervous system is of considerable interest. The impulse for movement in the voluntary muscles in the extremities is strikingly diminished. The patient may lie in the chamber for hours without moving his hands or changing his position. The desire to smoke disappears when voluntary respiration stops, even in patients who have been accustomed to smoke two packages of cigarettes daily. In many instances the relaxation is of such a nature that the patient does not require amusement."

Then again at a later date the doctor added that the machine not only rests the lungs but also the entire body and apparently the mind too. He said that the heart has its work decreased by a third. "Our subjects stop worrying. None feel bored."

43

"No, not at all," he replied. "But some people have claustrophobia to varying degrees, and so they are terrified at the prospect of being closed up in narrow compartments."

I wondered whether I had claustrophobia, decided I didn't, and crawled into the chamber. It is a sort of horizontal cylindrical structure with a dome which slides forward like that over the cockpit of a jet plane. But in this cockpit you stretch out flat on a surface made comfortable by a mattress. Then a partition, like a collar, slides down around the neck, separating the head and the body into two compartments. The dome is pulled back, closing the chamber, and the air compressor is switched on.

At the start I had been told to inhale each time the doctor—I could see him easily through the Plexiglas dome—raised his hand and to exhale as he lowered it. As his hand movements shortened, my respiration was to become shallower until he finally made a crosswise motion with his hands, like an umpire gesturing "safe." At this point I was to stop breathing entirely.

I did. It was a pleasant, soothing sensation; I didn't breathe for more than five minutes. It was probably the only five minutes during my entire lifetime when I made no movement whatsoever. But I was anxious to have Hazel take my place so that I could attempt to induce hypnosis upon a subject inside the pressure chamber. So I got out and she climbed in.

Her experience was a duplicate of my own. Then the microphone was turned on so that I would be able to talk to her from the outside. Here was the ideal opportunity: a completely relaxed subject, not moving, not even breathing. I could hardly wait.

Then when we were ready to undertake the experiment, the microphone refused to function.

It was a tremendous disappointment. We tinkered with the mike for several minutes but we finally had to give up. I'm still looking forward to taking another try at that experiment.

All my effort to become a good hypnotic subject should at least help to establish one point—not everyone can be *readily* hypnotized. And good subjects, so far as I know, cannot be distinguished by their behavior, their appearance, or their disposition.

It is generally agreed that there are certain factors which definitely affect susceptibility to the trance. Ordinarily, as has been stated, normal, happy individuals make the best subjects. As one hypnotist put it, the very best subjects seem to be the same ones who would be most likely to avoid the psychiatrist's couch.

I found that very anxious and nervous people are frequently difficult subjects, as are skeptics and "know-it-alls." There is little difference between the sexes or races, but some operators do contend that women generally make the best subjects. As to age, children are definitely easier to hypnotize than elderly people. In fact, susceptibility seems to diminish as the years go by. It is for this reason that one hypnotherapist has put forth the suggestion that all children be given instruction in trance induction before the age of fifteen.

Oddly enough, hypnotists and others having a fair degree of knowledge about hypnotism are usually poor subjects. Probably the people in this group cannot prevent themselves from criticizing or evaluating the technique of the operator who is trying to help them. Likewise, close friends and relatives of the hypnotist are usually not impressed by someone they know so well. A total stranger will generally obtain more effective results.

Alcoholics are generally easy to hypnotize, and so are those who stutter or stammer. (One respected authority, referring to hypnosis, declares that it is amazing that so many continue to suffer from stuttering when such a potent remedy is readily available.) Insomnia sufferers, on the other hand, are somewhat more difficult to help.

Contrary to my preconceived notions, real will power, if anything, would tend to make a subject better, because the will power could be utilized to co-operate with the hypnotist. Weak-minded or insane people, on the other hand, are extremely difficult, often impossible, to hypnotize.

My own conviction is that this major drawback of hypnosis—the fact that not everyone can be quickly hypnotized to an impressive depth—can be, and will be, overcome. Just as soon as a rapid, universal method of inducing a deep trance is developed, hypnosis will automatically become a therapeutic instrument of paramount importance.

And whether the key be psychological, mechanical, or electrical, the men of science will eventually spring open the lock. So far the big barrier has been the shocking absence of funds devoted to the scientific investigation of hypnosis. I was unable to find any record of a single grant ever having been made for the study of hypnosis itself.[8]

Meanwhile the experimentation is carried on by individuals. Many confine themselves to the therapeutic aspects of hypnosis; some explore the infinite potential of age-regression phenomena; and a few incessantly seek the perfect technique.

But there is still another facet of hypnosis, probably the most fascinating of all. It is concerned with probing the unknown realms of the mind, with the mysteries that have surrounded man for ages. I had never involved myself in this phase. Fate, however, had other plans; I was soon to take another step on the long bridge.

[8] There has been one grant for hypno-analysis, but none for hypnosis itself.

PART TWO

Another Step across the Bridge

CHAPTER 4

My wife and I were driving to Colorado Springs. It was a beautiful April day of Colorado sunshine, and giving a special touch of grandeur to the whole scene was the majestic Pikes Peak off to the northwest. Silently engulfed by this beauty, we had not spoken a word for fifteen minutes.

Suddenly I found myself humming a tune; oddly enough, my wife at that precise moment began to hum the very same tune. We had gone through several verses before we realized what was taking place. The same tune had occurred to both of us simultaneously, and we had been in perfect synchronization up to the point when, aware of the curious coincidence, we turned toward each other to register our surprise.

Hazel laughed. "Do you think that was telepathy?"

"No, not a chance," I assured her. "We were both simply affected by the same stimuli; these generated a similar chain of thoughts in our minds, finally creating the response, which in this case happened to be a certain tune."

"Husband gives wife the scientific treatment," mocked Hazel. "And perhaps the scientist can also explain why the response to the stimuli in this case was a tune called 'Once in a While' and why we hit upon it at the exact same instant, and also tell me just what every thought was in the chain leading to the final response."

"That's just where a lot of people get thrown off the track," I remarked. "After all, it might well be impossible to explain all these tiny details. Keep in mind that there are more than two billion people in the world, and the number of circumstances involving these people is infinite—astronomical! It would be even more astonishing, considering all these people and circumstances, all the accidents, crosscurrents, and intertwinings, if, out of this maelstrom, there didn't occur once in a while a few striking coincidences. It's nothing to get excited about.

"No," I added, "I can't buy telepathy."

"You didn't believe hypnotism was real either," she reminded me.

"Hypnosis is one thing. This telepathy stuff is another. And as for telepathy's first cousin, clairvoyance, that's strictly for the lunatic fringe!

"So I was wrong about hypnosis; that doesn't mean I have to be wrong all the time."

But once again, as though signaled forth by our little debate, events began to gang up on me. I was forced to scratch my head in wonder.

It all began with a dream. I dreamed that Mr. Haines, the general manager of Bernstein Brothers, came striding into my office in his usual brisk fashion and, just as I was about to speak into the mouthpiece of my dictaphone, shoved a stack of papers between me and the dictaphone. At the top of the papers was a check; he asked whether the check was made out in the right amount. When I nodded, he turned to go. But he spotted something on my desk. "I've been looking for this," he said. It looked like a letter; he took it and walked out.

Aside from the fact that it was a particularly clear dream, I paid no attention to it other than to comment about it to Hazel.

The following week, as I was about to start dictating, in came Mr. Haines, the general manager. He thrust his papers under my nose, asked whether the check on top was satisfactory, then started toward the door with his customary swiftness. But as he turned he saw a customer's order on my desk. "Hey, I've been looking for this," he said, picking up the order and taking it with him.

I reflected about this for a few moments, then I answered it with my old "necessity-of-coincidence" argument and got back to my dictation.

Within ten days I had another dream concerning our company and its general manager. This one was also crystal-clear, and more involved than the previous one. I dreamed that I walked into my office one morning and found my mother waiting for me. Before I even had a chance to express my surprise at this unexpected visit, the ubiquitous Mr. Haines swept into my office. He looked at my mother and then at me. He went back to the door, still having said nothing, and looked out of the doorway as if surveying the whole situation, apparently making sure that no one was listening. Then he slammed the door tightly shut.

As he turned from the door he reached into his inside coat

pocket and took out a letter. He walked toward me, holding the letter out for me. There the dream ended.

A week later I was discussing both of these dreams with my wife and a visitor from Denver. I explained how the first dream had subsequently materialized. "But if this second one comes to pass," I admitted, "I'll have to give some real thought to this whole business. The first one, after all, could have been nothing more than an accident. The manager is always popping into my office, and he frequently brings papers and occasionally a check.

"But this second dream. That won't happen. In the first place my mother wouldn't be sitting in my office early in the morning. And there would be no business at my office which would require the secrecy of closed doors. There haven't been any secrets at that office for more than sixty years. I can't possibly imagine what kind of letter the manager would be hiding in his inside coat pocket and why he would take the precaution to make certain that nobody overheard us discussing it."

The very next morning it happened.

As I turned into my office, there was my mother sitting by my desk. Somehow this failed to trigger the recollection of the dream; I wasn't thinking about it. We had scarcely had time to greet each other when Mr. Haines burst into the office and proceeded to re-enact all the details of my dream. As he shut the door and turned, the dream scenes vividly came alive in my mind and I knew exactly what would happen next. He would reach into his inside coat pocket, pull out a letter which was still in an envelope, and walk toward me with his right hand outstretched, holding the letter. He did precisely that.

At any rate, I would finally learn what was in the letter. Prior to taking it out of the envelope, however, I exclaimed, "Wait! Wait a minute! Before I even look at this letter I'll have to explain how I already witnessed this whole scene last week!"

They stared at me for a few moments; my mother seemed genuinely alarmed at this weird comment. I finally managed to throw some light on what I was talking about. Then I read the letter.

It was a medical report on my father. Our manager, it seems, had referred him to a physician for a medical check-up, and afterward Mr. Haines had asked the doctor for a report in order that our family might know the facts. All the ritual about shutting the door and making certain that nobody was listening was to insure against my father's overhearing his own report.

"Why are you afraid to let him know about this?" I asked after finishing the letter.

"Because it says that he's got something—a hiatus something," answered our worried manager.

"Hiatus hernia," I said. "That's not very serious. I was fearing the worst after the way you sealed the door."

Here it was again—a precognitive dream, one that predicted events which as yet had no existence. In this case the dream concerned a letter—one which had not even then been written. But these isolated cases by themselves would never have led me to a personal investigation. The incidents, however, kept right on piling up.

Next in the plot came Hazel's mother, Mrs. Higgins. She stopped at our house one Sunday morning just long enough to ask Hazel to join her. She was on her way to the ranch, she explained, to get a calf which had been missing for almost a week. "While I was working in the garden this morning," she went on, "your grandfather suddenly appeared to me in a sort of dream, even though I was wide awake. He told me that the calf would be found in a hole that had been washed out by floods at the edge of the big arroyo running through the ranch." Hazel's grandfather had been dead for more than two years.

Mrs. Higgins announced all of this in a matter-of-fact way, as though she actually expected to find the calf as the result of this incident. Hazel put on her jacket and left with her mother, but not before I scoffed at their willingness to waste their time.

When they returned within a few hours, the calf had been found in the exact spot that had been indicated. It had apparently been dead for several days. I muttered something to Hazel about her mother's probable use of deduction to decide where the animal was likely to be—and then attributing it to a "vision." Hazel didn't bother to answer.

Then even Hazel's cat got into the act. It's a Siamese cat named Tai. Somewhere along the line the cat had a litter of kittens; and through an indiscretion on Tai's part, the kittens were not exactly thoroughbreds. So Hazel's mother encountered no argument when she asked permission to take the kittens to her ranch about sixteen miles south of Pueblo.

The second day after Mrs. Higgins had left with the kittens, Hazel told me that Tai was missing; we couldn't find her anywhere. But the next afternoon the mystery was solved. Mrs. Higgins came to the house and told us that when she had gone out that morning to give the kittens their milk, who should be there on the doorstep, also awaiting breakfast, but the old gal, Tai herself.

Now Tai had never at any time been to the ranch. And if it makes any difference, she had never been in Mrs. Higgins' car, nor had she possibly been able to see even the direction in which Mrs. Higgins drove off that day with the kittens; Tai had been locked in the basement. Nevertheless, she had promptly found the way to her kittens, sixteen miles distant. No dope, this cat!

I learned never to relate these incidents to others, because they would inevitably respond with episodes which made my own look pretty slim. Very few people have had any experience with hypnotism, but it seems that almost everyone has encountered some form of extrasensory perception, whether it concerned animal stories or the death of a relative, which cannot be explained by ordinary principles. The complacent manner in which others accepted these things never failed to amaze me—it still does to this very day.

Meanwhile odd phenomena began to enjoy a current boom in newspapers, magazines, and books. *Reader's Digest*, for instance, printed an article entitled "Tales of the Supernatural," and later followed it up with "The Man Who Dreamed the Winners." Newspapers were telling the story of Lady, the Wonder Horse, an old mare who was demonstrating telepathic ability, finding missing people, and generally performing in a manner most unusual for both horses and people.

But the last straw, the final push that started me digging into the problem of extrasensory perception, came about accidentally and as a result of a hypnotic session. With a deep trance subject Bill Moery and I were conducting an experiment in age regression. When we were almost through, but before the subject had been awakened, I unconsciously toyed with a book on the shelf behind our subject. As I prepared to speak I inadvertently took the book into my hand.

"You have a book in your hand." This came from our hypnotized subject. Then he told me the name of the book.

Bill and I stared at each other, wondering who had asked him

53

and—what was more important—who was giving him the answers. Since, however, the books had been in view before the subject had been hypnotized, I tried something else, something he could not have seen.

"What do I have in my hand now?"

"Newspaper," he answered.

"What's the name of it?" I asked. I was standing behind him; his eyes, of course, were closed, and there was little possibility that he had seen this paper before the session or on any previous visits.

With little hesitation he answered, "*Wall Street Journal.*"

I looked at Bill across the room as I said to our subject, "Bill will hold up a certain number of fingers on his right hand; tell me how many fingers he is holding up."

Taking the cue, Bill put up his right hand (out of the subject's sight). He held up four fingers.

"Four!" shouted our subject.

After a few more striking demonstrations he abruptly announced, "That's all I know!"

When I inquired as to what he meant, he explained that when he knew something he simply knew it. "Then all of a sudden I don't know and it's all over," he said.

Bill and I relentlessly closed in; we wanted to get at the mechanics of this thing. What sort of signal tells you that you do know? Describe what takes place. Can you actually "see" these things, or are you picking up our thoughts? By what method can the mind be trained to do what you have just done? What is the sensation when this ability leaves you? We wanted any possible clue that we could extract.

But our subject's parlor performance was finished for that night. And during the few sessions we had with him at later dates, he was never again able to duplicate it. "When I know, I just know. Then all of a sudden it's all over."

Even after putting all these incidents together I could not be positive that they added up to anything. On the other hand, no genius was required to realize that here, at the very least, was a matter worthy of investigation.

Indeed, if these phenomena are real, regardless of how rare or how difficult to classify they may be, then they can change our entire concept of human nature. If these are realities which have been overlooked or omitted simply because they do not fit into the picture which modern science has painted, then we had better take another look at that picture. Maybe the picture's frame has been so dazzling as to have blurred our vision.

At any rate, I decided to stop being a blind skeptic. True science, after all, tests hypotheses; it is not supposed to cast aside any ideas which do not, at first glance, appear to fit our modern scheme of things.

Besides, it was clear that science, while solving the mystery of everything from the shape of our planet to the splitting of the atom, is still confounded by one of the most baffling of all puzzles: What is the human mind?

And so the bell rang for round number two. First had been hypnosis. Now came extrasensory perception, a term which refers to the ability to perceive things without using the senses.

I started with two questions: Were there any investigators seriously examining this problem? If so, what had they found?

At this point I recalled that one of my college instructors, back in the days when I was a freshman, had told us briefly about a fellow at Duke University who was performing experiments with a number of students in order to determine whether there was any scientific evidence in favor of telepathy. According to my instructor, this man was using specially designed cards and, in strict accordance with scientific method, was testing the ability of students to identify these cards without actually seeing them in any way. "The results seem to indicate," continued the instructor, "that we ordinary human beings actually have telepathic powers. Interesting."

Now, about fourteen years later, I was beginning to agree with my old teacher. It was interesting, all right. But I figured that this man at Duke had probably made a one-shot test merely to satisfy his curiosity, or to gather material for a magazine article. The odds were heavily against the possibility, it seemed to me, that this investigator would still be concerned with the same problem.

Just the same, I started inquiring about the "man with the cards" who had done telepathic experiments back in the thirties. I drew blanks until I came to my young medical friend.

"Oh! You must mean Dr. J. B. Rhine," he answered.

That was the first time that I had ever heard the name. But from that moment Dr. Joseph Banks Rhine became one of the most important names in my personal file.

"He's still at Duke University," added the doctor.

"But I suppose that, after all these years, he's no longer concerned with extrasensory perception," I said.

"Your guess is 100 per cent wrong," corrected the doctor. "Rhine has devoted his whole life to those studies; he's probably recognized as the world's number one authority on the subject, and his last book, *Reach of the Mind,* is generally regarded as a classic in this field. And Rhine is not the only one; there are scientists all over the world dedicating themselves exclusively to research in extrasensory perception."

And so I learned that there were indeed, both here and abroad, scientists keenly interested in these matters. As early as 1882, in a lonely protest against general indifference, a group of scholars in England had formed the English Society for Psychical Research for the purpose of investigating telepathy, telesthesia (clairvoyance), hypnotism, spiritualism—odd and unexpected phenomena which they felt it their duty to explain or to abandon as inane absurdities. This organization, fostering scholarly methods, is more active today than ever before, and has piled up an imposing record of experimental studies.

Following the lead of the British society, other scientists and explorers decided to tackle the same problem. And in 1930, together with three other members of the Duke University Psychology Department, the man who now appears to be the undisputed leader in this arena, J. B. Rhine, launched a full-scale attack. It was the first time in history that a group of university staff members had given so much attention to this subject.

Meanwhile literature in this field was beginning to build up. Books and reports were being contributed by the researchers of several nations. So off I went on another book binge, reading everything I could find on extrasensory perception.

It was interesting to note that in expanding my interest from hypnotism to extrasensory perception I had plenty of company. Indeed, there is a definite historical relationship between the two phenomena.[1] So close, in fact, was their relationship that for many years extrasensory perception was considered a by-product of hypnosis. Dr. Mesmer himself, the grandfather of modern hypnosis,

[1] See Appendix H.

once wrote that deeply hypnotized subjects can sometimes distinctly see the past and the future.

And so, historically at least, it is clear that hypnosis has been closely related to telepathy and clairvoyance. But since those early days, when hypnotists encountered extrasensory phenomena quite by chance, the investigation has come a long way, and some sort of digest is in order, because this is a matter with which we are all vitally concerned—and about which we shall be hearing more and more in the days to come.

In my own case I first became familiar with the terms that appear frequently in this work:

E S P : merely the abbreviation for extrasensory perception, which refers to the perception of an external event without the use of any known senses.

T E L E P A T H Y : the transference of a thought from one mind to another without the use of the senses.

C L A I R V O Y A N C E : the awareness of objects or events without the use of the senses—any direct apprehension of external objects.

(In short, telepathy involves communication between mind and mind; clairvoyance involves communication between mind and object.)

This is a good point at which to distinguish, by means of examples, between telepathy and clairvoyance, and to become acquainted at the same time with still other terms and principles which we shall encounter later.

If one person thinks of a number between one and five, and another person correctly perceives that number—and if this test is repeated without failure (and without trickery) for, say, one hundred trials—then we would certainly have a clear-cut example of telepathy.

In such a telepathic experiment the one who concentrates on the number is the "sender." The person trying to perceive the number is known as the "receiver," and the number is referred to as the "target." The receiver's response, in trying to name the target, is termed his "call," whether it be graphically recorded or merely oral. His correct calls are labeled as "hits."

In this instance, as with all cases of telepathy, the target is the thought or mental activity of another mind. But clairvoyance is the awareness, without use of the senses, of objects or objective events. A good example of clairvoyance is found in the book *Phantasms of the Living,* in which the experience of a ten-year-old girl is reported.

The girl was walking along a country lane when she suddenly had a "vision" of her mother lying on the floor at home. The perception was particularly clear and poignant—clear enough to include a lace-bordered handkerchief on the floor near her mother and sufficiently poignant to impel the girl to summon a doctor even before returning home.

It was not easy to convince the doctor that he should rush home with her, because her mother had apparently been in good health and was, furthermore, supposed to have been away from home that day. But the doctor followed the girl and, sure enough, there was the mother lying on the floor of the room the girl had described; and all the details, including the lace-bordered handkerchief, were just as the child had envisaged.

The doctor found that the mother was a victim of a heart attack and was of the opinion that she would not have survived if they had not arrived when they did.

This case would seem to be an especially good example of clairvoyance, rather than telepathy, because no one had witnessed, or even had reason to suspect, the event that took place. Yet the little girl had somehow "seen" the whole episode while she was walking along a country lane.

PRECOGNITION: prophecy; it is awareness of a future event which could not be inferred through the power of reasoning. This strange human faculty has also been the subject of recent scientific investigation, the findings of which will be discussed shortly.

PSYCHOKINESIS: the imposing term for what is more popularly known as "mind over matter." Taking the word apart, we have "psycho," which refers to the mind, and "kinesis," which is the Greek word for movement or motion. Can a man's mind directly influence the motion of material objects? Is it really possible for a dice player to "influence" those rolling bones? Researchers have an answer.[2]

PARAPSYCHOLOGY: the science concerned with the study of those mental manifestations—such as telepathy, clairvoyance, precognition, psychokinesis—which appear to transcend recognized principles. It is, in short, a division of psychology dealing with

[2] See Appendix K.

psychical research. The "para" standing in front of psychology (the study of the mind) means "beyond." So the literal translation is "beyond psychology."

Returning now to the matter of telepathy and clairvoyance, I was amazed to learn how much evidence there is for extrasensory perception—and that no other phenomenon in the history of science has had so little recognition for so much experimental research. Dr. Rhine and the Duke Parapsychology Laboratory, as a result of thousands of carefully controlled card experiments over a long period of time, had *proved* that telepathy and clairvoyance are realities.[3,4]

And I was even more surprised to note that these facts do not rest upon the Duke research alone. Corroborating experiments have been carefully carried out at numerous universities, including the University of Bonn in Germany; Cambridge, Oxford, and the University of London in England; and many American schools. More than ten years ago Professor Thouless of Cambridge had stated, "The reality of the phenomena must be regarded as proved as certainly as anything in scientific research can be proved." Recently Dr. Raynor C. Johnson, a physicist, wrote, "It is . . . a matter of the most profound and far-reaching implications to be able now to claim that telepathy, clairvoyance, and precognition are indubitable hard facts; that the evidence for them is as well-founded and reliable as for the basic facts of physics and chemistry."[5]

For those who have difficulty, despite the evidence, in accepting the reality of extrasensory perception, it might be helpful to use an analogy with hypnosis. The elusiveness of both phenomena is their distinguishing trait, the characteristic which renders impossible the assurance that any specific test will turn out successfully. Even though hypnosis, for instance, is now a universally recognized sci-

---

[3] See Appendix I for additional details of the Duke experiments.

[4] Despite angry denials from some quarters, the case for ESP stands as a solid scientific fact. Commenting on anti-ESP attacks, Yale Professor G. E. Hutchinson said, "The whole literature of parapsychology is disfigured by books and articles which are supposed to be critical evaluations, but which on examination turn out to be violent attacks by people who either have not read the works they are attacking or have willfully misunderstood them."

[5] R. C. Johnson, *Imprisoned Splendour* (New York: Harper, 1954). *See also* S. G. Soal and F. Bateman, *Modern Experiments in Telepathy* (New Haven: Yale University Press, 1954).

ence, still the most expert hypnotist cannot be positive that he will deliver a convincing demonstration during a given test. This factor, the elusiveness under test (or "show me") conditions, long delayed the acceptance of hypnosis and is now having a similar effect on extrasensory perception.

There are other points of similarity within these two phenomena: Both have histories bursting with conflict. Both fell first into the hands of fringe groups and much later came under the scrutiny of science. The bitterest foes of medical hypnosis were the doctors themselves; and those who strike hardest against parapsychology are probably the psychologists.

Nevertheless, resistance to the acceptance of hypnosis was finally broken by the fact that convincing, irrefutable demonstrations sometimes do occur. In the same manner general acceptance of extrasensory perception is inevitable. Indeed, just as there was no alternative to the ultimate acceptance of hypnosis, so there is no alternative to the acceptance of extrasensory perception.

The next problem confronting the parapsychologists was to determine whether the functioning of telepathy and clairvoyance is physical or non-physical. If extrasensory perception is purely physical—if the mind is strictly mechanistic—then the factor of distance (space) should have some measurable lawful effect upon its occurrence. The next step, therefore, was to design experiments to ascertain whether the mind truly transcended space. The results of these experiments proved conclusively that distance shows no effect whatever on ESP performance.[6]

But if the human mind can transcend space, this logically leads to a conclusion that I had long regarded as an impossibility: The mind must also be capable of reaching through time, because time, as we know it, is a function of space. It requires time to move through space. And if the mind does transcend time, then it possesses a most incredible power—prophecy.

I had long ridiculed those who had contended that it was possible for the human mind to perceive accurately a future event.[7] To me it was simply inconceivable. Perhaps I should have re-

[6] See Appendix J.
[7] Geoffrey Gorer, distinguished British anthropologist, wrote in his book *Africa Dances*, "It is my belief that African Negroes, without the inhibitions which time and a causal universe impose upon us, regularly dream the future as much as the past and as vividly, with the result that past, present, and future have no meaning to them as they have to us."

viewed more carefully the "history of impossibility." Throughout every age men have brushed aside as impossible ideas which have later become commonplace realities. And it is important to note that the scoffers are frequently prominent scientists, not just laymen. Simon Newcomb, eminent American scientist at the turn of the century, declared that it was impossible for any machine to fly long distances through the air. And an editorial in an eastern newspaper sized up the telephone like this:

A man about 46 years of age has been arrested in New York for attempting to extort funds from ignorant and superstitious people, by exhibiting a device which he says will convey the human voice any distance over metallic wires. He calls the instrument a telephone, which is obviously intended to imitate the word "telegraph" and win the confidence of those who know of the success of the latter instrument. Well-informed people know that it is impossible to transmit the voice over wires and that, were it possible to do so, the thing would be of no practical value.[8]

I should have remembered these things, but my hard core of conditioning had somehow never been penetrated by these considerations. Nor had I ever taken seriously any of the spontaneous instances of peering into the future. Such accounts—many by eminent and conservative observers—are abundant. Here is one sample from *Some Cases of Prediction,* a collection of a number of cases, together with verification reports, by Dame Edith Lyttelton, former president of the British Society for Psychical Research:

. . . A few weeks before the 1931 Schneider Trophy air race . . . I went to the cinema with my husband and a woman friend one evening; the news reel contained photographs of the British Schneider Trophy team. . . . We were first shown the team standing in a group and were then shown each member separately. I may say at this point that all the members were complete strangers to me. . . . I had no interest in the race whatever. . . . The team that year consisted of RAF men with the addition of one single Naval flying man, he stood out in the group by reason of his different uniform. . . . Then we were shown each man singly. As the photograph of this young man was thrown on the screen, I received a sudden terrific sensation

[8] A. M. Low, *What's the World Coming to?* (Philadelphia: Lippincott, 1951).

of shock, the shock of violent physical impact. I started so violently in my seat that my friend sitting next to me whispered, "What's the matter?" I answered in great distress, "He's going to be killed, he's going to crash." That was all. But either two, or three weeks later the newspapers came out with headlines "Schneider Trophy Fatality," the only Naval member of the team had crashed into the sea and had been killed instantly while on a practice flight. Those are the facts. My friend . . . can confirm them.

For many people such examples are unnecessary; most readers can supply their own experiences. Frequently these premonitions are concerned with forthcoming disasters, collisions, or deaths. As for me, I had always dismissed such reports as "coincidences."

For the parapsychologists, however, the matter was one neither for peremptory dismissal nor acceptance. It was for the laboratory. Again the famous ESP cards were employed, but this time the subjects were asked in advance to predict what the order of the entire deck of cards would be after they were shuffled a specified number of times; the shuffling would take place after a certain length of time. Later there were even more stringent conditions, including machine shuffling of the cards. The outcome: There is definite evidence for precognition, and it stands up against all alternative explanations.

"This man Rhine keeps fooling around with cards all the time," commented my father, who had been reading the *Reader's Digest* condensation of Rhine's book, "and I'll bet he doesn't even gamble!"

"Don't get the wrong idea," I answered. "This man isn't trying to break the bank at Monte Carlo. His card tests prove that the mind has a very real power that science has tended to overlook all these years. And don't be fooled by the fact that it now registers to only a slight degree. In Ben Franklin's time the big news about electricity was the fact that Franklin identified it with lightning by picking up a few sparks on the key at the end of his kite. But as more was learned about it electricity exploded into a force which revolutionized our way of life. And when the Wright brothers tried their new flying machine, the longest period of time they could keep a plane in the air was only fifty-nine seconds! Today the luxury Stratocruisers do a little better than that."

"In the same way this mind stuff, as we learn more about it, could become the mightiest power yet."

My father was quiet; he appeared to be reflecting upon my explanation. I was quite pleased with myself at having apparently impressed him with the significance of this pioneering work—pleased with him, too, for giving the matter thoughtful consideration.

Then suddenly looking over at me, he shook his head slowly and with obvious disgust. As he turned to walk away he left me with his final verdict: "That man will never make a dime out of it!"

It is true that there are no juicy financial rewards in store for the parapsychology pioneers. But this evidence that man is not, after all, merely a physical contraption is extremely significant. Our treatment of all things depends upon our understanding of their true nature. We can saw through a tree, cut it into pieces, and throw the pieces into a fire without the slightest compunction. We are convinced that the tree has absolutely no consciousness of the mutilation.[9] We have no hesitation in gleefully maneuvering a sharp hook into the mouth of a fish because we are convinced that the wriggling creature somehow does not sense what is taking place. Our treatment of dogs is on still a different plane; we can see that the dog is an emotional being, capable of love and loyalty.

But what of human beings? How shall we treat each other? The Nazis gave their answer at Dachau and Buchenwald. To them people were not so different from trees. Human beings could be dismembered and thrown into the furnaces. The Communists also have an answer: they think the human being is a transient, expendable machine, which must be sacrificed to the supremacy of the state.

But now at last there is scientific evidence that men are something more than bodies, that they have minds with freedom from physical law, that these minds have unique creative forces which transcend the space-time-mass relations of matter. The mind, in short, has been found to be a factor in its own right and not something which is centered completely in the gray matter of the organic brain. This new evidence, as it is developed, cannot help but strike hard against man's inhumanity to man.

[9] Not necessarily so, hints Sir Jagadis Chandra Bose, India's great scientist, whose amazing invention, the crescograph, registers spasmodic, painlike flutters when a tree or fern is pierced with a sharp instrument.

Before his death in 1923, Charles Steinmetz, the mathematical wizard and electrical engineer, told the world that science, when it finally turned toward spiritual discoveries, would make more progress in fifty years than in all its past history. If that great genius were alive today he would probably agree that the gong has sounded at last. The fateful half century has finally got under way.

CHAPTER 5

For me there was one disappointment in all the modern parapsychology literature. It concerned hypnosis. Practically nothing was being done to employ hypnotism in these controlled experiments. To quote one book: "To this day no one has determined whether hypnotism is of any service in the investigation of extrasensory phenomena. We found only that we could get results more quickly without it."[1]

This disturbed me. I could not conceive how the trance state could fail to affect the score of an experiment in telepathy or clairvoyance. The very history of these phenomena had been, as we have seen, wrapped up with hypnosis; the relaxation ascribable to the trance state should alone be a favorable factor. Then there had been my own experience with a subject under hypnosis. If such results could be developed unintentionally, would there not be at least a reasonable possibility of encountering similar results when they were purposely sought?

I spotted another comment by Rhine in a later book[2]: "There is much yet to be learned about how best to combine hypnosis with the exercise of these abilities." Yes, I thought, perhaps that was it. Perhaps the one big snag here was the failure to properly apply hypnosis to these tests. That gave me an idea.

So I sat down and wrote Dr. Rhine, telling him what I had in mind. I pointed out that I had been unable to find in his books, or any other books, any reports of tests conducted under *dual hypnosis*. In other words, in all these experiments only the person being tested for telepathic or clairvoyant perception had been in the hypnotic state. Why not, I asked, run some experiments after

[1] J. B. Rhine, *New Frontiers of the Mind* (New York: Farrar, 1937).
[2] Rhine, *Reach of the Mind* (New York: Sloane, 1947).

64

both the sender and the receiver had been hypnotized? In short, I suggested that I hypnotize one person in one room, that my friend Bill Moery hypnotize a second person in another room, and that we then ascertain, by means of controlled experiments, to what extent these two entranced subjects could communicate with each other.

Instead of the sender remaining in the waking state and only the receiver in the hypnotic state, it seemed a more logical test (of the effect of hypnosis) to place *both* under hypnosis. In this way, with both minds probably on the same subconscious level, communication between the two might be somewhat facilitated.

Dr. Rhine answered me promptly. "I do not know of any published work done with sender and receiver both under hypnosis." He added that he, too, was looking for a great deal more from hypnosis than had been obtained in the past. And in any event he urged that we proceed with our experiments in dual hypnosis.

So Bill Moery and I swung into action. We decided that, as the basis of the experiment, we would use five objects—a drinking glass, a knife, a bar of soap, a coin, and a cigarette. For each "run"— that is, for each round of twenty-five successive tries (or "calls") by the receiver—every one of these five objects would appear five times.

This meant that a list of twenty-five objects must be prepared before the test began. So that neither the sender nor the receiver should have any clue as to the order in which the objects would appear on the list, we would ask the witnesses to the experiment to establish the order in some random method. We asked only that each of the five objects—the glass, knife, soap, coin, and cigarette— appear five times on the list. We did not care how these "targets" were arranged. A sample listing of twenty-five targets, therefore, might appear as follows:

1. knife	7. coin	13. coin	19. cigarette
2. soap	8. glass	14. cigarette	20. knife
3. cigarette	9. knife	15. glass	21. knife
4. glass	10. soap	16. coin	22. coin
5. coin	11. soap	17. soap	23. glass
6. cigarette	12. cigarette	18. glass	24. knife
			25. soap

While the spectators were making up this schedule in one room,

Bill would hypnotize the sender in the kitchen. In still another room I hypnotized the receiver. After the sender was in the hypnotic state, one of the witnesses would hand Bill the list.

Also rigged up in advance was a simple two-way electric signaling device. By means of small electric bulbs Bill could signal me when his subject was ready to mentally "send" the first item on the list. I, in turn, could flash Bill as soon as my hypnotized subject, the receiver, was ready for number two on the list. And so on. This eliminated any conversation between the hypnotists or their subjects; even the light bulbs were beyond the visual range of the subjects (and their eyes, of course, were closed).

Noting that the first target on the list was "knife," Bill would place the knife in the hands of his subject, the sender, and direct him to concentrate on that item—the idea, in other words, was to convey mentally to the receiver in the other room that this particular object, now in his hands, was a knife. At the same time Bill would press a button; the resultant flash of light in my room would indicate that I should now ask my subject, the receiver, for his "call." As soon as the receiver made his call, I would record it on my pad, then I would signal Bill that I was ready for item number two.

This procedure would be followed until the sender had gone through the entire twenty-five. Never during any of this time would the receiver be given a hint as to whether he was wrong or right. To be sure, I would hardly be in a position to give such a hint since I myself had not the slightest idea as to the order that had been selected and handed to Bill. After the last call both subjects would be awakened, and then the sender's list would be compared with the receiver's calls, which were now recorded on my pad.

The first "guinea pig" was my wife. Bill hypnotized her—she was to be the sender—while in another room I hypnotized a second volunteer, who was the receiver. When both Hazel and my subject had been hypnotized, one of the witnesses gave Bill the paper listing the order of the twenty-five items. I received Bill's flash that he was now starting on the first target, and the show was on.

I explained to my subject that Hazel was now holding one of the five objects. Which one was it?

"Cigarette," he said. I wrote "cigarette" on my pad after number one; then I flashed Bill that we were ready for the next call. In a minute he returned my signal, indicating that Hazel now held the second item on the list. So I asked Walter for his next call.

This was our first effort, so naturally our technique had some rough spots. The first snag developed by the time we reached number five. When I asked Walter for his fifth call, he replied, "Soap." I recorded it.

I waited for the light which would signify that Bill was ready with the sixth object—waited, in fact, for a much longer time than usual. Finally I decided that I must have missed Bill's flash, probably having forgotten to look over at the light as quickly as usual. So I asked my subject for his sixth call.

"Soap," he replied again.

At this point I thought that I had better check with Bill to determine whether I had erred by going ahead with number six. I did so, taking Bill aside (in the presence of witnesses) and asking him what number five had actually been. "Soap," he said.

Then I asked what the sixth item had been. Bill registered surprise at this question, pointing out that he was still working on the fifth object. Indeed, the hypnotized sender, Hazel, still held the soap in her hand. Bill pointed out that I had never signaled that I was ready for number six.

It was true; the blunder was mine. So I suggested, since my subject was ready for number seven, that he leave the soap in the sender's hand, call it number seven, and we would go on from there.

When I returned to my subject and asked him for his seventh call, he responded with conviction, "Soap!" We proceeded from there and encountered no more hazards during the remainder of the run.

Afterward I asked the subject why he had insisted on calling "Soap" three times in succession. He answered that he could very clearly see that bar of soap—that nothing but soap floated into his perception during those calls. The term "float," incidentally, was his own expression. He explained that these various objects seemed to float into his perception on a sort of wave, and he described the wave with his hand.

Then we checked his score, counting all three soaps as only one hit. Even though he had correctly named the target three times, still it had been the same target, never having been changed in the sender's hands during all three calls. So we counted this as a single hit, and he had scored nine hits.

While this was not a spectacular score, it certainly would be extremely significant if it could be maintained. Furthermore, we had been particularly impressed by the soap incident. We determined, therefore, to pursue these experiments whenever we could find subjects—and sufficient time.

Within a month, using six different subjects, we had completed six runs or 150 calls. Our average had dropped a little but was still high. And even though this dual hypnosis routine had not resulted in a miraculous mental radio system, there had been certain factors which seemed especially significant. For one thing, when we added the "conviction" test, the results were surprising.

The conviction test was merely our term for the subject's adding, immediately after he made his call, a comment as to whether his perception on that particular call had been "clear" or "dim." For example, the subject might say, in answer to number seven, "Cigarette—clear," or, "Knife—dim." In this way we recorded the subject's personal conviction as to the perception of his own calls. Oddly, each receiver had an extraordinarily high accuracy on this conviction test.

Then there was something else, too. The number of "forward displacement" calls was out of all proportion. That is, the receiver had called an uncanny number of targets *in advance;* moreover, these advance calls had a striking tendency to be grouped together. For example, when asked for call number eleven, the subject might call the object scheduled for number twelve. Then, when asked for twelve, the subject would name the thirteenth object. And so on he would go, threading a pattern of advance calls. While these were scored as misses instead of hits, no Einstein was required to discern that these displacements were mathematically significant. But we had made too few tests to merit serious consideration.

CHAPTER 6

Meanwhile I was keeping Dr. Rhine at Duke informed on our work, and the correspondence between the doctor and myself began to assume hefty proportions. Dr. Rhine asked an extraordinary number of questions: Was the door closed between the two rooms during the experiment? . . . Was there any communication between trials as to the success of the trial just finished? . . . Will you make a comparative series of tests in which you have the same receiver in the hypnotic state go through the same number of runs with the same sender but with the sender in the normal state? . . . Do you have in mind also having the sender hypnotized and the receiver normal? There were many more, and most of these questions were concerned with precautionary measures to insure the accuracy of the experiments.

The hypnotic experiments continued until we had fourteen runs of twenty-five targets each, or a total of 350 individual trials. At this point Hazel and I decided to visit Dr. Rhine at his Duke laboratory. There were many questions he could answer for us, and besides, we wanted to meet personally this courageous scientist who had undertaken such a mammoth pioneering project.

At the airport, where Dad was seeing us off, his parting comment was, "I'll bet this Rhine isn't even listed in Dun and Bradstreet." As the plane took off, I was still trying to figure out whether he had been serious.

The following day Hazel and I were in Durham, North Carolina, more than two thousand miles from Pueblo, waiting in a high-ceilinged, book-lined room. While we were looking over Dr. Rhine's library, he walked in. Tall, handsome, and well built, he hardly fitted the picture that one imagines when thinking of the typical college professor. He wasn't even wearing glasses! Over his alert eyes were bushy black brows, revealing that his thick white hair had once been black.

Since I had already prepared a list of typewritten questions I wasted no time in asking them. And the doctor lost no time in answering; he seemed to have a prepared list of answers. I wanted to know about everything from experiments with prayer to his experience with Lady, the Wonder Horse. Hazel added questions too, and since we spent almost a week with Dr. Rhine we thought of more as we went along.

One question which inevitably pops up during a meeting between two people interested in parapsychology is "How did you become interested in these phenomena?" Naturally this was one of my questions for Dr. Rhine, and one night while we were having dinner together, he related an episode (also recorded in one of his books) which was a factor in his decision to plunge into the whirlpool of psychic mysteries. "When I was a graduate student at a large university," Rhine told us, "one of my most respected science professors related a typical psychic occurrence to which he had been in part an eyewitness:

"Our family was awakened late one night by a neighbor who wanted to borrow a horse and buggy to drive nine miles to a neighboring village. The man said, apologetically, that his wife had been wakened by a horrible dream about her brother who lived in that village. It had so disturbed her that she insisted he drive over at once to see if it was true. He explained that she thought she had seen this brother return home, take his team to the barn, unharness the animals, and then go up into the hayloft and shoot himself with a pistol. She saw him pull the trigger and roll over in the hay, down a little incline into a corner. No reassurance could persuade her that she had only had a nightmare. My father lent them a buggy (it was before the day of telephones) and they drove over to her brother's house. There they found his wife still awaiting her husband's return, unaware of any disaster.

"They went to the barn and found the horses unharnessed. They climbed to the hayloft, and there was the body in the spot the sister had described from her dream. The pistol was lying in the hay, where it would have fallen if it had been used as she had indicated and if the body had afterward rolled down the incline. It seemed as though she had dreamed every detail with photographic exactness. I was only a boy then, but it made an impression on me I've never forgotten. I can't explain it and I've never found anyone else who could," the professor concluded.

Rhine continued, "His story puzzled and impressed me when I heard it, and it has remained in my mind long years after most of the things he taught in class have been forgotten. It is not the story alone that I have remembered, but the fact that the man who told it, himself a teacher and a scientist, though clearly impressed by the occurrence, had no explanation whatever to offer; that he had lived all the years of his manhood believing such a thing had occurred and had done nothing, even to satisfy his own curiosity, about it."

When I, in turn, was asked to account for my own interest in these matters, I realized that I had never taken much time to give myself reasons. I supposed that my interest was something like that of the mountain climber in the novel, *The White Tower*. When asked why he insisted upon climbing a peak which had not yet been reached by man, he answered, "Because it is there."

Likewise, I just can't dismiss this stuff. It is there.

Our visit to Duke gave us an intimate glimpse of one of the world's most important scientists. Probably more than any other one person, Joseph Banks Rhine has managed to pry an opening under the most ponderous of all iron curtains, the mystery of man's own nature. His evidence is revolutionary; it calls for—indeed, it necessitates—a revision of many basic scientific concepts. The implications cut across psychology, medicine, philosophy, religion; they offer man, for the first time, an opening wedge in his efforts to understand himself and his fellow man.

And what a battle Rhine and his cohorts have encountered every inch of the way! During the early years, in fact, the research reports from his laboratory were far outnumbered by the articles of criticism directed against them. The first targets for criticism were the mathematical methods of evaluation used to determine whether the scores could be explained by chance. The decision which ended this part of the battle came in 1937, during the annual meeting of the American Institute of Mathematical Statistics, when the following press release was authorized:

". . . the statistical analysis is essentially valid. If the Rhine investigation is to be fairly attacked, it must be on other than mathematical grounds."

And a few months later Professor E. V. Huntington, distinguished Harvard mathematician, further clarified the mathematical issues involved in the ESP research in an article which appeared in the *American Scholar*.

Even so, it should come as no surprise that Rhine's evidence doesn't find the welcome mat spread before all the members of his own profession. Why should we expect Dr. Rhine to enjoy an immunity from the ridicule and strife that has plagued almost every pioneer from Giordano Bruno to Alexander Bell? Why should human nature suddenly go into reverse and smile upon a man who points out that all is not just as we have been taught for three centuries? Men of science are, after all, human beings, basically the same kind of beings who opposed Galileo, Mesmer, Newton, Pasteur, Semmelweis. Evidence which does not fit neatly into the current pattern is regarded, or perhaps disregarded, with disdain. A Yale professor, Dr. G. E. Hutchinson, a member of the National Academy of Sciences, summarized the situation as follows:

"The reason why most scientific workers do not accept these results is simply that they do not want to, and avoid doing so by refusing to examine the full detailed reports of the experiments in question."

The skirmishes, issues, and tests surrounding Rhine extended even to his bookselling efforts. The salesmen of his own publishing house had to be convinced. Take, for instance, the following account from a former executive of Farrar and Rinehart, the publisher of Rhine's first popular book:

"Dr. J. B. Rhine's first book for the general reader on extrasensory perception, called *New Frontiers of the Mind,* was to be published in the fall of that year [1937]. In spite of a couple of interesting articles in Harper's Magazine, the knowledge of extrasensory perception at that time was confined to a small number of people who had followed the earlier Duke work with interest. Ninety-nine out of every hundred Americans were highly skeptical, and it became evident to the editorial department that in spite of the book's selection by the Book-of-the-Month Club and in spite of a growing interest in the subject, the half dozen or so key salesmen of the firm's staff were far from comforted. It was evident that unless something drastic were done, the book would be sold without full confidence and enthusiasm by our representatives. John Farrar's solution of this problem was characteristically simple. He called me into his office, explained the problem as he saw it, and instructed me to give the sales force a demonstration of the truth of extrasensory perception. . . .

"At the time of sales conference none of the now familiar Duke extrasensory perception testing cards were available and, in any event, any demonstration with them would have partially failed of its object since the cards were unfamiliar to the salesmen and would have been viewed as a piece of magician's equipment rather than a fair test of the thesis of the book. Accordingly, I summoned the boys into a vacant office and had one of them produce a pack of cards which, like one or two other salesmen in my experience, he happened to have in his desk. I told them that I was going to prove that there was such a thing as extrasensory perception and I asked each of the six to shuffle the pack and cut it. They did so with a thoroughness which I can remember appallingly as I watched. I then told them the truth that there are fifty-two cards in a standard playing deck such as that one, that the chance that I would correctly identify the top card on the pack by suit was one in four and by suit and number one in fifty-two. I pointed out that the mathematics on the second card were somewhat more complicated. The chance of my being right by suit and number was of course one in fifty-one; the chance of being right by suit was slightly more than one in four. The chance of being right by suit and number of the first two cards in the sequence was, according to me, estimated to be one in fifty-two times one in fifty-one, a very large figure, which would be multiplied again by fifty if I were right about the third card, and so on. They admitted that these figures were correct, and I had them put the pack in front of me, closed my eyes and, as nearly as I can describe the process, learned that the first card was, as I remember it, the jack of diamonds. One of them turned the card over and it was the jack of diamonds. I must confess the fact that I was surprised at this point, but enormously heartened, and with new confidence, I proceeded to call off correctly the next four cards by suit and number. At the end of that time there was a very heavy silence in the room and I realized that the point had been made. Instantly I felt something begin to evaporate from whatever area of the mind is involved in a feat of this sort, and when one of them asked me "just one more to see if I could," I knew I could not. However, I called the nine of clubs and the card was actually the ten of clubs and at that point I stopped. . . ."

Rhine's middle name should have been "careful." He found time during our visit to elaborate on this "careful" principle. In the field of parapsychology, he warned, the word "careful" must be the watchword to an even greater extent than in any other endeavor. Parapsychologists, he indicated, must always tack up the "careful" slogan whenever they worked, much in the manner in which Thomas Watson of the International Business Machines company posts his "Think" signs.

Proof that he practiced what he preached was provided when I questioned him on the matter of spirit survival. "What do you think, Doctor—is there any part of a human being that survives after death?"

On his lips I could see the trace of a smile. But all I could hear was "careful" phraseology, which, when summed up, said, "We must reserve final judgment."

"But at the moment," I objected, "I'm not asking for a scientific verdict. I'm only asking for your personal opinion."

This time the smile was more distinct, but the words remained "careful." Many times, he pointed out, we see a piece of property that we should like to own, but we must not consider that the property belongs to us until the actual purchase has been made. I gave up.

At the time I was quizzing Dr. Rhine on the survival question I hadn't the vaguest notion that one of my own hypnotic experiments—the discovery of Bridey Murphy—would eventually provide me with interesting evidence on this very issue of survival.

We spent several days at Duke. Then, having made our pilgrimage to the capital of parapsychology, we started home again, fully charged with determination to carry on with our experiments. Hazel had even made sketches of some of the laboratory equipment; maybe, she suggested, we could start our own junior laboratory at home. It sounded like a good idea.

Our intentions were good, therefore, as we arrived home. And we probably would be still running dual hypnosis experiments to this day if it were not for one little incident.

One day a man came walking into my office. He looked very much like any other man. But this fellow sent me racing across the long bridge—and into the biggest adventure of all.

PART THREE

The Big Step

CHAPTER 7

When I was a sophomore in high school I read Maugham's *Of Human Bondage*. There I found a wonderfully articulate statement of the materialistic philosophy that had been crystallizing within me ever since I had been old enough to ask questions. The principal character, Philip, had been given a Persian rug by an artistic reprobate, who assured our hero that by studying the carpet he would be able to comprehend the meaning of life. Long after the donor's death Philip was still puzzled. How could the intricate and illusory pattern of a Persian rug solve the problem of life's meaning? But later he suddenly got the point. The answer was obvious. Life had no meaning.

Ah, now there was a boy with common sense. This Philip character was practical. And since he had been created by no less a master than Somerset Maugham, I now had real authority for my own beliefs. It was just as Philip said: "The rain fell alike upon the just and the unjust, and for nothing was there a why and a wherefore."

Why couldn't everyone, I wondered, see just as Philip did that life was meaningless, without purpose—and that death peremptorily ended the whole show? And why all the argument about the possibility of life after death? Anyone could plainly see that a dead body was very dead indeed. How could anyone seriously believe otherwise? Three hundred years of science had failed to prove the immortality of a single soul. So why try to make something out of nothing?

I was fifteen years old then.

But this pattern of thinking had started as early as the first grade. If I hadn't noticed it before, then I surely observed during my first year at school that there were glaring inequities among the kids in the class. Keith, for instance, was brilliant; he knew all the answers. He was taller and huskier than the others; any girl would willingly tell you that he was the best-looking boy in the class. And he was the best all-around athlete, could play anything. To top it all, his parents seemed to have plenty of money; he

77

dressed better, lived in the biggest house, and his father drove the biggest car.

Orlando, on the other hand, had been short-changed in every department. The poor lad was so dull that the most elementary exercise was beyond him. On the playground he was so clumsy that he soon picked up uncomplimentary nicknames. And there was no denying that he was unattractive to look upon, really an ugly kid. His clothes, because his family lived in poverty, were so shabby and ill-fitting as to draw derision. Then one day a truck ran over Orlando, and he died in pain a few weeks later.

I would ask my mother the "why" of these things. Why did the Keiths have everything while the Orlandos had been blessed with nothing but misery? My poor mother did her best to answer, but it was clear that she was bewildered too.

This was also the beginning of another kind of education. I was learning that the grownups didn't have all the answers. Before this I had always been comforted by the feeling that no matter what the problem the grownups would have the solution. Now even that solace was fading away. Not only didn't they have all the answers, but many that they did offer, I was later to learn, were dead-wrong.

In any event, in those days it seemed that any philosophy which embraced a meaningful pattern was strictly a myth. How could there be any sort of divine justice which would permit, apparently without reason, one person to have intelligence, health, beauty, and wealth while it consigned to another stupidity, sickness, ugliness, and penury? If there really were a larger plan, it seemed to me, it was either too ineffective or too imperfect to do anything about these grave inequities, and in either case there might as well be no plan.

I had gone to Sunday school every week. But I never did realize that we were actually expected to *believe* the Bible stories. I had always taken for granted that they were merely moral tales, like *Aesop's Fables.* David's slaying of Goliath, for instance, was just like the tortoise's defeat of the hare. I didn't comprehend that there was actually supposed to have been a real person named David. And when Moses struck a rock and water gushed out, that was solid proof that these were mere myths. Not even my father could get water from a rock. So a fable it had to be. And Sunday school, I figured, was just another parental device to keep us in school one more morning.

It never occurred to me that my parents were sending me to church to learn about immortality. When I quizzed my mother about related topics, I could tell that she was as puzzled as I. And as for my father, he was so busy working night and day, making it possible for me to wear clothes like Keith's, that I was sure he had no time to think about any kind of philosophy. I came, therefore, to my own conclusion: Religion and immortality are fables. Life is an accident—an accident that begins at birth and ends in death.

That was a long time ago.

But it was not so terribly long ago that I was in college, and there my earlier convictions were confirmed. The most brilliant student I knew wasted no time in assuring me, and anyone else who would listen, that "religion is a have for the have-nots." For the ignorant, for the downtrodden, for all the unfortunates, he steadfastly maintained, faith in immortality is something to cling to. A last hope. But we who were at the college level were supposed to be too enlightened to accept such a superstitious credo.

And if there were any college professors who had a different view, they managed to keep it a secret. Looking back, I grant that there must have been, as a matter of simple statistics, those who would not concede that religion is a "have for the have-nots." But they never spoke up; perhaps the whole question was taboo. Or maybe it was reserved for the divinity school, and there was a gentleman's agreement not to bring up this topic before ordinary students of finance. At any rate, it was clear that most of the instructors dreaded being drawn into any discussion concerning man's true nature.

My "higher" education, therefore, only substantiated my first-grade concepts. I found myself quoting my atheistic companion, deriding those who could be so foolish as to believe there might be a meaning to life, and generally reveling in my smug "intellectual superiority."

Just before graduation the last assignment in public speaking class provided an ideal opportunity to summarize my position. The subject of our final speech was to be a biography, anyone's biography. Some in the class made the obvious conventional choices: Lincoln, Edison, Ford. A few clever lads came up with surprises like Rudolph Valentino and Jesse James.

But for me this was a chance to get a professional hearing for my cynical, iconoclastic views. So I selected a character who would fit my theme—Solomon Grundy.

Solomon Grundy
Born on Monday,
Christened on Tuesday,
Married on Wednesday,
Took ill on Thursday,
Worse on Friday,
Died on Saturday,
Buried on Sunday.
This is the end of Solomon Grundy.

As if Solomon's career hadn't been fleeting enough in the first place, I chopped him down still further. I gave him just three days. In my abridged version Solomon entered the world on Monday, took sick on Tuesday, and rigor mortis set in on Wednesday. No use keeping him around for a whole week.

Explaining that every man, whether it be Napoleon or the half-witted campus caretaker, is a Solomon Grundy, I spent my allotted time in pointing out that all biographies were essentially the same. Man is born: he makes motions and noises; then he dies a meaningless death. So why should I not choose for my subject, I argued, the pattern for the lives of all men—Mr. Grundy?

When I finished the discourse I sat down and awaited the judgment of my professor. It came with two words: "Thoughtful composition."

Here, I reasoned, was tacit approval of this brand of philosophy. And it had come from a man with several degrees. The higher the education, it seemed to me, the more confirmed became this sort of thinking.

It is no wonder, then, that my opinions as I left college began to harden into a "so what?" attitude, and the whole game appeared somewhat pointless. No matter what goal I set for myself, those two words—"so what?"—would loom over the goal posts. I would think of the end result, imagining that the job had already been accomplished, and then the "so what?" would pop up again. It wasn't a very pretty picture; it led to the grave, nothing more.

Years later my experiences with hypnosis and subsequently with extrasensory perception hinted that there might be a glimmer of something more. But I still hadn't gone far enough to make a real dent in all my previous conditioning.

This, then, was the background, the philosophical setting, when a man named Val Weston walked into my office.

CHAPTER 8

I had been answering the mail and was just removing a cylinder from the dictaphone when a voice behind me said, "Pardon me. My name is Weston. I'm with the Department of Commerce."

I turned around. He was a six-footer, built like a wrestler who keeps himself in shape. He explained that his division was keeping a list of the steel products available from every distributor in his area. Such a list, during the post-war period of steel shortages, might be helpful in establishing allocations, in spotting various items for which defense industries were searching, and for general co-ordination.

He was in the office about fifteen minutes. But during that short time the telephone rang repeatedly and a parade of employees and others zipped in and out. Nevertheless, I managed to give him the information he wanted, and I thought that I had seen the last of him as he went out the door.

Five minutes later he was hustling back into my office, his eyes sparkling with obvious interest. He said, "I understand that you are interested in hypnotism and extrasensory perception."

I wondered how he had suddenly picked up that bit of knowledge until he explained that he had encountered my father just before leaving the building and he reconstructed the conversation for me.

I admitted my hobbies to Weston, and the two of us promptly became engrossed in a general bull session. It turned out that he had long been interested in the same matters. And he had really been around. He had been in the Orient, was very well read; and as he was about fifteen years my senior, his education in these fields was somewhat more extensive than my own. To be sure, he had plenty to tell me. But in that madhouse getting it told was no simple task. Our conversation was chopped up by numerous interruptions, until at last we gave up. But not before arranging to get together that week end.

Weston had a cabin at Rye, Colorado, a picturesque mountain village in the Greenhorn range, just an hour's drive from Pueblo. Hazel and I drove there the following Saturday, and we resumed our session where we had left off a few days before.

For a first name, Weston used Val. His real name was Percival, but I suppose that one doesn't go around calling a king-sized male by the name of Percival. Having been in China and India, he had a rather keen understanding of Eastern philosophy and religion. He had interviewed yogis and fakirs and had witnessed performances which sound incredible to us occidentals no matter how frequently we are told about them. While his reading background was surprisingly comprehensive, he evidently preferred works with a philosophical flavor.

I was decidedly impressed. He was well informed regarding the subjects in which I was interested. Hazel and I were fascinated; the time was flying by.

And then the roof fell in.

Abruptly, and without warning, he swung into a ridiculous subject: reincarnation!

For a few minutes I continued to listen; I wanted to make sure whether he could possibly be serious. He was.

Reincarnation—oh no!

How could this intelligent-looking man, apparently normal in every other respect, be talking in earnest about a subject so preposterous!

Interrupting Weston, I reminded him that it was growing very late; it was time for Hazel and me to get back to town. I wasted no time in getting out of there, practically pulling Hazel with me.

All the way home I kept muttering words like ". . . and he seemed so intelligent . . . just can't tell by looking at someone . . . have to be more careful in the future. . . ." Hazel paid no attention; she was fast asleep by the time we rolled into our driveway.

About a month later business brought Weston to Pueblo again, but I contrived to be "just too busy" to see him that day.

He very likely sensed that I was avoiding him. And simple deduction would have disclosed that the reason was his reincarnation rantings. He couldn't have failed to observe that I had been intensely interested until he had slipped into the you-have-lived-before-and-will-live-again theme.

I suppose it was because he was aware of my reason for dodging him that he sent me two books. I had heard of neither. One was called *There Is a River*, by Thomas Sugrue, and the other, *Many Mansions*, by Dr. Gina Cerminara. I noticed that both were concerned with a man named Edgar Cayce (pronounced Casey), who had died only a few years before (1945).

Although I didn't know it then, picking up those books was a signal for the beginning of a new phase in my life. It was an act that ultimately forced me to dig into fields that I had always regarded as ridiculously out of bounds.

The books started off so sensibly and interestingly that, for a while at least, my attention was diverted from where they were leading me. Edgar Cayce's story, as it began, was not so very different from thousands of others who had lived at the same time. He was born on a farm near Hopkinsville, Kentucky, in 1877. Although he had little formal education—having gotten only as far as the ninth grade in a country school—there was one book he had mastered: the Bible. He reread the Bible every year.

He didn't take to the farm, so while still in his teens, he moved to town and worked at various sales jobs from stationery to insurance. Up to this point, then, we still have a conventional pattern: A devout Christian farm boy goes to the city and struggles to earn his living at whatever job he can find. But here the Cayce story shifts abruptly.

A severe attack of laryngitis when Cayce was twenty-one finally resulted in the loss of his voice. All medication was ineffective; he just couldn't talk. This depressing condition cut short his saleswork and kept him at home for several months, where he brooded over his apparently incurable ailment. Finally, however, he went to work as a photographer's apprentice, a job that would not be so demanding on his voice.

Then one night a traveling hypnotist came to the town. He heard about Cayce's condition and offered to attempt a cure through hypnosis. Cayce was willing, and while under hypnosis it was proved that he could speak perfectly. But as soon as he was awakened he reverted to the former condition and couldn't talk. Again and again the hypnotist tried, not forgetting to employ the post-hypnotic suggestion that Cayce would be able to speak normally *after* he awakened, but to no avail. Cayce could talk while in a trance, not afterward.

The professional hypnotist moved on to his next engagement. The following day, however, a local resident, an amateur hypnotist named Al Layne, who had witnessed the whole affair, came to offer a suggestion: If Cayce could talk while under trance, then why not go into a trance once more and this time, if Cayce could still speak normally while in such a state, let him try to describe the nature of his affliction? Perhaps he could give some clue as to the root of the trouble, some indication or sensation that would identify the cause.

Because all other remedies had failed, Cayce was ready to try almost anything. He went into a trance, then was asked to explain his vocal difficulty, which he did. These were his words:

"Yes, we can see the body. In the normal physical state this body is unable to speak due to a partial paralysis of the inferior muscles of the vocal cord, produced by nerve strain. This is a psychological condition producing a physical effect. This may be removed by increasing the circulation to the affected parts by *suggestion* while in this unconscious condition."

Layne made the suggestion outlined by Cayce—that is, he told the sleeping Cayce that circulation to the vocal cords would increase and the condition would thus be removed. Cayce's chest and throat turned pink, finally scarlet. Several minutes later he said, "It's all right now. The condition is removed. Make the suggestion that the circulation return to normal and that after that, the body awaken."

Layne followed instructions. Cayce awakened; he spoke normally for the first time in many months.

Layne was delighted. Soon he came up with another idea. If Cayce could diagnose for himself, there was a bare possibility that he might be able to do the same thing for the young hypnotist, Layne, who had long suffered from stomach trouble. Agreeing to the experiment, Cayce again went under hypnosis; this time he diagnosed Layne's ailments and told him what to do about it, recommending certain drugs, diet, and exercise.

Following these directions, Layne improved remarkably within a few weeks. He bubbled with excitement. Not only was he getting well, but he was certain that Cayce possessed a rare gift. When in a hypnotic trance Cayce spoke like a physician, using accurate physiological and medical terminology. In both these cases, furthermore, his prescriptions had included measures which, although overlooked in prior medical examinations, had been surprisingly successful.

Layne, therefore, was eager to determine whether they could help others who were suffering from poor health. Cayce, though, was not so easily persuaded. In the first place he knew nothing about medicine, had never read a single book on the subject. He couldn't understand how this stuff could be pouring out of him. (Keep in mind that Cayce had total amnesia for the entire period of the trance; he had to be told what he had said after awakening.) Furthermore, success in his own case might have been accidental; and Layne's improvement, he reasoned, might possibly be attributed to imagination. And since Cayce apparently had no control over what he said while in a trance, he might give directions that would be harmful rather than helpful.

But Layne's exuberance would not be quashed. Playing upon Cayce's natural desire to help others—young Cayce had always wanted to be a preacher and was thwarted by financial circumstances—Layne finally inveigled a promise to attempt a few experiments. Cayce wanted it firmly understood, however, that this would be an effort to help only those who requested, and genuinely needed, assistance.

He made it quite clear, furthermore, that he would accept no money or payment of any kind.

Thereupon were launched the approximately thirty thousand "health readings" of Edgar Cayce. This title was applied by Layne, who was now having all of Cayce's trance utterances recorded *verbatim*. Very soon it had become plain that the strange faculty of the "sleeping doctor" was most uncanny, indeed.

Oddest of all was the fact that the person requesting the reading need not even be present. It was learned that it was possible to conduct readings at a distance provided Cayce was given the exact name of the person and his location at the time the reading was made. If a person, for instance, were living in an apartment in New York City, he could request a Cayce health reading by giving no more than his address, his name, and a statement that he would be in his apartment at, say, 2:00 P.M. on a certain date.

At the appointed time Cayce would loosen his tie, take off his shoes, and lie down on a couch. Having already learned to place himself in a trance, he would close his eyes and move his clasped hands, palms upward, over his forehead. Then, apparently receiving some subconscious flash, he would move his hands down and cross them over his solar plexus. After he had taken several deep breaths, his eyes would begin to flicker, indicating that he was slipping into a trance state. At this point Layne (or Mrs. Cayce or some other person) would read the following statement, which had been adopted as the standard opening:

"You will now have before you [individual's name], who is located at [street, address, town, state]. You will go over this body carefully, examine it thoroughly, and tell me the conditions you find at the present time, giving the cause of existing conditions; also suggestions for the help and relief of this body. You will answer questions as I ask them."

Within a few minutes Cayce would begin to speak. Ordinarily he would begin, "Yes, we have the body," and he would continue describing the person, diagnosing the ailment, and recommending steps that should be taken for relief. When it is realized that the letter requesting the reading included none of the person's symptoms, nor even a hint of any sort, this bizarre talent grows even more electrifying.

It is interesting to note that in the event the person asking for the reading was not at the designated location, Cayce would say, "We don't find him. The body is not here." At other times he would voluntarily give a detailed description of the room, often making such comments as, "Big dog in the corner . . . The body is just leaving now—going down in the elevator . . . We find the mother praying."

Most important, however, was the fact that sick people were getting well after Cayce's diagnoses; cures were effected, moreover, even with cases which had been regarded as incurable. A young girl in Alabama, for instance, had been committed to a mental institution as hopelessly demented. A later Cayce reading, however, disclosed the curious fact that an impacted wisdom tooth was impinging upon a nerve in the brain. The slumbering diagnostician suggested that the tooth be extracted. Subsequent dental surgery confirmed the reading, and the girl made a complete return to sanity.

One of the most famous and widely investigated cases was that of little Aime Dietrich of Hopkinsville, Kentucky. The child's mind had failed to develop since an attack of grippe at the age of two; she was, furthermore, seized with convulsions every day by the time she was five. Numerous specialists had been consulted, and the last one had assured the anguished parents that the child was the victim of a rare brain disease which must invariably prove fatal.

Not completely reconciled to their tragedy, the parents turned to Edgar Cayce as a last resort. The humble, uneducated photographer's apprentice was almost too timid to step in where famous physicians had failed. Nevertheless, he did respond to the Dietrich summons, and the outcome is well-documented history.

While in a trance Cayce said that just before the child's grippe attack she had fallen from a carriage and that the grippe germs had settled in the injured area; this had caused all the trouble. He stated that a return to normality could be made through certain osteopathic adjustments.

The girl's mother then remembered the fall from the carriage but she didn't understand how this could possibly have any bearing on the case. In any event, the adjustments were made, and for the first time in three years the girl began to show signs of recovering. Later the father gave the following testimony before a notary public:

At this period our attention was called to Mr. Edgar Cayce, who was asked to diagnose her case. By autosuggestion he went into a sleep and diagnosed her case as one of congestion at the base of the brain, stating also minor details. He outlined to Dr. A. C. Layne how to proceed to cure her. Dr. Layne treated her accordingly every day for three weeks, using Mr. Cayce occasionally to follow up the treatments as results developed. Her mind began to clear up about the eighth day and within three months she was in perfect health, and is so to this day. The case can be verified by many of the best citizens of Hopkinsville, Kentucky.

Subscribed and sworn before me this eighth day of October, 1910. (Signed) D. H. Dietrich, Gerrig Raidt, Notary Public, Hamilton County, Ohio.

As the cases accumulated, many doctors became interested in the miracle man of Virginia Beach. Some began to use him for diagnosing their own most puzzling cases. One doctor in Delaware, who had utilized Cayce's talents for years, attested that the diagnostic accuracy had been better than ninety per cent. A New York doctor agreed with this, and was even inclined to raise this figure.

It should not be inferred from this, however, that Cayce had a perfect batting average. He had his share of strike-outs. There were readings which failed to match the situation, diagnoses which did not seem to fit the case, instances of off-the-target performance. Overall, though, his record was phenomenal.

Remembering that the two books had been sent to me by Val Weston, I was wondering, as I started reading the first one, why he wanted me to know about the medical clairvoyance of Edgar Cayce. As I continued to read, however, Weston's motive became obvious. It seems that Cayce finally focused his incredible ability upon another problem. And the latter clearly was the matter to which Weston was directing my attention.

It was in the third chapter of *Many Mansions* that I first read the absorbing account of how Edgar Cayce happened to plunge into reincarnation. Perhaps the best manner in which to share with the reader some of the impact that struck me at that time is to borrow from those same passages in *Many Mansions*. The book's author, Dr. Gina Cerminara, entitles her third chapter "An Answer to the Riddles of Life," which begins:

> For twenty years of humanitarian activity, Edgar Cayce's clairvoyance showed itself to be reliable in literally thousands of instances. One feels the need of reminding oneself of this fact when coming to the next development in his strange career.
>
> At first his powers of perception had been directed inward, to the hidden places of the human body. Not until many years passed did it occur to anyone that these powers might also be directed outward, to the universe itself, to the relationship of man and the universe, and to the problems of human destiny. It happened in the following way.
>
> Arthur Lammers, a well-to-do printer of Dayton, Ohio, had heard about Cayce through a business associate, and his interest was sufficiently roused for him to take a special trip down to Selma, Alabama, where Cayce was living at the time, to watch him work. Lammers had no health problem of his own, but he was convinced, after several days' observation of readings, that Cayce's clairvoyance was authentic. A well-informed, intellectually alert man, he began to think that a mind able to

perceive realities unavailable to normal sight should be able to shed light on problems of more universal significance than the functioning of a sick man's liver or the intricacies of his digestive tract. Which philosophic system, for example, came closest to the truth? What was the purpose, if any, of man's existence? Was there any truth in the doctrine of immortality? If so, what happened to man after death? Could Cayce's clairvoyance give answers to questions like these?

Cayce didn't know. Abstract questions concerning ultimate matters had never crossed his mind. The religion he had been taught in church he accepted without question; speculation as to its truth in comparison with philosophy, science, or the teachings of other religions was foreign to his thinking. It was only because of his generous desire to help suffering people that he had continued to go into a sleep so unorthodox. Lammers was the first person who saw other possibilities in the faculty besides the curing of disease, and Cayce's imagination was stirred. The readings had seldom failed to answer any question put to them; there seemed no reason why they should not answer Lammers' questions.

Consequently Cayce accepted Lammers' invitation to visit him in Dayton in order to determine what the readings had to say about these philosophical inquiries. It was decided, since Lammers had recently become curious as to whether there could be any truth in astrology, to ask the sleeping Cayce for Lammers' horoscope.

The subsequent reading indicated that the answers to Lammers' queries were not a matter of astrology; it was implied, for instance, that certain qualities and tendencies of Lammers had not been the result of a particular sign of the zodiac. Instead—and here comes the revelation that burst upon me with atomic force— these factors could be more specifically attributed, stated the reading, *to a previous lifetime* on earth, when "he was once a monk."

Oh, oh! There it was again, I said to myself. When the persistent Weston perceived that I was unwilling to listen to his reincarnation rhapsody, he had attempted to implant his propaganda by sending me a book. Well, I wouldn't be trapped. Muttering imprecations, I shoved the book aside. This stuff is not for me, I kept assuring myself.

To Hazel I raged against reincarnation, the book, and even

Cayce himself. But Hazel scarcely looked up from her own reading; she merely remarked something to the effect that I would be getting back to the book again sooner or later and that I might as well pick it up now. I did.

Taking up where I had left off, I was glad to learn, at least, that Cayce had also found himself in consternation. He simply did not understand this reincarnation business. He was afraid at first that it might be anti-Christian. As to this part of the Cayce story, let's refer again to *Many Mansions:*

Cayce's inner turmoil is not difficult to understand. He had been brought up in an atmosphere of strict, orthodox Christianity, with no instruction in the teachings of the great world religions other than his own. At that time, therefore, he was unaware for the most part of the many profound points of similarity between his faith and other faiths, and had had no opportunity to appreciate the ethical and spiritual light which burns in lamps other than that of his own form of Christianity. He was particularly uninformed with regard to that cardinal teaching of Hinduism and Buddhism—reincarnation.

He was repelled, in fact, by the very word, confusing reincarnation, as some people do, with the doctrine of transmigration of souls—namely that man returns to earth, after death, in an animal form. . . . The readings themselves soon disabused Cayce of this confusion. Reincarnation, the readings explained, does not mean the return of human beings to animal form; it is not merely a superstition of ignorant people. It is a thoroughly respectable doctrine, both from the religious and the philosophic point of view. Millions of educated people in Indian and Buddhist countries believe it intelligently, and guide their lives by its ethical principles. There are, to be sure, many sects in India and the East that teach the transmigration of the human soul to animal forms; but this is only a misinterpretation of the true reincarnation principle. Even Christianity has garbled and mistaken forms; one must not permit a narrow acquaintance with the distorted versions to close one's mind to the possibility of truth in the original.

Lammers was able to add to the clarification given by the readings themselves. Reincarnation means *evolution*, he explained: the evolution of the spirit of man through many successive lifetimes on earth—sometimes as a man, sometimes as a woman, now as a pauper, now as a prince, here belonging to one race, there to another—until finally the spirit has reached the perfection enjoined on us by Christ. The soul is like an actor who takes different roles and wears different costumes on different nights; or like a hand that puts on the glove of a material body for a little while, and when the glove is threadbare, slips out and later dons another glove. Any number of men of intellect in our hemisphere have accepted this idea, and written about it. Schopenhauer thoroughly believed in it. So did Emerson, Walt Whitman, Goethe, Giordano Bruno, Plotinus, Pythagoras, Plato.

Consoled to some extent, Cayce was persuaded to continue his probing of this other dimension in man—to give more readings, that is, on the subject of past lifetimes. As the new brand of readings grew in number—they were called "life readings" for lack of a better name, and ultimately totaled about twenty-five hundred —Cayce's doubts began to dissolve. Historically the readings rooted out information which almost always surprised the unschooled Cayce, to whom they would be read after he awakened. In one instance Cayce told a man that he had been a stool-dipper in a previous incarnation. No one present, however, had the slightest hint as to what a stool-dipper was. But digging for facts unearthed the answer that this referred to the job, in the early-American witch-hunting days, of strapping alleged witches to stools and dipping them into a pool of water.

In another case a man was told that during his previous incarnation he had been a Confederate soldier in the Civil War, and the reading gave his former name and address. Naturally the man was anxious to learn whether he could actually find records which would verify this account, and so he began his search. Finally tracing the records to the state historical library, he found that there had, indeed, been such a person, that the person had lived where Cayce specified and had enlisted in Lee's army as a color-bearer in 1862.

Aside from these historical confirmations, there was another phase, the psychological, which in many respects was most convincing. In the cases involving psychological analyses the predictive accuracy of the Cayce readings could be checked during the present lifetime. Even for people he never saw, Cayce forecast character delineations, talents, physical defects, assigning their origin to previous incarnations, when they had, according to Cayce, begun to develop.

CHAPTER 9

From this recording of the Cayce story, however, it should not be deduced that I accepted the whole matter without further question. Far from it. Granted that the books I read had seemed sensible and forceful; nevertheless, the whole thing was still not quite comprehensible to a mind that had been so long trained in another school. I was ready to concede that there must have been a man named Edgar Cayce and that this man had somehow managed some remarkable performances. But that was all.

I did, however, concur in the thought set forth by Dr. Cerminara on the very last page of her book:

If reincarnation is indeed the law of life whereby man evolves and becomes perfect. . . . Surely it is worth the attention of serious-minded men to investigate a possibility the establishment of which could be so clarifying, so lifegiving, and so transformative. If indeed the soul of man has many mansions, now, of all times, is the time we need to know that truth . . .

Yes, I could agree that here was a matter which at least merited further consideration. Hazel agreed too. So, armed with three questions, we flew off on the first part of our search—we would chase down the Cayce story, trying to learn for ourselves just how much truth it contained. Our aim was to seek out doctors, lawyers, businessmen—anyone who could give us his firsthand experience with Cayce. Each interview would start with these questions: First: Could Cayce have been a fraud? Next: What about his medical diagnoses? Could he really diagnose clairvoyantly for strangers who were miles away? Last: What about this reincarnation idea?

Our first stop was Virginia Beach, Virginia, the central office of the Association for Research and Enlightenment, an organization formed by friends of Edgar Cayce some time before his death. The primary purpose of the association is to integrate research in science, religion, and philosophy, with particular emphasis on demonstrating that these are all spokes in the same wheel.

There we met Edgar Cayce's son, Hugh Lynn, who, incidentally, inherited none of his father's psychic talents. Young Cayce, an official of the association, still maintains all the Cayce data, publishes a monthly bulletin as a means of keeping in touch with the members, lectures on various aspects of his father's work.

As I reflect upon my first meeting with Hugh Lynn Cayce I wonder why he didn't run me out of his house. My skepticism, together with blatant charges that some of the claims made for his father seemed to me to be excessive, would not have won any Dale Carnegie awards. But Hugh Lynn's pleasant manner never faltered; he had apparently grown accustomed to people like me popping into his office just to tell him that they suspected it was all nonsense.

Hugh Cayce cordially answered all our questions and then, at our request, led us to a sizable vault where all his father's readings were filed. Hazel and I studied the case records, follow-ups, testimonials, and other data, stopping once in a while to fire more questions at Hugh Lynn. Then we flew off to New York to get to the core of our Cayce inquiry—to put our three basic questions to those people on the list already compiled.

There was no doubt regarding the answer to our first question. There had been nothing fraudulent about Edgar Cayce. Quite to the contrary, he had been a pious, sincere Christian who personally held himself responsible for helping others to the very best of his ability.

My question as to whether Cayce might possibly have been a fraud was greeted with answers ranging from laughter at my ignorance to shocked indignation at my presumptuousness. One Manhattan manufacturer, livid with rage at such a question, stood up and ordered me out of his office. "How can you even use the word 'fraud' in the same sentence with the name of Edgar Cayce?" he roared. "That man saved my life; time and again he helped my friends, my family, and thousands of others. How dare you ask such a question?"

At a safe distance I hastily apologized, explaining that my purpose was not to make charges but only to check certain points. Somehow I managed to pacify the enraged tycoon, and then he proceeded to outline his own fascinating experiences with Cayce. It was easy to understand why some of his reports, although they were well documented and attested by several witnesses, had not found their way into any of the books about Cayce. They were simply too fantastic! The authors had reasoned, I suppose, that it would be hard enough for the readers to believe the less extravagant Cayce accomplishments.

At any rate, when we had finished quizzing all those who were on our list, the answer to question number one was patent: Cayce most assuredly was no fraud.

In getting the answer to our second question, which concerned Cayce's diagnostic ability, my real purpose was to learn whether his clairvoyance had been genuine. I still could not get into my head the conception of a man who could lie down in Virginia and describe accurately the detailed events of a scene taking place in New York at that very moment. There are many who take for granted the possibility of clairvoyance. To me, however, the whole idea had always—before my studies in extrasensory perception—been incredible. And I was still without conviction that reliable clairvoyance could be repeatedly demonstrated under test conditions.

Hazel and I started first with what the doctors had to say about Cayce. In this respect the Sherwood Eddy report,[1] was particularly enlightening. In addition we made our own inquiries; we were delighted to find that doctors who had known Cayce and had utilized his unique faculty were quite willing to discuss the matter at some length. These medics, corroborating the Eddy poll, agreed that Cayce's accuracy, *on patients whom he had never even seen,* ran between 80 and 100 per cent. One doctor insisted that he had never known Cayce to make a single mistake in diagnosis, and for many years he had turned to Cayce for assistance with his most difficult cases.

We didn't stop with the doctors. We wanted to get the story directly from some of the people who had been helped. But no matter where we went—from lawyers to authors to steelworkers —it was the same old story: Cayce worked wonders.

A lawyer recounted an example of the Cayce accuracy. A friend of the lawyer had broken his leg. Recognizing it as an opportunity to test Cayce, the attorney telegraphed for a reading on the friend, asking what should be done about the badly fractured right leg. After the reading he received a telegram from Cayce which

[1] Sherwood Eddy's book, *You Will Survive after Death,* includes reports by doctors who used Cayce readings for their patients over a number of years.

stated that nothing was wrong with the right leg. At first this appeared to be an error on Cayce's part, but the lawyer soon realized that he had referred to his friend's "right leg" when it was actually the left leg which had been fractured. When the error was corrected, a second reading followed, and this time the sleeping clairvoyant described the injury in detail, specifying the treatment that would be the most effective. "Remarkable!" concluded the attorney, and he shook his head in wonder while he reflected on the incident.

Once again we encountered cases which will probably never be printed in a book. But printable or not, all the cases added up to a clear-cut affirmation on the question of Cayce's clairvoyant ability.

When we came to our last question—"this reincarnation idea"— our job was somewhat more complicated. Aware that this question was somewhat nebulous, we reinforced it with further inquiry: "Did you have a Cayce life reading? If so, has it in your opinion proved sound? . . . Were any of these readings obviously ridiculous? . . . Did you by any chance find the life readings as convincing as the health readings? . . . What sort of evidence emerged from your reading or from any others about which you may have knowledge? . . . Is there someone else to whom you can refer us on this particular issue?"

Here was a matter on which clear-cut verdicts could hardly be expected. In contrast to the health readings, the accuracy of which could frequently be checked immediately, the Cayce readings involving previous lifetimes produced evidence of a different nature. If the reading, for instance, referred one to an existence a few hundred years previous, it was no easy matter to pin down the details for a positive verification. It was true, however, that historical records frequently yielded confirmation of obscure personalities and details as specified in the readings.

As one busy executive put it, "No, I don't have the ironclad, loophole-free brand evidence. All I know is that I found my own reading very impressive. Cayce told me things about my own character and personality, bringing in various other circumstances, that I have not only found to be accurate, but also very helpful. I believe the whole principle set forth by the Cayce readings, and I try to live my life accordingly."

We interviewed a very charming woman who told us that she

had asked for Cayce readings for each of her two sons shortly after their birth. Both readings were made more than twenty years ago, yet the detailed projections made by Cayce, which were based, he had indicated, on their former earth experiences, have proved singularly true, even to the extent of predicting skills, traits, hobbies, interests, and professions.

But to me the most surprising aspect of our survey was the unexpectedly large number of sound, sensible individuals who accepted reincarnation with complete respect. While I was bashfully hiding behind terms like "reincarnation stuff," the people we interviewed were guilty of no such pussyfooting. To the contrary, they spoke out forcefully, with neither hesitation nor embarrassment, pointing out that careful thought would almost inevitably lead one to admit the possibility of this other dimension. They began, in fact, to make me see the whole thing a little more clearly. One engineer, for instance, put it this way:

"We know for a fact, beyond any possibility of dispute, that the range of vision of the human eye is very limited. The ether is literally filled with substances which cannot be seen by the human eye. We know, for example, that the room in which you and I are now sitting is filled with radio waves and television waves; these waves are passing through walls and all the matter in the room, including our bodies. Yet to our eyes these waves are invisible. The same is true of X rays, ultra-violet rays, alpha rays, beta rays, gamma rays, cosmic rays, and atomic radiation. Nobody doubts the reality of these forces—an X ray can burn us up, and atomic radiation can destroy us. Nevertheless, the finite human eye is blind to all these energies; it has a very narrow band of vision.

"Is it not also possible, then, that the force which animates our bodies is a sort of *high-frequency electromagnetic charge* which is beyond the very narrow range of our eyesight? You can call this high-frequency charge by whatever name you prefer—psyche, mind, spirit, soul. But in any case the fact that it cannot be perceived by our weak little eyes should not be given undue weight.

"Edgar Cayce—and millions before him[2]—simply added another dimension. He said, in effect, that this high-frequency electromagnetic charge still remains intact upon death of the physical

[2] Approximately one *billion* people accept the principle of reincarnation.

96

body. The old heap of matter, the body, is worn out, and so it is discarded, buried. But the inner charge—the psyche, I usually call it—persists, and this is the substance which incorporates the consciousness, the memories, the impressions of a lifetime.

"Cayce maintained, furthermore, that this 'electrical' charge could later be infused into an embryo or body which is about to be born.

"Maybe it will help you to look at it this way: When my television set is working, the screen is alive with pictures and the speaker is noisy with sound. But the prime energy which is responsible for all this action is nothing more than invisible television waves. We can't see those high-frequency waves; nevertheless, we know that they are present.

"Now when my TV set wears out—when the tubes are shot, the transformer shorted—we still have no question that the high-frequency waves are yet very much in existence. And if a new TV chassis is moved in, those unseen television waves are once more transformed into a kind of energy which can be seen by our eyes and heard by our ears. That high-frequency force was there all the time, but it could not be registered by worn-out—dead—equipment.

"To carry the analogy a little further, let us consider an excellent TV set in perfect operating condition. Even though that set is perfect it will deliver neither picture nor sound—no, not even a commercial—unless those invisible high-frequency waves enter it."

I liked the engineer's analogy. This kind of language—rather than metaphysical terminology, with which I could never quite feel at ease—made it simpler for me to see the picture.

After all these interviews regarding the Cayce story I was eager to resume my company's business. One of my assignments on this eastern trip was concerned with checking the company's investment portfolio with a top-notch New York security analyst, who is sometimes referred to by his coterie as the Wizard of Wall Street. With this representative of the stock market, I was sure that I could shake loose from the subject of reincarnation and get my mind back to more mundane matters, such as the possibility of American Telephone and Telegraph's increasing its traditional nine-dollar dividend—and whether Montgomery Ward, with more than eighty-two dollars of net current assets for every share of stock, was a particularly attractive offering in view of its current market price of only sixty dollars per share.[3] Yes, this conference should leave Edgar Cayce and his theme far behind.

But no such luck.

I had been with the Wall Streeter only about half an hour when I spotted on his desk a book of short stories by Kipling. During a lull in our conversation, therefore, I dropped a comment merely intended to fill the void. I said what everyone already knew—that Kipling was a master of the short story. The security analyst, of course, agreed. He said, furthermore, that he had just been reading a particularly interesting Kipling story entitled, "The Finest Story in the World."

"It's about reincarnation," he said.

Here we go again, I thought.

From this point, naturally, it didn't take me long to summarize my own current interest in the topic, and I soon learned, to my amazement, that this financier's reading interests had not been confined to the *Wall Street Journal.* He had long been curious about the problem of rebirth, and he quickly recommended several reference sources, suggesting that I check them myself. One of the sources he cited was to be found in the third chapter of John in the New Testament, in which Nicodemus (a leader of the Pharisees, a Jewish sect) questioned Jesus about spiritual truths. The Wall Street analyst was able to quote the words of Jesus without even turning to his New Testament:

"Except a man be born again, he cannot see the kingdom of God."

Then again: "And no man hath ascended up to heaven, but he that came down from heaven, even the Son of man which is in heaven."

When I left the financial district I took the subway and headed for the New York Public Library. I wanted to check the Kipling story—the one about reincarnation. I had read a lot of Kipling but I could not remember any reference to reincarnation.

But sure enough, there it was: "The Finest Story in the World." And a fine tale it is, too.

While I was still in the library I thought it would be a good

[3] As of autumn 1952.

idea to check the card file to learn whether there might be any other interesting contributions on the same topic. I came across an interesting definition: *Reincarnation is a plan whereby imperishable conscious beings are supplied with physical bodies appropriate to their stage of growth.*

As I continued checking I was stunned at what I found.

The reincarnation researchers had really invaded the place! There were literally hundreds of references—books, poems, researches, anthologies. In almost every conceivable form of literature the scholars of rebirth were having their say. And one of the first statements I read—written by Professor T. H. Huxley—seemed to be pointed directly at me: "None but very hasty thinkers will reject it [reincarnation] on the grounds of inherent absurdity."

My check on the card file turned into an extended study which started at that moment and has never stopped. I was surprised again and again by encountering great names whom I would never have expected to be even remotely interested in the matter of reincarnation. Even the archcynic, Voltaire, had something to contribute: "It is not more surprising to be born twice than once; everything in nature is resurrection."

Another very earthy chap, none other than the brilliantly versatile Benjamin Franklin, made several allusions to the reincarnation principle and even suggested, at the age of only twenty-three, that his own epitaph should read as follows:

> The body of Benjamin Franklin,
> Printer,
> Like the cover of an Old Book
> Its contents worn out,
> And stripped of its lettering and gilding,
> Lies here, food for worms,
> But the work shall not be lost,
> For it will, as he believed, appear once more,
> In a new and more elegant edition,
> Revised and corrected
> by
> The Author

As to the poets, it appeared that they had enrolled almost *en masse* into the ranks of the believers. Included in the list were

Tennyson, Browning, Swinburne, Rossetti, Longfellow, Whitman, Donne, Goethe, Milton, Maeterlinck. John Masefield, England's Poet Laureate, wrote:

> I hold that when a person dies,
> His soul returns again to earth.
> Arrayed in some new flesh-disguise:
> Another mother gives him birth.
> With sturdier limbs and brighter brain,
> The old soul takes the road again.

Literary notables, philosophers, and thinkers had made their contributions too. Cicero, Virgil, Plato, Pythagoras, Caesar, Bruno, Oliver Wendell Holmes, Victor Hugo, Thomas Huxley, Sir Walter Scott, Ibsen, Spinoza—they were all there. Schopenhauer defined his position in no uncertain terms: "Were an Asiatic to ask me my definition of Europe, I should be forced to answer him: It is that part of the world which is haunted by the incredible delusion that man was created out of nothing, and that his present birth is his first entrance into life."[4]

There were, moreover, repeated references to the subject of reincarnation as found in the New Testament. At least one book was devoted exclusively to that theme.[5] The author wrote, "That reincarnation, not only in the case of men, but also as the law of life that applies to all men, is distinctly taught in the New Testament has been shown. To dispute this point is to deny that the authors of that collection of writings meant what they said in unmistakable language. To reject what they said is to impugn their teachings."

One of the most interesting books I found was a studious, thoughtful report called *The Problem of Rebirth* by the Honorable Ralph Shirley. The book is almost a full-scale consideration of the subject's many facets, and it presents a number of impressive cases.

One of the most extraordinary of these cases is that of little Alexandrina Samona, a doctor's daughter, who died when she was only five years old (March 15, 1910). The mother was particularly distressed over the loss of her daughter, and her grief was aggravated by the realization that in all probability she would have no more children. As a result of a miscarriage and a subsequent

[4] *Parerga and Paralipomena.*
[5] James M. Pryse, *Reincarnation in the New Testament* (1900).

operation (before Alexandrina's death) doctors seriously doubted that she could ever again become pregnant.

Three days after the child's death the mother had a dream. In this vivid dream Alexandrina came to her mother and made an effort to mitigate the woman's sorrow. "Mother, do not cry any more," implored the girl. "I have not left you for good. I shall come back again little, like this." Then Alexandrina (in the dream) made a motion with her hand which apparently intended to convey the idea that she would come back again as a baby.

This was not much solace for the skeptical mother. In the first place the doctors had already made it clear that the odds were against the possibility of her ever bearing another child. Furthermore, she had no respect for the principle of reincarnation, which would seem to be involved here. Her grief, therefore, continued unabated.

Nevertheless, the dreams persisted. Much to her surprise, moreover, she learned on April 10 that she was again pregnant. Still, though, Mrs. Samona was doubtful. In view of her poor health and the opinion of the medics, she felt she could not successfully give birth to another child. But Alexandrina (again in a dream) insisted, "Little Mother, do not cry any more, as I shall be born once more with you as my mother, and before Christmas I shall be with you again."

Then, at a later date, the girl added something which made the mother more skeptical than ever: "Mother, there is another one as well within you." The girl made it clear, in short, that when she was born this time she would be accompanied by a little sister. Naturally this seemed ridiculous to the ailing mother. She doubted that she could bear one child, let alone two. Furthermore, there had never been twins in the family.

On November 22, however, Mrs. Samona gave birth to twin daughters. One was altogether unlike the first Alexandrina; but the other, whom the parents again named Alexandrina, bore an astonishing resemblance, both physically and mentally, to the deceased child.

Alexandrina II was, like the first, left-handed, she had the same disposition, likes, dislikes, idiosyncrasies, and speech habits. And, like the first Alexandrina, she had hyperemia of the left eye, seborrhea of the right ear, and a slight facial asymmetry.

An even more impressive incident developed when the twins

were ten years old. A family trip to Monreale had been proposed, the mother adding, "When you go to Monreale, you will see such sights as you have never seen before."

"But, Mother, I know Monreale," replied Alexandrina. "I have seen it already." When Mrs. Samona protested that she couldn't have yet made this trip, the girl stubbornly persisted in her contention. "Oh yes, I went there. Do you not recollect that there was a great church with a very large statue of a man with his arms held open on the roof? And don't you remember that we went there with a lady who had horns, and that we met some little red priests in the town?"

Finally the mother remembered that some months before the death of the first Alexandrina the family had, indeed, made the trip, taking with them a lady suffering from disfiguring excrescences on her forehead. Just before entering the church at Monreale they had met with a group of Greek priests whose robes were decorated with red ornamentation.

The family recalled that all these details had made a particularly deep impression on Alexandrina I.

The Honorable Ralph Shirley then goes on to list a considerable number of attestations and corroborations by eminent persons and officials who were acquainted with the circumstances as they developed. He concludes: "It is obvious that the doctor took all pains to secure evidence on the question at issue which should satisfy, if not the most bigoted skeptic, at least the most intelligent scientific investigator."[6]

There were scores of provocative cases. One example, still without satisfactory explanation, was presented in a book by the late Professor Flournoy of the University of Geneva. More than half a century ago this psychologist called attention to a Swiss girl who, while in a trance, claimed to have lived before in the kingdom of Kanara during the fifteenth century. Furthermore, the girl, who had never finished grammar school or been outside the canton of Geneva, spoke perfect Hindu words and phrases and gave forth a plethora of detail about Kanara and a very obscure prince named Sivrouka. A scholar verified the proper usage of her Hindu; and a researcher in Calcutta confirmed the accuracy of her political and

[6] Attestations in corroboration were printed in *Filosofia della Scienza*, January 15, 1911.

historical knowledge, which seemed to be available only in a little-known book of the history of India which had been written in Sanskrit and was admittedly beyond the reach of the Swiss lass.

Still reeling under the word-beating delivered by the allies of the students of reincarnation, I returned to my round of New York business chores. But no matter where I went, the subject doggedly pursued me. A friend in the real estate business called my attention to a curiously interesting article which he had clipped while still in high school. It concerned an eleven-year-old Indian girl named Shanti Devi, who claimed, and demonstrated with an impressive degree of evidence, that she could remember myriad details from her "previous lifetime" on earth.[7]

When she was only four years old the girl began to make intermittent references to her former existence as the wife of Kedar Nath Chaubey, in Muttra, another city of India. By the time she was eleven, her numerous offhand remarks, including the comment that she had died only twelve years ago after giving birth to her second child (just one year before her entry into this lifetime), finally assumed such proportions that a lawyer, a publisher, and a teacher took interest in the case. This group, after learning that her former "husband" was still alive, arranged a series of tests.

Shanti Devi quickly proved that she could recognize and give the correct addresses of all principals involved in her "prior incarnation," and that, although she had never in this lifetime been in the house in Muttra, she could describe in detail everything there with which a woman who lived there twelve years ago would have been familiar. Then she gave her "husband" a description of their life together that none but the dead wife could have known—a description so intimate that it brought the husband to tears. "It was as though that wife, now twelve years dead, stood again beside him."

But the *coup de grâce* was delivered when the girl claimed that she had hidden some money in a corner of an underground room at the old house in Muttra. After she was taken to the house, she pointed to the location, then dug up the box. Finding no money inside, she was disappointed, because she insisted that she

---

[7] The Shanti Devi case is also reported in *The Problem of Rebirth*, by the Honorable Ralph Shirley.

had left some there. At this point the "husband" admitted that he had taken the money from the box after the wife's death!

Just before taking off again for Pueblo I stopped at a bookstore to pick up something to read on the return plane trip. I reached for a book by a widely known English psychiatrist.[8] Scanning the table of contents, I stopped at Chapter XVI. The chapter's title: "Reincarnation Outflanks Freud."

Turning quickly to this part of the book, I observed that the doctor had for many years been conducting age-regression experiments with hundreds of subjects. But instead of stopping when the subject's memory reached back to infancy or birth, *the doctor had kept right on going*, probing still farther back, investigating the mystery of memories before birth.

Such a thought had never even occurred to me before. I had conducted age-regression experiments with dozens of subjects, but naturally I had always stopped when the subject returned to infancy. That was the end of the line, I had figured. But now I was learning that some hypnotists don't stop there; they just keep right on going!

Well, I was a hypnotist. I had some excellent subjects who were capable of age regression under hypnosis. What was I waiting for?

There and then I decided to find out about this pre-birth aspect of the memory for myself.

CHAPTER 10

Returning to Colorado, I realized, after one quick glance at my desk, that it would probably be several weeks before I could find time to launch any new experiments in hypnosis. The desk was stacked high with what appeared to be endless letters, reports, inquiries, complaints, advertising proofs, salesmen's cards, and catalogues.

There was an unusually large batch of headaches. Our shipping manager, for instance, had shipped a truckload of corral wire to

[8] Dr. Sir Alexander Cannon, author of *Power Within* (New York: Dutton, 1953).

Trenton, New Jersey, instead of Trenton, Nebraska. . . . A packing-house superintendent in the East wrote that the beef hoists we shipped him would lift cows into the air all right; but we had overlooked, he insisted, installing reversing devices so that he could get the animals back down again. . . . A farmer in Muleshoe, Texas, angrily called our attention to the fact that his pump, which had been guaranteed to deliver forty thousand gallons per hour, would not produce "enough water to irrigate a postage stamp."

And during my absence there had been, as usual, a parade of salesmen through the office, urging that we add their products to our line. There were, now that uranium mining was booming in Colorado, a dozen different offers from manufacturers of Geiger counters and other radioactivity-detection instruments. An inventor wanted backing for his electric cattle-branding iron and for his automatic farm gate that would open upon the approach of an automobile and then close mechanically after the vehicle had passed through.

But somehow, little by little, the mountain on my desk leveled out and the headaches dwindled to no more than a daily dose. At last I could carry out my plans for hypnotic experiments with "memories before birth."

First I would have to select a subject, and for this purpose I had decided that I should consider only those who were capable of a somnambulistic trance—that is, those subject to complete amnesia during the trance. So I gave some thought as to the best subjects I had encountered during the past year. Immediately Milton Colin came to mind; he was twenty-two years old, intelligent, pleasant—and he could fall into a deep trance within the first few minutes of hypnosis.

But he had just gone off to the Navy.

Then there was my wife. But Hazel already knew too much about the whole business. She had helped me chase down the Cayce story, had read many of the same books as I, and would undoubtedly know in advance the purpose of the experiment. No, she was not the likely candidate.

Finally I remembered Ruth Simmons. I scarcely knew Ruth and her husband, Rex, but I recalled how quickly and deeply she had become entranced during two earlier demonstrations—long before I knew anything about the possibility of memories before birth. Furthermore, she had remembered absolutely nothing afterward that had taken place during the trance; she was, in short, a somnambulistic subject. It was doubtful, moreover, that she knew anything about reincarnation, and she would certainly know nothing of my recent research. Ruth Simmons, I decided, was the logical subject.

But getting the Simmonses to come to the house was no easy job. In the first place I was forced to compete with bridge games, cocktail parties, and club dances, which had become standard routine in their lives. Then, too, Rex, who knew practically nothing about hypnosis and wasn't eager to start learning, took no delight in the prospect of having his wife put into a deep trance; and I had told him frankly, in extending the invitation, that I was going to hypnotize Ruth.

Finally, however, sandwiched between a Thanksgiving formal dance and a cocktail party, a date was set: November 29.

When the Simmonses arrived—and after the preliminaries outlined in the first chapter—I set about the work of the evening. Into the microphone of the tape recorder I spoke the following introduction:

This is Saturday, November 29, 1952. The time is 10:35 P.M. It's a clear, very cold night. Present are Mr. and Mrs. Rex Simmons, and Mr. and Mrs. Morey Bernstein. The hypnotist is Morey Bernstein and the subject is Mrs. Rex Simmons, age twenty-nine. I have hypnotized this subject twice previously within the last six months, and during one session I took her back on an age regression to the age of one.

Ruth was made comfortable in a reclining position on the couch. Then I lighted a candle and turned off all the lights with the exception of one lamp.

I asked Ruth to take seven very deep breaths, to inhale as deeply as possible, and to empty her lungs as completely as possible with each exhalation. As soon as she had finished with the deep breathing, I held the lighted candle at about a 45-degree angle above and in front of her head and not more than eighteen inches from her eyes.

I explained that while she was staring at the candle flame I would soon begin to count. When I began with the count of "One," I told her, I wanted her to close her eyes and imagine that she could see the candle flame in her "mind's eye." Then when I said, "Number two," she should, I suggested, open her eyes and once more look into the candle flame. And while she was looking at the flame, I added, I would eventually toll the count of three, at which signal she was to again close her eyes and once more pick up the image of the flame in her mind.

A recording of the session at this point would have read thus: "Keep your eyes on the candle flame. You will notice, as you look at the flame, that one portion of the flame is especially bright, a sort of glowing central heart of the flame. Focus your attention on that bright, glowing core of the flame, and in a few moments I shall begin to count.

"When I count 'One,' you will close your eyes but you will continue to see the candle flame in your imagination. Even in your imagination you will focus upon the brightest portion of the flame. And while I talk to you, you will become sleepier and sleepier, because that flame is becoming for you a symbol of sleep. The flame means sleep; the flame means sleep. Your subconscious, even now, is beginning to associate the image of the flame with the process of sleep. In your subconscious the flame is becoming a signal for sleep, deep sleep. Whether you actually look into the flame or merely see the flame in your mind's eye, you will grow sleepy—your limbs will become heavy, your eyelids will get heavier and heavier, and you will want to drift off into a pleasant sleep. The flame means sleep. Flame and sleep. Flame and sleep.

"Then when I reach the count of two, you will again open your eyes and look directly at the flame of the candle. But even as you do you will notice that the very glance at the actual flame makes you even sleepier; it will impress even more deeply into the subconscious that the flame means sleep, that the flame is a symbol of sleep, that the flame is a signal for you to grow sleepy and to drift into a pleasant, relaxing sleep.

"And so I will reach the count of three, at which time you will again close your eyes and pick up the image of the flame in your mind's eye. By this time you will be very, very sleepy. You will keep your eyes closed and drift into a deep, pleasant, relaxing sleep as I continue to talk to you."

Then I asked my subject, who was already drowsy, whether she clearly understood my instructions. In a sleepy voice she indicated that she understood.

So I started the counting, monotonously repeating after each count all the suggestions designed to set up the association between "flame and sleep." (I am not at all convinced that monotonous repetition is essential to trance induction, but it is the stock in trade of most hypnotists, and I didn't care to deviate on this occasion.) Finally, after the count of three, Ruth's head fell to one side on the pillow; her breathing was deep and regular.

At this point I employed a technique for deepening the trance. After that came the ordinary age regression. The tape recorder plays it back like this:

TAPE I

". . . Deep asleep . . . deeper and deeper asleep . . . deeper and deeper asleep. Now we are going to turn back. We are going to turn back through time and space, just like turning back in the pages of a book. And when I next talk to you . . . when I next talk to you . . . when I next talk to you, you will be seven years old, and you will be able to answer my questions. When I talk to you next, you will be seven years old, and you can answer my questions. Now. Now, you are seven years old. Do you go to school?
Yes.
What school do you go to?[1]
Adelphi Academy.
All right. Who sits in front of you?
Uh . . . Jacqueline.
And who sits behind you?
Verna Mae.
Verna Mae what?
Booth.
Do you know any boys in the class?
Uh-huh.
What is the name of one?
Donald.
Donald what?
Barker.
And what is your favorite study? What is your favorite subject?
Uh . . . reading. Reading.

[1] Readers who have heard the phonograph record made from the original tape should be reminded that the record was necessarily edited to keep within time limitations (and to eliminate proper names and identifying references).

Can you read well? Are you a good reader?

Fair.

All right.

Fair.

All right. Now rest and relax. We're going to turn even farther back through space and time. We're going back now to the time when you were five years old. We're going back to the time when you were five years old. When I talk to you again, you will be just five years old. Now, now you are five years old and you can answer my questions.

Do you go to school?

Uh-huh . . . yes.

What is the name of the school?

Adelphi Academy.

In what town do you live?

Brooklyn.

What grade are you in?

Kinder . . . garten.

All right. Who sits in front of you?

No one.

Why is that?

Oh . . . we sit at long tables. . . . Nobody sits in front of me.

Who sits on your left?

Uh . . . Violet.

Violet who?

Crosby.

And who sits on your right?

David.

David. David who?

Daniels.

All right. What is your favorite game?

Ummm . . . ummmmmmm . . . hopscotch.

Who is your best friend?

Jacqueline.

All right. What is your favorite toy?

Bubbles.

All right.

Doll. Doll.

Oh, I see. Bubbles is a doll?

Uh-huh.

What is your favorite dress? Do you have any dress that you like better than the others?

Uh-*huh!*

Which one is it?

It's a black velvet one . . . it has little tiny bows on the pockets . . . black velvet dress and big pockets. . . . I can put my hands in, with bows on it.

All right. All right. Now rest and relax because you are going still farther back in space and time. When I talk to you again, you will be three years old, you will be three years old. Now, now you are three years old. Now, do you go to school?

No.

You do not go to school?

Uh-uh.

What is your favorite toy?

Ummmm . . . dog.

Toy dog or a real dog?

Real one.

What is its name?

Buster.

All right. Do you have any dolls?

One little colored doll.

Do you know what it looks like?

Uh-huh.

Tell me what it looks like.

It's colored like a colored baby . . . has black hair painted on its head . . . and it has a green and white polka-dot dress. No shoes. It has a diaper . . . it's dirty . . . didn't wash it, didn't wash the diaper, nobody washed it. . . .

That's very good.

Dirty.

Do you have any playmates?

Just my sister.

What is your sister's name?

Helen. . . . Helen.

All right. Don't you have any other playmates?

No.

Isn't there a little boy or girl who lives next door?

No.

What church do you go to?

No church.

All right. Now I am going to talk to you again in a few moments. The next time I talk to you, the next time I talk to you, you will be only one year old. Now, now you are one year old and you can answer my questions.

Now, how old are you?

One.
Do you have any toys?
Yes . . . some blocks and a . . . uh . . . a cotton dolly and I tore her dress and sucked on her . . . got her all dry and funny-looking.
What is her name?
Jus' Baby.
What do you say when you want a drink of water?
Wa . . . wa.
What do you say when you want a glass of milk?
Uh . . . can't say that.
Rest and relax. Now I will not ask you any more questions for a while. But I want you to think about what I am saying. I want you to think about the things I am saying. You are going back . . . back . . . back, 'way back into time and space. Now, for instance, you are going to be six years old. Think about the time you were six years old. Think about the time when you were six years old. And now slip on farther back to when you were five years old. Think about that. See yourself. See some scene. See some scene in which you were five years old. You don't have to tell me about it, just think about it, and see it in your mind. Now go on back farther, four years old. See yourself, see something that took place when you were four years old. Now go on back farther, still farther. Three years old, see yourself when you were three years old. And now back still farther. Two years old, two years old, two years old. And now still farther back. One year old, one year old. See yourself when you were one year old. See some scene. Watch yourself. Be looking at yourself when you were one year old. Now go on even farther back. Oddly enough, you can go even farther back.

I want you to keep on going back and back and back in your mind. And, surprising as it may seem, strange as it may seem, you will find that there are other scenes in your memory. There are other scenes from faraway lands and distant places in your memory. I will talk to you again. I will talk to you again in a little while. I will talk to you again in a little while. Meanwhile your mind will be going back, back, back, and back until it picks up a scene, until, oddly enough, you find yourself in some other scene, in some other place, in some other time, and when I talk to you again you will tell me about it. You will be able to talk to me about it and answer my questions. And now just rest and relax while these scenes come into your mind. . . .

Now you're going to tell me, now you're going to tell me what scenes came into your mind. What did you see? What did you see?

. . . Uh . . . scratched the paint off all my bed. Jus' painted it, 'n' made it pretty. It was a metal bed, and I scratched the paint off of it. Dug my nails on every post and just ruined it. Was jus' terrible.

Why did you do that?

Don't know. I was just mad. Got an awful spanking.

What is your name?

. . . Uh . . . Friday.

Your name is what?

Friday.

> [I was under the impression that she had said "Friday."
> The others in the room, as they later told me, also thought
> she said "Friday." But we were soon to learn otherwise.]

Don't you have any other name?

Uh . . . Friday Murphy.

And where do you live?

. . . I live in Cork . . . Cork.

Is that where you live?

Uh-huh.

And what is the name of your mother?

Kathleen.

And what is the name of your father?

Duncan . . . Duncan . . . Murphy.

How old are you?

Uh . . . four . . . four years old.

And you scratched the paint off your metal bed?

Yes . . . scratched the paint off.

All right. Now see if you can see yourself a little older. See if you can see yourself when you're five, or six, or seven, or see yourself when you're an older girl. Are you a girl or are you a boy?

> [Since I was of the opinion that the name she had given
> sounded like Friday, I suddenly reflected that this Friday
> Murphy person might have been a male.]

A girl.

All right. Do you see yourself when you are older?

Yes, I do.

What are you doing now?

Playing . . . playing house . . . playing with my brother.

What is your brother's name?

Duncan.
What is your father's name?
Duncan.
I see. How old are you when you're playing house with your brother?
Eight.
What kind of a house do you live in?
Uh . . . it's a nice house . . . it's a wood house . . . white . . . has . . . has two floors . . . has . . . I have a room upstairs . . . go up the stairs and turn to the left. It's very nice.
What is the name of the country in which you live?
It's Ireland.
I see. Do you have any other brothers or sisters?
Have one brother that died.
What did he die from?
He was sick. Had some kind of black something . . . black something. I don't know.
How old were you when he died?
I was four . . . just four. He was just a baby.
I see. Do you have any sisters?
No.
Do you know how old your brother was when he died?
No. Just a . . . not one . . . yet. Don't know.
Now that you are eight years old, do you know what year it is?
No.
You don't know what year it is?
Eighteen something. Eighteen-oh . . . 1806.
Eighteen hundred and six?
Uh-huh.
What do you have for breakfast? What do you eat for breakfast?
Oh . . . uh . . . eat . . . uh . . . milk . . . milk. . . .
Anything else?
Muffins.
Muffins?
Muffins. Eat muffins and jam, 'n' milk and fruit. Muffins mostly.
Where does your father work? Where does your father work?
He's a barrister . . . downtown . . . a barrister . . . in the town and the village.
What town?
In Cork . . . in Cork.

[The word "barrister" stunned all of us. Knowing Ruth Simmons, we were struck by the incongruity of this word issuing from her.]

All right. You say he goes downtown and what?

He's a barrister. He's a smart man.

What games do you play?

Play hide-and-seek. Look, and Duncan finds me.

Duncan finds you.

Uh-huh. Can't find Duncan. He knows better places than me to hide.

Duncan is older than you, isn't he?

Yes.

How much older?

He's two years older than me.

Now tell me about your father. Is he a tall man or a short man?

He's tall.

What color hair?

Sort of reddish, like mine.

Your hair is red?

Uh-huh. It's real red.

[Ruth's hair decidedly is not red. It's brown.]

And what is your name?

Friday.

Why did they name you Friday?

Bridey . . . Bridey.

Oh, I see, Bridey. Why did they name you that?

Named me after my grandmother, Bridget . . . 'n' I'm Bridey.

I see. All right, now tell me about your mother. Is she a big woman or a little woman?

Just medium . . . she is.

What color hair?

Black.

Tall or short?

She's just medium.

And what is her name?

Kathleen.

Uh-huh. What are the names of any of your neighbors?

Don't have any neighbors . . . live outside the village. . . .

All right. Now, see if you can see yourself when you're a little older. Get older than eight. See if you can see yourself growing up. See if you can see yourself when you were about fifteen years old. . . . Can you do that?

Uh-huh.

Do you have a job about the time you are fifteen years old? Are you working anyplace?

No.

Do you stay at home?

Well, I go to Mrs. . . . Mrs. . . . Mrs. . . . uh . . . Strayne's Day School, and I stay away from home all week.

[Actually this name sounded like Mrs. *Drain*. During a later tape, however, we were informed of the spelling above: *Strayne*.]

Oh, you're going to school.

Uh-huh.

What are you studying?

Oh, to be a lady . . . just *house* things . . . and *proper* things.

I see. Do you ever get married?

Yes.

What is the name of the man you marry?

Marry . . . Brian.

Who?

Brian.

Is that his first name or last name?

First name.

What is his last name?

MacCarthy.

[The spelling of both "Brian" and "MacCarthy" was derived from a later tape.]

All right. What does he do?

His father is a barrister too, and he goes to school. And we get married. He goes to school at Belfast.

Uh-huh. And is the marriage a happy one?

Yes.

You don't have any fights?

Oh, some. Mostly just . . . little fights.

But you like Brian?

Oh yes.

Do you have any children?

No.

You never have any children?

No. No children.

I see. Do you always live in Cork?

No . . . go to Belfast.

[At this stage the Irish brogue was growing more pronounced. The words "go to Belfast" were rushed together and accented in a manner that seemed fresh from Erin.]
Go to Belfast?
Uh-huh. Brian goes to school in Belfast. His parents live in Cork, but his grandmother lives in Belfast, and we live in a cottage in the back of her house while he goes to school.
Then he always provides well for you?
Yes.
But you have no children?
No children.
Do you live in Belfast?
Yes.
Do you like Belfast as well as Cork?
No.
Do you have any friends in Belfast?
Yes.
What are their names?
Mary Catherine and her husband . . . his name is Kevin. Have children, and we love to go over there.
What church do you go to?
I go to St. Theresa's.
St. Theresa's.
Uh-huh . . . in Belfast.
What is the name of the priest? What is the name of the father?
Father John. Father John.
Do you know your catechism?
Oh . . . oh . . . married a Catholic. . . . Don't know as I should. Don't believe . . .
Oh, weren't you a Catholic when you were little?
No.
What were you when you were little?
I was a Protestant.
What kind of a Protestant?
Went to a little church. It was a . . . just a . . . non-sectarian sort of thing.
All right. What are some Irish words? What are some Irish words?
Oh . . . oh . . . you want to know. Oh, there's a colleen 'n' a . . . oh . . . I try to think of the word for the ghost. . . . What do you call a ghost? Oh, I think . . . *mother socks* . . . oh. There's a . . . oh . . . a *brate!*

[After "colleen"—and before "brate"—she spoke another word. But the tape recorder does not play back this one word clearly enough to transcribe. The "mother socks," judging from the manner in which she used it, would appear to be a sort of oath which she muttered in exasperation while trying to think of more words.]
What's that word?
Brate.
What does that mean?
Aw, that's a . . . little cup . . . that you drink out of, 'n' you wish on it. Very . . . very Irish, you know. Just something we think about all the time . . . wish on it. Drink and just wish on a brate. . . . Oh, I can't think.
Are there any prayers . . . Irish prayers . . . with Irish words?
We always say the prayers from the Bible just . . . at our house.
Can you say any of them now, say any one prayer now?
Say the prayer we say before our meal:

> Bless this house in all the weather.
> Keep it gay in springy heather.
> Bless the children, bless the food.
> Keep us happy, bright and good.

That's before we eat.
All right. Now is there anything else that you can tell us about Irish customs, customs or traditions in Ireland, that you would like to tell us about? Have you ever been to a wake?
Oh yes, been to the wake before the funeral. Oh, it was . . . it was with Brian, 'n' his uncle 'n' . . . they all stay up . . . and they're all very unhappy. It's always the day before, you see. It's always the day before they take 'em to *ditch* them . . . in the grounds, and they all sit around and weep and drink tea, and everybody's unhappy. Then the next day they *ditch* them.
What do you mean, ditch them?
Puts 'em in the ground! . . . for good.
[Here again the brogue was especially distinct.]
I see. Are there any other Irish customs or traditions that you can tell us about?
Oh . . . dance when you're married.
What do they call it?
Oh, it's just an Irish jig thing; you dance and they put money in your pockets . . . to buy . . . it's a party and everybody gives

their money and that way you have a gift, you see. It's just people that wouldn't send you other gifts.

All right. Is there anything else at all that you'd like to tell us about Ireland?

It's beautiful.

All right. Rest and relax. Rest and relax. Clear your mind completely. Go even farther back. Go back again to that time when you were a little girl in Ireland, and go right on back, past that, beyond that, go on back, back, back, even beyond that. You're going back into another lifetime before the one in Ireland. Going back, back, still farther back, still farther back, still farther back, and oddly enough, strangely enough, some scene will come into your mind. When I talk to you next, you'll remember a scene in which you were included. Although you may not look the same, you'll know that it will be you, and you'll be able to tell me all about it. Now you think for a few moments, and you'll be surprised that a scene will just pop into your head. Now, I'll talk to you again in a little while.

[I then gave her about three or four minutes to think. I don't know whether she really needed this intermission. But I did. All this time I had been holding the small microphone, occasionally transferring it from one hand to another, near Ruth's lips. Besides, the impact of the whole thing was beginning to reach me.]

Now there is some scene that you remember. There is some scene that you remember. Tell me about it. Tell me about it.

Dying . . . just a little baby.

Dying?

Uh-huh.

Who is dying?

Me.

Where are you? Do you have any idea?

It's in a house, and my head . . . sickness.

What country, do you know?

It's . . . America.

Do you know your name?

No.

Do you know how old you are?

Just a baby . . . a little baby.

What is your mother's name?

Uh . . . Vera.

What is your father's name?

John.

What is the last name?

Jamieson.

[I have no idea as to the correct spelling; this is just a guess.]

What state do you live in?

. . . New Amsterdam.

Do you happen to know what year it is?

No.

But you know you're in America?

Yes.

How do you know?

It was . . . knew I was.

And did you die?

Yes.

All right. Now clear your mind. Clear your mind and forget about that. That will not bother you, and you'll go still farther back. You will go still farther back, back, back, back, back, and you will see another scene. And as soon as you see another scene, as soon as you see another scene, you can tell me about it.

[No answer.]

Do you see another scene?

No . . . no.

Nothing comes into your head?

No.

All right, let's go back to the time you were in Ireland. Do you see yourself again in Ireland and Cork?

Yes.

All right, what is your name?

Bridey.

What is your last name?

Murphy.

What is the name of the man you married?

Brian.

Brian what?

MacCarthy.

[She was practically spitting out these answers, as though she was a little annoyed at my repeating these old questions.]

All right. Now see yourself in that lifetime, and see yourself up to the time of your death. And tell me, tell me as an observer so that it won't disturb you, tell me how you died.

Fell down . . . fell down on the stairs, and . . . seems I broke some bones in my hip too, and I was a terrible burden.

Were you old?

Sixty-six.

[The first part of the above answer she gave quickly, as though she was well aware that she had died in her sixties. But the "six" came more slowly, indicating that there was a little more difficulty in remembering her exact age.]

How did you finally die?

Oh, just sort of . . . withered away.

You didn't want to live?

No . . . I was such a burden. Had to be carried about.

Was Brian still alive?

Yes . . . he was there.

Did he take good care of you?

Yes. He was so tired all the time, though.

He was?

Yes.

In what city were you living when you died?

Belfast.

Do you remember the day you died?

Uh-huh. 'Twas on a Sunday.

And you remember it?

Yes, Brian was to church, and it upset him terribly that he wasn't there. He left me, deserted me. But he didn't think I was going that fast. A lady came to stay with me so he could go to church . . . and I died.

[This answer brought about a wholly unexpected turn in the questioning. It had never even occurred to me that I might explore her memories as to what took place after her death. But now at least some probing in that direction was necessitated, I felt, by the comment that Bridey had just made.

She had said, "Brian was to church, and it upset him terribly that he wasn't there." This statement puzzled me. If Brian had not been present at the scene of her death— if he had been in church—then how could Bridey have known that he was "upset" to learn that she had died during his absence?

There was only one possibility. If Bridey had somehow been conscious of what took place after her death, then her comment would be understandable. I decided, therefore, to pursue this point.]

How old were you?

I was sixty-six.
Were you in pain when you died?
No, just tired.
I see, just tired. You wanted to die?
Yes.
Did you believe that you would live after death?
Yes.
Can you tell us what happened after your death? Can you tell us what happened after you died?
I didn't do . . . like Father John said. I didn't go to purgatory!
[In looking back this answer seems particularly meaningful. Instead of replying with a listing of her activities—or any sort of statement about what she did—Bridey instantly charged back with an emotional outburst, declaring what she did *not* do!

It was as though, contend several of those who listened to the tape recording, Bridey had been particularly concerned with this purgatory problem. It is possible, the listeners speculate, that she had been developing considerable apprehension over the purgatory question as she lay on her deathbed. Hence the reaction to her pent-up anxiety, "I didn't do like Father John said. I didn't go to purgatory!"][9]
Where did you go?
I stayed right in that house . . . until John died.
And could you see John all that time?
Uh-huh.
Was Father John dead too?
Oh, he died. . . . I saw him. I saw him when he died.
And then you talked to him?
Yes.
I see. Well, when Brian died did he join you?
No. . . .
He didn't?

[9] For readers, whether of the Catholic Faith or not, the following quotation (taken from the book, *Purgatory*, by Reverend F. X. Schouppe, S.J., Chapter Three, page five) may help to clarify the theological definition of the word purgatory: "The word *Purgatory* is sometimes taken to mean a place, sometimes an intermediate state between hell and heaven. It is, properly speaking, *the condition of souls* which, at the moment of death, are in the state of grace, but which have not completely expiated their faults, nor attained the degree of purity necessary to enjoy the vision of God."

No. Didn't see . . . watched him . . . lots of times until Father John died, then I left the house.

Oh, I see. When Father John died, you left the house?

Yes.

But you stayed in the house until Father John died?

Yes, he came to visit Brian, and I stayed.

All right. When you left the house, where did you go?

. . . Uh . . . I went . . . home to Cork . . . and I . . . saw my . . . brother.

Which brother?

Duncan. And he was still alive! . . . And *so* old!

[Indeed, Duncan would have been old, probably in his seventies. And since Bridey likely had not seen him for many years—she had been living in Belfast—it is logical that her first reaction would have been one of surprise over the change which had taken place in Duncan.]

He was still alive?

Yes.

And you stayed in the house there?

Yes, I stayed in Duncan's house.

Did you ever let Duncan know that you were there?

No, he wouldn't . . . he wouldn't answer me.

How did you try to speak to him?

I would . . . I would stay there by the bed and talk, and he would never see me.

He would never see you. Well, did he finally die?

Yes, he died.

And then did he join you?

No. There were lots of people there I didn't know.

Lots of people you didn't know?

Yes, but I didn't see everybody I knew. Father John I saw! . . . 'n' I saw my little brother that died too.

[I had almost forgotten about Bridey's little brother, who had died when he was "just a baby."]

Oh, you saw him?

Yes.

Did he talk to you?

Yes, he talked to me, but he didn't know, I had to tell him I knew who he was.

[Presumably the baby would not have recognized this sixty-six-year-old woman; she had to tell him who she was. On the other hand, Bridey recognized him at once; apparently he still looked the same.]

Oh, he didn't know?

No.

Then did he recognize you?

Yes, he said he just remembered me, some things about me, but he didn't remember anything about my mother or the house or . . . He remembered some things about Duncan too: Duncan would push him off the little cradle side and tip it over, and he would fall. And he remembered some things.

What was it like? Did you like where you were?

Yes.

Was it better than your life on earth?

No.

It wasn't?

No, it wasn't full enough. It wasn't . . . just . . . couldn't do all the things . . . couldn't accomplish anything and . . . couldn't talk to anybody very long. They'd go away . . . didn't stay very long.

[Here Bridey's voice became plaintive, almost pained. It is at this point that numerous listeners—to the tape recording—have suggested that Bridey might well have been in purgatory, after all, without even having realized it.]

Did you ever have any pain?

No.

No pain. I see. Did you ever have to eat anything?

No.

You never had to eat?

No, never ate, never sleep, never sleep . . . never get tired there.

Well, tell me how you finally left that world.

Oh . . . I . . . left there and I was . . . born . . . and I lived in America again. I was born in Iowa . . . I . . .

In Iowa?

Yes . . . I was . . .

[Here she was referring to her birth in 1923, in Iowa.]

Do you remember how you became born again, do you remember how it was possible for you to be born again? Tell us about that.

I was . . . oh, I was just . . . I don't know how it happens, but I just remember that suddenly I wasn't . . . just in a . . . just a state . . . then I was a baby.

Did anybody select the body that you inhabited? Did anybody select the body?

I don't know about that.

How did you know what body, how did you know what country to go to, how did you know all those things? Who took care of all those details?

Don't know. . . . It just seems like it just happens . . . and you just don't remember and . . . you remember most things and then . . . all of a sudden . . . I remember just being a baby again.

> [Bridey was never able to relate the details of the rebirth process—And I have had other interesting subjects since Bridey, but none have thrown any light on this one issue. Other investigators, though, claim somewhat better results.]

Then you remember that you died when you were little. . . . No . . . not when I was in Iowa.

> [This was simply an effort purposely to trip the subject, something I have resorted to at various points throughout the series of sessions. It never worked; she always held her ground.]

Not when you were in Iowa?

No.

What did you do then?

I lived.

You did? And what did you do there?

Oh . . . I just lived there for one year.

What was your name?

Ruth.

Ruth what?

Ruth Mills [maiden name].

I see. I see. Then you must have lived in the spirit world a long time before that.

Um . . . oh . . . I don't know.

In all that time you were never able to talk to anyone on earth?

No. Tried to.

Well, could any of the people in that spirit world, could any of the people in that spirit world talk to any of the people on the earth?

Don't know.

You never saw it happen?

No. . . . Tried. Lots of people wanted to talk to people, but they just wouldn't [listen].

I see. Now, tell me about this time you were a baby in New Amsterdam.

Yes.

That was before this lifetime, wasn't it?

Yes.

Was it after the lifetime in Ireland or before the lifetime in Ireland?

It was *before*.

It was before the lifetime in Ireland.

Yes.

Then before you were Ruth Mills you were in Ireland. Is that right?

Yes.

You lived in Ireland, and you married Brian MacCarthy. You died when you were sixty-six years old, and then you spent a long time in the spirit world, and then you were born in America as Ruth Mills. Is that correct?

Yes. That's right.

Let's talk again about the time you were living in Ireland. Let's talk again about the time you were living in Ireland and you got sick. You hurt yourself; you fell down and hurt yourself, and you finally died when you were sixty-six years old. You remember that, don't you?

[By now it should become painfully clear that I had no organized pattern for this first session. I skipped about from one phase of her history to another, abandoning one line of pursuit when I would temporarily run out of questions, and then returning again after I thought of more questions.]

Yes.

All right. I want you to tell me again what happened after your death. What happened after your death? Where did you go?

I stayed at my house . . . stayed there with Brian.

Could you watch them bury you? Could you watch them bury your body?

Yes, I watched them ditch my body.

You did?

Yes. They ditched it.

They ditched it? Did they have a wake for you?

No, because I'd told Brian I didn't want anybody to be unhappy and . . . mourn . . . for me.

I see.

I was a burden and . . . I would be happy to just go to sleep.
And you watched them ditch you?
Yes. I did.
Did you try to tell anybody that you were watching them?
No, I was tired.
You were still tired?
Yes.
I didn't know that you had feelings in that life.
Not for long.
Not for long?
No.
Then there was no pain?
No pain.
And you didn't have to eat?
No.
And you didn't sleep?
No. No sleep.
How did you spend all of your time?
Oh . . . just . . . watching. . . .
Did it seem like it was a long time, or did time mean anything?
No . . . doesn't mean anything.
You didn't pay any attention to time?
No . . . doesn't mean anything.
You didn't pay any attention to time?
No . . . no night or no day . . . like you had it . . . Brian . . .
What did you say?
No night and day like Brian had it.
Did Brian get married again?
No. He *wouldn't*.

[An interesting way of stating it. She did not answer that
Brian *didn't* marry again; she flatly replied that he
wouldn't—the sort of answer one might expect from a wife
who was sure of her husband's nature.]

Do you remember when he died?
No. I would remember, but I went away when Father John
died.
You went away when Father John died?
Yes. I stayed there until Father John died, then I went home.
Well, did you join Father John then?
Oh, I saw Father John for a while, and I talked to him.
Where was he?
He was there in the house. He used to come and visit.

In Cork?

No . . . with Brian, and I would see him . . . and he would come back there. He liked to visit with us, and he always came back.

Well now, who died first, you or Father John?

I did.

And then some time later he died? And then you immediately joined him? Is that right?

Yes, he came to the house . . . he came where he wanted to come.

But Brian didn't know that Father John and you were there, is that right?

Yes.

And you couldn't seem to tell him that?

No, I couldn't. [Almost a tense whisper.] He wouldn't listen.

Well, did the people who died go to different places?

Yes . . . there were . . . no it's just one place, but . . . it's spread out.

How did you talk to each other?

Just like . . . we always did.

I see. The others could hear you?

Yes, they could hear me.

But the people on earth, like Brian, could not possibly hear you?

They won't listen!

They wouldn't listen? Do you think that if they would have tried to listen they could have heard you?

Yes, I think so.

But you're not sure?

No. I just wanted them to . . . so bad.

Well, didn't anybody in this spirit world ever teach you anything? Didn't you ever go to school, or didn't anybody ever give you any instructions of any kind?

No. Was just sort of a . . . transitory thing. Just a period, just something that happened.

But you did realize that you didn't die, after all, when your body died?

I always wanted to tell Brian, but he was so worried.

He was worried?

Was . . . afraid he didn't say enough prayers or . . . go to church enough or something all the time.

I see. I understand. Now, for a moment let us go back to

when you were a baby in New Amsterdam, when you died as a baby in New Amsterdam. Do you recall that?

Yes, I do.

In what country was New Amsterdam?

Was in America.

New Amsterdam in America.

Yes.

Uh-huh. You know what that is called now?

No. . . .

Is it still called New Amsterdam?

No.

What is it called now?

New York.

Uh-huh.

New York now.

[This is a good example of the shifting point of orientation of a subject in a hypnotic age regression. As Dr. Lewis R. Wolberg, famous medical hypnotist and psychiatrist, says, "Regression is never stationary, constantly being altered by the intrusion of mental functioning at other age levels."

In this case the subject first replied that she did not know the present name of New Amsterdam. But after a few moments of reflection she was able to utilize her present knowledge.]

How old were you?

Don't know . . . just baby.

[The entire New Amsterdam episode is without value from the standpoint of veridical checking. She cannot give us dates or even use her own name. The sequence, therefore, is of interest only in so far as it fits into the whole pattern.]

All right. Now, rest and relax. Clear your mind completely, because you're coming back to the present time and place. You're coming back to the present time and place. Now you're at the present time and place. You're perfectly relaxed, you're perfectly comfortable. You feel very, very pleasant, pleasant —a soothing, comfortable sensation. I shall start counting toward five. When I reach the count of five, you will awaken and feel fine. One . . . two . . .[10]

[10] Information regarding phonograph records (made from the actual tape recordings of the Bridey Murphy hypnotic sessions) can be obtained by writing to the Wholesale Supply Corporation, Box 458, Pueblo, Colorado.

CHAPTER 11

Even though the next day was Sunday, I went to the office while Hazel was still doing the breakfast dishes. For many years I had been in the habit of spending a few hours at the office each Sunday; after six days in that madhouse I suppose the novel prospect of working in undisturbed serenity pulled me down there on the seventh day. I was particularly enjoying the Sabbath calm that day: no telephones, no salesmen, no customers, no equipment breakdowns, no interruptions of any kind.

Then there suddenly came a thunderous rumbling from the main entrance doors downstairs. I knew exactly what that noise meant. Ordinary people knock on the doors. But this deafening, furious shaking of the doors, in earthquake-fashion, was done by no ordinary human being. It had to be Stormy Sam MacIntosh.

It was.

I managed to open the doors before he ripped them out of the frame, and then Stormy Sam flew right by me, leaving one of his typical greetings: "Only an idiot would work on Sunday, you idiot!"

Sam MacIntosh is an industrial engineer. Although he is well known in industrial circles throughout the Southwest—he was the field engineer for a major manufacturer during the last two decades—he makes his home in Pueblo. Lean and handsome, he's especially tall, about six feet four or five.

The stormy Scotchman raced to the back end, the electric motor section. He was looking for, he somehow explained between bursts of cursing, a 25-horsepower, slow-speed, high-torque, totally enclosed motor for hoisting duty.

Accepting no help from me, he found the motor he wanted, then walked briskly to the switchboard, plugged in a downstairs phone, called long distance for the mine "super," and completed arrangements to have a truck pick up the motor that afternoon. Regarding me as though I were completely helpless, and muttering profane epithets against the whole human race, he went to the invoice register, made out the charge for the motor, and filed the invoice in its proper place.

Finally, his job done, he turned to me. "Say, Dr. Saxon tells me that you've been doing some work in hypnotic age regression. Sounds interesting. Have you done anything more lately?"

How can a fellow win? Even in the midst of the ulcers factory and high-torque motors the old subject keeps creeping in.

I talked in general terms for a while, not mentioning a word about the newest development. But he was showing more interest by the minute, and he obviously had more knowledge of the subject than I had supposed.

Abruptly he announced, "Mary and I will be over to your place tonight to hear some of your tape recordings." Just like that. Mac-Intosh was not one to fool with formalities; he merely decreed. Of course, he had done business with me for years; and his wife, Mary, an avid gardener, had long been exchanging plants and advice with Hazel.

That evening, after Sam and Mary MacIntosh arrived, I decided that, instead of playing an ordinary age regression, I would put on the Bridey Murphy tape of the night before. While our guests settled back and listened, Hazel occupied herself by drawing up a ranch-style house plan. And I started on a layout for a full-page advertisement in the *Record Stockman*, a cattlemen's publication. Having heard the recording before, we didn't intend to give it our full attention again.

I looked up only once during the first part of the tape, the ordinary age regression. Mary MacIntosh was retaining her customary composure, and Sam was as sternly serious as usual. Later, when the recording came to that point where we go "over the hump"— that is, where the regression moves back into the period before the subject's birth into the present lifetime—I made it a point to observe Sam and Mary again.

As the Bridey Murphy story commenced, they both hunched forward. Mary's jaw dropped; Sam's eyes narrowed. I said nothing. And Hazel was oblivious to all of us; she had just finished the rough floor-plan sketch and was now starting on the elevations for the ranch home she probably would never have.

The take-up reel on the tape recorder turned slowly, around and around, and eventually brought Bridey Murphy to that portion of the tape which is concerned with St. Theresa's Church in Belfast.

Listening almost subconsciously, I gave most of my attention to the advertisement on which I was putting the finishing touches.

Suddenly we were all jerked to attention by Stormy Sam, who was on his feet, shouting, "Turn that thing off!"

Bewildered, I walked over and pressed the "stop" button on the recorder. I could hardly see any reason for his brusque command. Had he been somehow offended? I turned to him for an explanation.

"You two," said Sam, "may have something of momentous significance here. Yet you sit there doodling like a pair of dolts."

"Relax, Mac, we've already heard it," I explained.

"Heard it! Heard it! Wake up, Rip van Winkle! I'm not talking about listening to it. I'm talking about doing something about it."

When he saw that I was still puzzled—and after labeling me with a few more of his pet names—he went on, "Pretty soon, regardless of what precautions you take, people will start talking about this. Then you'll get your first real taste of how much mayhem can be committed by rumors, gossip, and chatter.

"By some you will be regarded as just a harmless darn fool. But others will dub you a fanatic, a troublemaker, a crackpot, or a lunatic. You'll be getting phone calls and letters from mediums, cultists, and faddists. To top it all, there will be those who are offended in the mistaken impression that you are questioning various religious beliefs."

There were a few moments of silence while I considered his point. Then I asked, "Well, what can I do about it?"

"Unfortunately, not very much. But there are a few things. First you and Hazel must have nothing personally to do with the checking of individual identities in Ireland—the ones that are involved in this tape. Leave that to an independent agency. In other words, keep your nose away from any Irish knowledge. In fact, keep as aloof from this work as you possibly can. Just be the middleman, the fellow with the tape recorder.

"And make a lot more tapes with this girl; check, double-check, and cross-check her while you're interrogating her. Get facts, facts, facts."

While Mac was glibly suggesting "a lot more tapes," I was thinking of all the trouble I had in arranging a single session. "And if I follow all your suggestions," I asked, "then all my troubles will be over?"

Stormy gave out with a smile, an expression that is almost foreign to his face. "No. But do what I suggest anyway."

"Incidentally, Mac, I didn't know that you were interested in re-incarnation."

He stiffened. "I'm not!" Then he softened a little and added, "But years ago I did a paper on child prodigies. I've never quite gotten over it. Mozart wrote a sonata when he was four and an opera by the time he was seven. I remember that a twelve-year-old Swiss boy had been appointed inspector of the Grand Maritime Canal by the Swiss Government because of his mechanical genius. And what about Samuel Reshevsky, the chess champion? When he was only five years old he simultaneously took on three European chess champs and whipped them all.

"A two-year-old kid in Massachusetts," he continued, "could read and write. By the time he was four he could speak four languages, and a few years later he could tackle any kind of geometry problem. And some time ago the *Reader's Digest* ran an article about Blind Tom, the Negro slave, who played his master's piano brilliantly the first time he ever put his hands on it.

"How," he asked, "can a mind that's only a few years old write sonatas, solve complicated mathematical problems, and play championship chess? There must be some other factor, something we don't see."

I had often wondered about the same thing myself. I had observed, moreover, that in almost all these cases there had been no apparent hereditary justification for these transcendent capacities. Then, too, those fields in which the prodigies exhibited their proficiency were *old* ones—music, mathematics, chess, languages.

Before the MacIntoshes left that night, Sam helped me to draft some questions for the second session—that is, if I could ever catch and hold my subject long enough for another session. In making up the questions we kept in mind that it would be asking too much to expect that she would remember historical and political details.

Memory is, after all, vitally concerned with association. And association is indissolubly linked with emotion and interest. You may have no difficulty, for instance, in recalling the scene of your graduation from high school even though it may have taken place more than twenty years ago. If asked, though, who was the governor of your state at the time of your graduation, you will likely draw a blank. Even though the same amount of time has elapsed in both cases, and you were probably reading the governor's name in the newspaper almost daily, your mind registered one event and apparently dropped the other.

I was once asked whether the numeral six on my wrist watch was an Arabic or a Roman numeral. Without referring to my watch, even though I look at it several times each day, I could not remember which type of number it bore. Later, looking at my watch, I was embarrassed to notice that, as is the rule with most watches, it had no number six; the second hand took its place.

So memory is primarily dependent upon neither frequency of observation nor the passage of time. Rather, the essence of memory is *interest*, of which a fundamental element is *emotion*. In short, the greater the emotional impact of an event the sharper the memory of it.

The same thing is true, I have found, in my hypnotic experiments. While hypnosis enormously extends the memory, it does not perform the magic of conjuring images which held no emotional content for the subject. Hypnosis lifts a curtain and permits the "eye" of the mind to penetrate to depths which are ordinarily inaccessible to the conscious mind. But even at this "distance" the mind (under hypnosis) will still remember in vivid detail only those incidents which were charged with at least some degree of emotion; it still tends to "forget" events which held no interest.

Careful not to expect the impossible from "Bridey Murphy's" memory, therefore we made out a list of questions. Not a long list. Since "Bridey" had been somewhat exhausted after the long first session, I knew that the second session must be somewhat shorter. And owing to my belief that an ordinary present-life age regression was the right sort of "warm-up" for a past-life regression, not too much time remained for the quiz period.

I now realized, moreover, that, in addition to limiting the length of the session, there was something more I could do in order to bring "Bridey" out of her trance in a less fatigued state. I could simply use the post-hypnotic suggestions that she would, after she awakened, feel "even better than before she went to sleep," "completely relaxed," "comfortable and rested." It might even be a good idea, I thought, to give her a five-minute rest period before awakening her, suggesting that the five-minute sleep would be equivalent to one full hour of deep slumber.

As I had anticipated, pinning down the Simmonses long enough to make tape number two was no cinch. But at last, a week before

Christmas, Rex called me. He and Ruth were having guests that night, he told me, but if I wanted to bring my recorder over to their house and make another tape some time during the evening I could come ahead.

I went.

On December 18, 1952, at 9:30 P.M., after having impatiently plodded through an hour of social functioning, I got the second session under way in the presence of witnesses. The hypnosis and the simple age regression went smoothly. After that a transcription of the tape reads as follows:

TAPE II

And now you're going to go on farther back, you're going to slip back, back, back. Surprising as it may seem, you'll find that you can go on farther back. You'll find that you can go on farther back—back—back. Your memory will go on back—back—back. And your memory will find yourself; you will find a scene in which you were included, perhaps in some other lifetime, some other age, some other time, some other place. You will pick up that scene which includes you; you will see that scene clearly. I will talk to you again in just a few moments, and when I talk to you again, some scene in which you took place will have popped into your mind. You will see it clearly, and you will be able to tell me about it. Now, now, what scene is in your mind? Tell me about it.

Going to go on a trip.

Going to go on a trip?

Uh-huh.

Where?

To Antrim.

To where?

Antrim.

Antrim?

Uh-huh.

Where's that?

It's at the seashore.

That's at the seashore?

Uh-huh. There are cliffs . . . 'n' . . . white, bright cliffs . . . and there's a red stone . . . black ones . . . from the glens . . . and other . . .

> [It will be noticed that the subject has this time reverted to a different scene from the one she initially recalled dur-

ing the first session. At that time she saw herself scratching the paint off her bed at the age of four.]
And with whom are you going on this trip?
With my mother . . . my father.
And what's your mother's name?
Kathleen.
What is your father's name?
Duncan.
And how old are you?
I'm ten.
And you're going on a trip?
Uh-huh.
A trip to Antrim?
Antrim.
Uh-huh, and it's by the seashore?
Yes.
Just the three of you are going?
Oh, my brother too.
Which brother?
Why, Duncan—my brother Duncan.
I see.
Uh-huh.
All right, now, tell me about Antrim. Tell me about it. Describe it—what's it like?
It's a seashore town. There's cliffs there. The water runs, the streams run down real fast and they make . . . little rivulets in the ground to get to the sea . . . and there's cliffs . . . and the cliffs are real white . . . 'n' Father says sandstone ballast, black ballast . . . just . . . from the Glens of Antrim.
Where is your other brother?
My other brother—little brother . . . he's dead.
He's dead?
Yes.
How old was he when he died?
Oh, he was a baby . . . just a little baby . . . I don't know. . . .
From what did he die?
He was . . . sick of . . . I don't know what was wrong with him. He died . . . when he was just a little . . .
What disease did he have?
He . . . I don't know . . . I don't know.
All right. What is your name?
Bridey.

Bridey what?

Bridey Murphy.

Are you sure that that is your name, or do you really have some other name?

I was named after my grandmother.

You were named after your grandmother?

Uh-huh.

What was her name?

Bridget.

All right. Now tell me what town you live in.

I live in Cork.

In Cork. Now tell me whether Cork is north or south of Belfast.

'Tis south of Belfast.

South of Belfast?

Uh-huh.

About what is the distance between Cork and Belfast?

Uh . . . uh . . . it's in a different province. Uh . . . Belfast is . . . no . . . Belfast is . . . uh–uh . . . in a different province. . . . I don't know how far away it is.

Can you tell me, can you tell me as you go from Cork to Belfast—can you tell me any of the names of the towns, the names of any towns or villages that you pass or go through?

You go through Carlingford . . . Carlingford.

All right.

. . . There's a . . . there's . . . Carlingford is a lake too . . . a lough . . . Carlingford, in Carlingford.

All right.

There's a lough . . . a lough . . . a lake . . . uh . . . see . . .

All right. Is there anyplace else that you can tell us besides Carlingford and that other place that you go through or go by on your way from Cork to Belfast . . . on your way from Cork to Belfast, what other place?

. . . You go through the Glens of Antrim to go up North. . . .

All right. Now can you give us the names of any rivers in Ireland? Any rivers in Ireland?

There's Lough Carlingford and Lough Foyle are two . . . two. . . . Don't say "river," say "lough."

Oh, I see, "lough" is the word for river?

Uh-huh.

I see, lough. All right. Give us the name of some mountain in Ireland.

. . . Mountain . . . there's a famous one. . . . What is it? . . .
Oh . . . I can't remember the name, but it's very famous.

Very famous mountain?

Oh, very famous. It has a lot of—Ireland has lots of hills. I don't remember, but there's one very famous one. . . .

Well, tell us the name of a well-known lake.

Foyle . . . Foyle is a lake . . . a lough . . . !

A lough?

Yes, lough.

Is a "lough" a river or a lake?

Don't say "river."

Don't say "river"? all right, lough. Now what is the name of that famous mountain?

. . . Uh . . . I can't remember. . . .

Can't seem to remember the name of the mountain?

No, I know, but I can't remember.

You know it, but you can't remember it. All right, perhaps you'll think of it later. What does your father do?

My father is a barrister.

What does a barrister do?

He practices . . . legal . . . business.

All right, practices legal business. All right. When did you first meet Brian? Can you tell us about how old you were when you first met Brian?

. . . I was seventeen.

Did you meet him in Cork or Belfast?

I met him in Cork.

All right. How did he happen to be at Cork?

His father is a barrister too . . . and his father and he came to our house.

Brian came to your house?

Uh-huh.

When you were seventeen?

Uh-huh.

What school were you going to when you were seventeen?

I was going to a day school.

What was the name of the day school?

. . . Mrs. . . . Mrs. . . . uh . . .

What was the name of the day school? Mrs. what?

. . . Uh . . . uh . . . uh . . .

[During the making of the first tape she had given us the name of the day school—Mrs. Strayne's—but here she is unable to remember it. This example does not stand alone; throughout the series of tapes there are several instances which indicate that the subject's memory is sharper at one stage than another. This might be accounted for by difference in the depth of trance, vagaries of memory, or differences in point of orientation of the subject.

In my opinion—and the opinion of witnesses—Ruth achieved her deepest trance during tape number one and tape number five.]

Did you go to any other schools before you went to that day school?

No . . . I went there all the time, and when I got bigger I stayed there.

You lived right there?

Uh . . . for the week time.

And then you went home for the week end?

Yes.

Did you like Brian when you first met him?

No.

How old was Brian?

Oh . . . he was nineteen.

He was two years older than you?

Uh-huh.

I see. But you didn't like him when you first met him?

Oh, he was all right. He wasn't anything.

Well, how did you get engaged to him?

He came back in the summer and worked in his father's office, and I just . . . went with him. . . . 'Twas just taken for granted, I think.

I see. Did you like anybody else before you met Brian?

. . . Uh . . . no.

All right. What was the name of Brian's father?

Brian's . . . he . . . he was John.

John what?

MacCarthy.

All right, you had two friends by the name of Mary Catherine and Kevin.

Yes.

Where did they live?

In Belfast.

What was their last name?

. . . Uh . . . Mary Catherine and Kevin . . . *Moore.* . . .

All right, Mary Catherine Moore, Kevin Moore, is that right?

Yes.

All right, all right. Now tell us about your death. Do you remember your death?

Yes, I . . . remember . . . I just . . . I just went to sleep . . . I just went off . . . on a Sunday . . . it was a Sunday.

It was a Sunday?

Uh-huh.

Uh-huh. About what time of the day was it?

It was while Brian was at church.

While Brian was at church. How old were you?

I was sixty-six.

All right. Can you tell me, can you tell me what are the three essential elements of the Mass in the Catholic Church? What are the three essential elements of the Mass? Can you remember that?

No.

[At this point I was plainly disappointed. Regardless of whether Bridey had been a Catholic, she still should know—or at least so it seemed to me—something as fundamental as the three essential elements of the Mass. After all, I reasoned, she was married to a Catholic; consequently she should have picked up this much information. I don't know why, but I had somehow assumed that this was something quite elementary and generally known.

A few days later, however, Stormy MacIntosh straightened me out as to this idea. To prove that I was wrong, he asked several people to name the three essential elements of the Mass. Not a single one could comply. Then I asked the answer of the person who had suggested the question in the first place. To my surprise, he, too, failed to give the whole answer.]

Can you ever remember attending Mass?

No.

Didn't Brian make you go whenever he went?

No.

Oh, he didn't?

No.

Oh, I see. Now, we would like to check, we would like to check any records, or any other indications, that prove you lived in Ireland at that time. Where could we find, where could we find some records, or any other indications, that would prove you lived in Ireland at that time?

. . . Uh . . . there would be some articles in the Belfast *News-Letter*.

The Belfast *News-Letter*?

About Brian?

Yes. And he taught at the Queen's University for some time . . . you know, the Queen's University at Belfast.

Uh-huh. And his name appeared in the paper?

Yes, on several times.

Uh-huh.

Belfast *News-Letter*.

Where else would we find any records of it? Was there a marriage certificate?

Oh . . . I believe there was . . . sure . . . there was banns published. It was . . . Father John had the banns published.

Uh-huh.

What's a band?

[I was under the impression that she had said "bands." But one of the witnesses quickly spelled the word for me.]

Oh, it's something in the church . . . you do it before you get married, you . . . you . . . know it's an important bulletin or something, you tell the people that you're going to get married.

[From one of the witnesses: "B-a-n-n-s."]

Oh, I see. All right.

That's the church. . . .

What was your address? Can you possibly remember your address in Belfast?

Uh . . . uh . . . uh . . . uh . . .

Can you tell us anything about the neighborhood? What side of town, and so forth?

Oh, it was near town, it was near a road, some road . . .

What was the name of that road? Did it have a name?

It was . . . about . . . twenty minutes from St. Theresa's . . . walking distance.

What was the address at Cork, can you remember that address?

That was . . . the Meadows.

The what?

Just the Meadows.

Uh-huh.

All right. I want you to remember your lifetime in Ireland about the time you were forty-seven years old. About that time did you have plenty to eat?

There was . . . a . . . I remember . . . we did.

You did?

Uh . . . there was trouble.

There was trouble?

Uh, there was trouble.

What kind of trouble?

Well, the people in the South . . . uh . . . they didn't want to have anything to do with England. They . . . all they . . . want to send *no* representative, have nothing to do with them. We . . . people wouldn't talk Gaelic. Grandfather wouldn't talk Gaelic, he would say, "Gaelic is fit only for the tongues of the peasants. Don't speak Gaelic; it's fit only for the tongues of the peasants."

Your grandfather?

Yes.

What was his name?

His name was . . . Duncan too.

Duncan too?

Uh-huh.

All right. Do you remember any wars, any war or wars, that the people in Ireland were engaged in during your lifetime? Do you remember any wars?

Oh . . . I remember . . . about Cuchulain.

[This name, as she said it, sounded like Cooch-a-lain. The spelling was later verified by a friend.]

About what?

Cuchulain. He was a warrior.

He was?

Yes.

An Irishman?

Yes . . . he was the bravest, and the strongest, and when he was seven . . . seven years old, he could slay big men.

Is that right?

Uh . . . when he was seventeen he could hold *whole* armies.

Did you ever see him?

No.

Where did you hear about him?

My mother told me about him.

I see. Did you ever hear anything about America? During this lifetime did you ever hear anything about America?

Uh . . . yes . . . some . . . somebody went there. They went to . . . America.

Who went there?

141

Some friends of my mother and father, and they went to Pennsylvania.

To stay?

Yes.

Did they write to you?

They always wrote to my mother . . . 'n' my father.

What were the names of those friends?

. . . Uh . . . Whitty.

Whitty?

Whitty.

    [I haven't the slightest idea whether this is the correct spelling. This would seem to be the phonetic spelling.]

That was their last name?

Uh-huh.

And they went to Pennsylvania.

Uh-huh.

Did they like America?

Uh-*huh*.

They wrote your mother that they liked America?

Uh-huh.

I see. Now you say you were sixty-six years old when you died?

Uh-huh.

And you died while Brian was at church?

Yes, I died while Brian was at church. [Very faintly.]

All right. Now I want you to rest. I want you to rest and relax, be completely comfortable. Now, we'll return again to your lifetime in Ireland, return again to your lifetime in Ireland, return again to your lifetime in Ireland. What was the name of that famous mountain in Ireland?

    [No answer.]

Can you remember the name?

I just can't remember.

Just can't quite remember?

No, I just . . .

Well, give us the names of some other loughs.

Loughs! [Correcting pronunciation.]

Loughs, all right. Give us a few, two or three.

Lough Munster.

Lough Munster? All right, what else?

Lough . . . There's a lough for each . . .

Lough what?

For each . . . of the provinces. There's . . . four provinces
. . . Munster, Ulster . . . Ulster. . . .
Ulster. Remember any other?
Uh . . . uh . . . two more.
Can't remember the other two?
No.
All right. Let's go up to the time of your death, up to the time
of your death. How old were you?
Sixty-six when I died.
All right. What happened after you died? Tell us about what
happened after you died. Did you watch them bury you?
Oh, I watched them. I watched them ditch my body.
You watched them ditch your body?
Yes.
And you saw Brian?
Oh yes, I saw him. He was there.
Where did you go? After you died?
I went home. I stayed in the house and watched Brian.
You watched Brian?
Uh-huh.
All right. How did Father John die?
Father John . . . he just died in his sleep.
Died in his sleep?
Yes.
You didn't watch him die, did you?
No, I didn't watch him die.
But he came to you after he died?
Yes, he did, and we talked. . . . He had a pleasant death.
He had a pleasant death?
Uh-huh.
Well, where did Father John go when he left you? When he
left the house there, where did he go?
He said he was going to his home.
He said he was going to *his* home?
Uh-huh.
Do you have any idea where Father John could be now? Is
he living on this earth?
I don't know. . . . He's living. He lives.
He lives?
He lives.
How do you know?
I just . . . know that you live.

But do you know *where* he lives? Do you have any idea where he lives?

No . . . I don't know. I went back to Cork and I didn't see him.

I see. All right, while you were in this spiritual world, while you were in this spiritual world did you hear anyone call it the astral world? Did you hear anyone call it the astral world?

Astral world.

Did you ever hear that name?

Yes, I've heard that.

All right, we will refer to it as the astral world. We will now refer to it as the astral world. In this astral world did you have any feelings or emotions?

You were just . . . satisfied; you weren't . . . you . . . I felt bad when . . . when Father John died, but he came to me and we talked, and it was not like the grief you have here.

Not like the grief you have here?

No, it's . . . nothing to be afraid of.

Did you have any pain in that astral world?

No. No.

No pain? Did you have any attachments of any kind, any family attachments, relatives?

No.

No marriages?

No.

I see. Do relatives stay together?

No. No . . . we . . . it was . . . no, my mother was never with me. My father said he saw her, but I didn't.

Oh, you didn't see your mother?

No.

Your father, though, told you that he saw her.

Yes.

I see. Was there any such thing as love and hate?

No.

You neither loved nor hated?

No . . . loved those that you left.

You didn't hate anyone?

No.

You said that you couldn't talk very long with anyone in that astral world, that they would go away. You said that you couldn't talk very long because they would go away. Where would they go?

They would just . . . journey . . . just a passing phase . . .

you just . . . you have no time. There's . . . nothing's important . . . you just . . .

All right. You said that you went from your house at Belfast in this astral world, you drifted back to Cork. How did you get from Belfast to Cork?

. . . I just willed myself there.

You did what?

Willed myself there.

Willed yourself there. How long did it take to get from Belfast to Cork?

I don't know. It wasn't any time.

It wasn't any time? In other words, when you thought about being in Cork you were there in Cork?

Just almost.

Uh-huh. All right. While you were in Cork in this astral life, in this astral world, did you know what was going on at Belfast, back at Brian's house, could you tell what was going on in Belfast at Brian's house?

No.

You didn't know?

I didn't . . . watch. You could.

You could watch?

You could . . . but . . . I didn't watch. I just stayed there . . . you could see . . . just *anything*.

You could see anything you wanted to see just by wanting to see it?

Just willing it . . . so you just think . . . you see everything.

I see. Could you ever tell, while you were at Belfast, could you ever tell what Brian was *thinking* about? Could you tell what he was *thinking* about?

Oh, I knew when he missed me. I knew when he needed me . . . 'n' . . . he missed me after Father John didn't come to the house.

He missed you then?

Yes. He . . . was lonesome before, but they would talk, and he had somebody. . . . After he died, he was lonely.

After he died, what?

After Father John died, he was lonely.

I see. Could you read his thoughts then, could you read his thoughts all the time?

. . . If I thought of it I could think of . . . I could know what he wanted and think.

When you saw your brother, your little brother that died—

when you went back to Cork you told us that you saw your little brother that died.

Yes.

How did he look? Did he look like a small child, or did he look like a grown-up adult?

He was just little.

Just the way he looked when he died?

No, he was . . . he was just a child, but he wasn't . . . he could talk.

I see. Could he talk when he died?

No, he was . . . no, he couldn't when he died . . . he was just a baby.

Uh-huh, but he could talk when you saw him?

Yes, he could talk then.

How was he dressed?

No clothes.

No clothes. All right. And you remember talking to your little brother. Do you remember anything he told you?

Yes . . . he told me that . . . Duncan and I would run through the room and . . . push over the cradle, and Duncan would tip him out, and he'd cry, and Duncan would run and hide and my mother would think I did it.

Well, didn't that hurt him when you tipped over the cradle?

It was on the ground. It was . . .

Oh, I see.

Just a little thing. He would just roll out.

Didn't you and Duncan like your little brother?

Oh yes. We liked him, but he . . . he was always so sick, and my mother was always with him after he came.

What did he die of, your little brother?

. . . Don't know. . . . I can't . . .

What did he die of?

. . . I can't remember. . . . He was just a baby, I know, but . . .

All right. In that astral world, in that astral world did you ever have any changes in temperature, any hot or cold?

No.

No heat, no cold. Did you ever have any wars of any kind, any fights of any kind?

No.

No wars, no fights?

No.

All right. In that astral world did you have a sense of smell,

146

and touch, and hearing, and seeing? Did you have all those senses? In the astral world could you touch things?

No.

Could you smell things?

No. You could see. . . .

You could see.

And you could . . .

You couldn't smell? You couldn't touch?

You could hear.

But you could hear. All right. Now you told us that there was always a sort of light in your astral world, there was always a sort of light but that you could see the night and day, you could see the night and day that Brian was having while it was always light where you were. Is that right?

Uh-huh.

That light that you had, that light, you could see it clearly, and you could see when Brian was having night and day, is that correct?

Yes.

But could you touch or feel or sense the light that you were having in the astral world? Could you sense that light in any way besides seeing it? Could you sense that light in any other way besides seeing it?

No.

You couldn't.

No.

All right. How could you tell you were having light all the time? How could you tell? How could you tell that Brian was having night and day?

I could see him, and I could see him go to bed, and I would sit there by the bed . . . and they just accept the night and day.

Well, then you knew it was night because he was going to bed, but did you actually see a change in color?

No. No, I just knew it was night. He accepted it.

Oh, I see. He accepted it, but you couldn't see it?

No.

I see. All right. Was there anything, were there any things in that astral world such as death, disease, or old age? Were there any such things as death, disease, or old age in that astral world?

There was no death, there was just a . . . passing of . . . you passed from that existence . . . you passed . . . to another existence. That's all, there was no death.

Any disease?
No.
Any old age?
No. There were old people there; I was old. I was . . .
Did you get any older?
No. I was sixty-six.
I see. All right, now rest and relax, rest and relax, and let's go back once again to that astral world. In that astral world did you ever have to obey any regulations or laws of any kind? Did you ever have to obey any regulations in that astral world?
No.
No laws, no regulations?
No.
Nobody guided you, nobody gave you instructions?
No.
You just went where you willed to go?
Yes.
You did what you willed to do.
Uh-huh.
You rest and relax, rest and relax, rest and relax, and let those scenes come into your mind long before the lifetime in Ireland. Those scenes will come into your mind. Those scenes will come into your mind, and I'll talk to you again in just a few minutes, and you will tell me about them. Just rest and relax and let those scenes come into your mind. [Switch to other side of tape.] Rest and relax, rest and relax, and just listen to my voice. Just listen to my voice. You remember the astral world, and you remember Father John, and you remember your life as Bridey Murphy. You remember your lifetime in Ireland as Bridey Murphy. And you remember being a very small girl in that life-time. Now you're thinking even farther back, back, back, and back. You're going farther and farther back. Now some scene is coming into your mind, some scene in your mind that you can tell me about. Go ahead and tell me about it. Go ahead and tell me about the scene that is in your mind. . . . Tell me about the scene. What is in your mind?
I don't know.
You don't know? You don't see a scene?
No.
No scenes at all?
No.
Nothing farther back?
No. . . .

148

No scenes come into your mind. Do you see any scenes in which you were a child?

. . . In Ireland . . . I was a child . . . a little girl . . . in Ireland. Reading . . . reading . . . in a book.

You were reading a book? Do you remember the name of the book?

Uh-huh.

What was the name of the book?

It was *Sorrows of* . . . *Sorrows of* . . . *Deirdre.*

Sorrows of whom?

Deirdre. [She pronounced this as Dee-ay-druh.]

All right. How old were you when you read that book?

I was . . . eight.

What was the book about?

It was about Deirdre . . . and she was . . . beautiful girl and . . . she was going to marry . . . this king . . . this King of Scotland . . . and she didn't love him . . . and this boy came and saved her. She was in a dungeon . . . and they ran away . . . and they were betrayed and brought back . . . and they killed him and she committed suicide. The story of the *Sorrows of Deirdre.*

You read that when you were eight years old?

No, it was my mother read it.

Your mother read it?

It's a story that everybody reads in Ireland. It's the *Sorrows of Deirdre.*

Sorrows of Deirdre. Do you know who wrote it?

. . . No . . . I just know I heard it.

Your mother told it to you?

Yes, and . . . the *Tales of* . . . *Emer.* [Or *Emir.*]

The tales of whom?

Emer.

Emer?

Uh.

And what were those about?

It was about the most beautiful girl in Ireland . . . and she had . . . she had six gifts.

She had six gifts?

Uh-huh.

Can you remember what they were?

. . . Gift of beauty . . . and the gift of song . . . and the gift of pleasant speech . . . and the gift of . . . wisdom . . . and the gift of needlework . . . and the gift of . . . chastity.

The gift of chastity. All right. All right. What else do you remember about that lifetime in Ireland when you were a little girl?

. . . Uh . . . I remember . . . pulling the straws off the roof.

Pulling straws off the roof?

Uh-huh.

You had a straw roof?

No, it was . . . the barn was . . . thatched roof.

Thatched roof.

Was pulling the straws off . . . and my father was so mad. . . .

All right. Now I want you to think back, back, back before this Irish lifetime. Just drift on back. If you make no particular effort you'll find that you can drift on back. I want you to drift on back, and you'll find yourself in New Amsterdam. You'll find yourself in New Amsterdam. Drift on back until you pick up a scene in New Amsterdam. Now, do you have a scene in New Amsterdam?

Uh . . .

Do you see a scene in New Amsterdam?

Uh . . . uh . . . uh . . .

Don't see a scene?

Uh . . . arm hurts.

Your arm hurts?

Uh-huh.

When you were in Amsterdam?

Uh-huh.

Why did it hurt?

Oh . . . sick.

You were sick? With what?

. . . Uh . . . uh . . . arm hurts.

Your arm hurts? Why does your arm hurt?

Uh . . . my leg hurts.

Your leg hurts. All right, it hurt you then, but it doesn't hurt you now, it doesn't hurt you now. All right, now let's forget about the lifetime in New Amsterdam. Let's forget about that and go back to Ireland.

[Because the subject seemed painfully disturbed, I quickly suggested another scene, one that would divert her from the New Amsterdam sequence. Then I concluded the session in the usual manner.]

CHAPTER 12

Between the second and third session Stormy MacIntosh and I had a new thought. If this girl had really lived that lifetime in Ireland, if she had really been Bridey Murphy, we reasoned, then perhaps she had had some special talent or ability that could either be demonstrated during the trance or brought out later by means of a post-hypnotic suggestion. Maybe she could play the piano or some other instrument; she might even have been able to play chess. We hoped, in short, that we could evoke from Bridey Murphy the execution of some skill or ability which is not presently within the capacity of Ruth Simmons.

So in preparing for our third round with Bridey we set up our plans accordingly. Then, entreating the Simmonses to reserve a few hours before I left for New York on January 26, I was granted the evening of January 22, 1953.

The following is the transcription of the third recorded session (after the customary ordinary age regression):

TAPE III

Let's go back before you were born in this life. Let's go on back, back, back before your birth. Do you remember that? Do you remember the existence before you were born into this life?
. . . I just . . . remember being . . . just waiting to . . . oh . . . oh . . .
Go ahead and tell me about that, waiting to what?
. . . To be just . . . oh . . . oh . . . you just wait.
Where were you waiting?
I just . . . waiting where everybody waits.
Waiting where everybody waits? What do you call that place where everybody waits?
It's just a place of waiting.
Oh, I see. All right, well now, in that, let us call it the astral world or spirit world, in that astral world or spirit world who told you that you were going on to another existence? Who told you that you were going to be born again?
Some . . . women.

Some who?

Women.

Women?

Yes.

What did they call them? . . . Or don't you remember what they called them?

> [After Bridey's comments in the earlier tapes regarding the astral world, I looked up the report of another in-investigator who is doing some of these same kinds of hypnotic experiments. From his material I derived a few more questions about the astral world.]

Oh . . .

Did they have any name at all?

I don't remember.

Now in this astral world, the spirit world, could you tell the difference between males and females? Was there any sex, in other words?

No.

I see. But you could tell a man was a man, or that a woman was a woman?

You just knew.

You just knew, I see.

All right. Now here is a question that I want to ask you. While you were there in that astral world, in that spirit world, were there times when you could remember all of your previous lifetimes?

I don't remember.

You don't remember?

I . . . remember some things, but I . . .

Now there are some things that you remember. Just pick out anything, just pick out anything you remember and tell us about that.

. . . Uh . . . I . . . remember . . . dancing . . . dancing . . .

Dancing with whom?

By myself.

Dancing by yourself?

I was . . . practicing . . . jig.

> [As she was soon to explain, she was referring to her dancing when she lived in Ireland.]

You were practicing a jig?

Uh-huh. I was a good . . . dancer.

You were a good dancer.

Yes, as little girls go, I was a good dancer.

Now, were you remembering that you danced in the astral world or you were in the astral world and you could remember that you once danced?

I was remembering I could dance.

You did dance in the astral world?

Oh no.

Oh no. I see. All right. Now, there in that astral world, in that spirit world, were there any insane people?

I didn't see any.

You didn't see any. All right, that's good. Now, also, while you were in that astral world, in that spirit world, could you tell the future for the people on earth? Could you look at the people on the earth and see what was going to happen to them?

Yes.

You could?

Yes.

You could see the future?

Yes.

I see. What makes you say that you could? Give us an example.

Because I . . . I just . . . seems like before . . . you were born . . . you would know you would pass . . . just see things that were going to happen . . . and I saw a war . . . some man there said there was going to be a war. It was before I was born . . . before I was born. And he . . . he said . . . be a war . . . there *was* a war before I was born . . . they could see . . . people knew what was going to happen . . . if you were there.

[Bridey Murphy MacCarthy died in 1864; Ruth Mills Simmons was born in 1923.]

I see. All right.

But that doesn't concern you.

It didn't concern you. I see. Well, that's very interesting, very interesting. Now, rest and relax, rest and relax. Be perfectly comfortable. Rest and relax. You will not get tired. Now I want you to remember farther back, just very easily without any effort, you just remember back, back, back, and you will pick up a scene, a former scene, when you lived on the earth. Now just go on back before you were in that astral world, go on back to before you were in that astral world and you will pick up a scene and you will tell us about it.

. . . Uh . . . birthday party.

Birthday party? All right.

. . . Seven years old.

153

You're seven years old?
Uh-huh.
Is it your birthday party?
It's my birthday.
I see. And what is your name?
Bridey.
All right. Who was there at your birthday party?
. . . Ah . . . my mother . . . and my father . . . and my brother.
All right, who else?
Just the family.
How about your little brother? Was he there?
Oh no! He was dead.
He was dead? What was the name of your other brother? What was the name of the brother who was there?
Duncan.
Duncan, I see. What was the name of your mother?
Kathleen.
Kathleen. And how about your father, what was his name?
It was Duncan too.
Duncan too, I see. And your father, Duncan, what did he do, what was his business?
He was a . . . barrister.
A barrister?
Yes.
In what town?
In Cork.
Is that where you lived, in Cork?
Yes.
I see. All right. Now you were seven years old and were having a birthday party. Do you remember who else was there? Was there anyone else besides the family?
Oh . . . it was . . . Mary was there . . . she did the cooking.
Mary who?
Mary . . .
Remember her last name?
. . . No . . . no . . . I don't remember.
Well, all right, I want you to get a little older in that same lifetime. Get a little older, see yourself getting eight, nine, ten, eleven, twelve, older and older. See yourself going to that day school that you told us about before. See yourself at the time of going to that day school. Did they teach you anything about politics?

Oh no!

Oh no?

They don't teach that . . . they don't.

Well, now, let's go on farther, and remember yourself getting older all the time, and then you met and finally married. . . . Whom did you marry?

Brian.

All right. Now, at the time of the marriage, you must remember the wedding; tell us what date that was, just the year, the date. What year was that?

It was eighteen . . . eighteen . . .

Now you say first you were in Cork, and then you got married in Belfast. How did you travel from Cork to Belfast? What kind of automobile did you drive from Cork to Belfast?

No automobile.

No automobile?

I traveled in a carriage.

In a carriage?

I traveled in a livery.

In a what?

In a livery carriage with horses.

With horses?

Yes.

All right. Now, what towns or places did you go through from Cork to Belfast?

. . . Oh . . . I went . . . oh . . . through . . . Mourne. . . .

You went through where?

Mourne.

Mourne?

Mourne. I went through . . .

What else?

Oh . . . through Carlingford and . . . we went through . . . oh . . . through . . .

Give us another place. Give us one more place that you traveled through before you got to Belfast.

. . . Oh yes, Balings [Baylings?] Crossing.

All right. Now that's enough. Don't strain your mind any more. Just relax. Take it easy, relax completely. About how old were you when you met Brian?

About . . . about . . . sixteen.

[Here Bridey says she was "about sixteen" when she met Brian. On the second tape when I asked about how old she was when she met Brian, she replied that she was seventeen.]

All right. Did Brian live in Cork or Belfast before you were married?

He lived with his grandmother.

Where?

In Belfast.

I see.

His mother was dead and . . . his father was a barrister too.

His father was a barrister too. You had some friends named Mary Catherine and Kevin. What was their last name? Mary Catherine and Kevin what?

Moore. Moore.

Do you happen to remember the name of the road on which you lived in Belfast?

. . . Road . . . road . . .

. . . All right, let's not try to remember that, forget about that. Now, could your grandfather speak Gaelic?

Grandfather *wouldn't speak* Gaelic.

Wouldn't speak Gaelic?

. . . Said . . . Gaelic is just for the tongues of the peasants. They wouldn't speak it.

I see. But did you know any Gaelic words, you yourself, Bridey Murphy, know any Gaelic words?

. . . Oh . . . just . . . oh, like *banshee?*

Yes.

Yes . . . and . . . like . . . oh, banshee and . . . oh . . . oh . . . *tup!*

What?

Tup.

What's that?

T-u-p. Tup!

What does that mean?

Tup . . . oh, you're a tup! . . . You're . . . you're just a sort of a rounder, just a . . . it's mostly not very good grammar. They don't speak proper.

I see. All right. Now, you had a newspaper in Belfast, what was the name of it?

Belfast . . . Belfast *News* . . . Belfast *News-Letter.*

All right. Belfast *News-Letter.* By the way, did they teach you how to read at that day school you went to? Did they teach you how to read?

They read to us.

They read to you.

They read to us, and we had to take things home and . . . our mother was supposed to teach us . . . oh, a lot of it, but they read to us and we learned to read the . . .

You learned to read a little there, did you?

Yes, a little.

I see. In all this reading did you ever read about the Queen; any time that you read from that time that you went to the day school until the end of your life there, did you remember reading about the Queen?

I don't remember about. . . reading about. . . Queen.

All right. Now, here is a question I want you to think about. While you were in that lifetime as Bridey Murphy, or Bridget Murphy, and you were married to Brian, did you have any particular talent? Could you dance? Could you play the piano? Could you play chess? Could you play any other games? Can you tell me about that?

I could dance.

You could dance?

I could dance.

Were you known as a good dancer?

Oh, I was just . . . my family thought I was a good dancer, and . . . it wasn't . . . I just danced for the family.

You just danced for the family.

Uh-huh.

Was there any particular dance that you liked best?

I liked the Morning Jig.

Is that what you called it, the Morning Jig?

Yes.

Can you remember that clearly?

Yes.

I want you to go through that Morning Jig in your mind, just go through it in your mind, go through it in your mind and you will be surprised that after you awaken tonight you will be asked to do that and you can do it very easily. Go through it in your mind. You will not do anything now, just relax comfortably now and remember the Morning Jig. Remember all the little steps, remember the Morning Jig. You'll find it's easy; let it go through your mind, just let it fill your whole being, and later you will be able to do the Morning Jig very easily. Now, I'll give you just a few moments when I won't speak to you and you will be remembering with pleasure and comfort, watching yourself doing the Morning Jig. You will remember, you will remember doing the Morning Jig. I will not talk to you for a few moments. You remember that. You will enjoy the pleasant thoughts and memories of the Morning Jig. . . .

All right, all right. Rest and relax, rest and relax, and you will find it easy to talk to me and to answer these questions. Now, did you have any other talents? Did you play any kind of musical instrument?

Played the *lyre*. [She pronounced it leer.]

You played the lyre?

Uh-huh.

Did you play well?

Oh, just fair. I played the . . . for two years I studied. I played just fair. Duncan played better.

Duncan played better? Uh-huh. Do you think you could play a lyre now if you had one?

I think so.

You think so? All right. Could you play anything else? Could you play chess?

No.

Couldn't play chess?

No.

Play any other games?

Played fancy.

Played fancy. What was that?

We played that with cards.

Played fancy with cards. What sort of a game?

'Twas a game with a board . . . only two could play.

Only two could play?

Duncan and I would play, and . . . we would go around the squares. The cards would tell you how many times you would move.

Oh, I see.

. . . Ooh, the first one to get back, we would always get a muffin and have something for surprise. It would be our own little special reward. He would give me something of his I wanted. If I would lose, he would take something of mine that he wanted . . . a book or some candy, or something I had that he wanted. We just made it that way for our winning.

I see. Now, you used to cook for Brian, didn't you?

Oh yes.

Was there any particular dish, favorite dish, that he liked or that you liked to make him?

Boiled beef with onions was his favorite.

Boiled beef with onions?

Boiled beef and . . . I would cook it all day.

Was there any other particularly Irish dish that he liked?

That's Irish! Boiled beef and onions is a *good* Irish dish.

[Here Bridey was decidedly indignant; she appeared thoroughly annoyed that I might be questioning whether boiled beef and onions is an Irish dish.]

Yes, yes I know. Was there anything else?

He liked potatoes *any* way, just any way you fixed potatoes. He would eat them. If you made a cake, he'd like it. I always fooled and joked because I told him I could make a cake and he would eat it with potatoes.

Do you remember the names of any companies in Belfast, any places where you traded, any stores, any companies, any businesses of any kind in Belfast? Do you remember any?

I remember . . . the rope . . . company. There was a big rope company.

A big rope company?

Yes, a rope . . . they made rope.

They made rope.

Yes, and there was a tobacco house . . . was a . . . oh . . .

What?

It started with a J . . . J . . . J—something tobacco house.

Anything else? Any other companies, businesses, stores, banks? The names of any of them. Just give the name of one store or bank, or anything you want. Give me the name of one.

There was . . . a . . . Caden House. It was a . . . place for . . . uh . . . women's apparel, things that the ladies would . . . blouses and camisoles and . . . and . . .

What was the name of it?

The Caden's House.

How did you spell it?

. . . C, it's a C-a-d-e-n-n-s.

Did you ever go downtown in Belfast?

Oh yes . . . I did.

You remember what it looks like, don't you?

Oh yes. . . .

All right. Do you remember Queen's University?

Yes, I remember.

Why do you remember Queen's University?

Brian taught at that school.

Did you ever go out there with him?

Oh no.

You never did?

No.

Uh-huh. All right. Can you remember some more Irish words? Last time you told us, for instance, brate. You told us about a brate. Can you remember any typically Irish words, like brate, something that means something in particular to the Irish? Tell us some more Irish words.

Oh . . . oh . . . oh . . . brate. . . . I told you about the . . . ghosts.

What are they called?

They're . . . that's the banshee. That's Gaelic . . . that's how people would say that there was . . . when somebody would die, that would be the wail of the banshees. That's . . .

All right. What is a lough or a loch?

It's a . . . water. . . . It's . . . oh . . . a spot of water. . . .

Is it called loch or lough?

My mother says "lough."

Your mother says "lough"?

Yes, it's "lough."

What does Brian say?

Oh . . . just . . . he calls it "Loch [Lock] Carlingford."

"Lock Carlingford"?

Yes. Mother says "Lough" . . . I always said "Lough."

You always said "Lough."

He says "Loch Carlingford."

I see. All right. That's very good. Had you ever been to Dublin?

No.

Never been to Dublin?

No.

What were the Meadows in Cork?

There's . . . where I lived.

All right. Did you ever hear of Cuchulain?

Yes. I heard of Cuchulain.

What about him? What did he do?

He was . . . just a sort of hero . . . we read about him. He was a hero of Ireland. He did everything. He was the bravest . . . my mother read he was the bravest, and . . .

Your mother read about Cuchulain?

Yes, he was the bravest, strongest warrior.

All right, who was Conchibar? Did you ever hear of him?

Conchibar . . . Conchibar . . .

Never heard of him?

160

No.

All right. Now, let's forget about all that and go up to the time of your death. Now, the thing that we want to know there is about what year that was. Now, you told us that you attended your own funeral. You watched them bury you. Is that right?

Yes.

All right. If you remembered that, you must remember what year it was. Perhaps they had it marked on the grave or on the tombstone, or wherever they marked it. You probably saw it. Now, what year was that?

It was . . . eighteen . . . uh . . . six . . . one-eight-six . . . four.

One-eight-six-four?

Was on the tombstone . . . one-eight . . . I think . . . I see one-eight-six-four [1864].

Are you looking at the tombstone now?

Yes.

What does it say? Read the whole thing, besides the numbers. What does the whole thing say?

. . . Ah . . . Bridget . . . Kathleen . . . uh . . . M . . . Mac-Carthy. . . .

Maybe those first numbers tell you when you were born. Are those first numbers saying when you were born?

One . . . seven . . . nine . . . eight.

That's good. Now, how about the other set of numbers?

[At this point she made a gesture with her hand while she said, "There's a line."]

One . . . there's a line . . . a line and then . . . one-eight-six and four.

All right. Let's forget about it. Rest and relax. Clear your mind entirely. Clear it completely. Now we're going to come up through time and space. We're going to come back up through time and space, come back to the time when you were Bridey Murphy, come back to that time. Come back to the time when you were in the astral world, when you were in the spirit world. You remember that. Then you were born again in Iowa. Now we're at the present time and place. I want you to relax and feel fine. I want you to take a deep breath, and that deep breath will be very relaxing; it will be just like getting an hour's sleep. You'll feel so fine and relaxed. Now rest and relax. Be completely comfortable, very comfortable. After you awaken, you will remember very clearly the Morning Jig that you used to do in your Irish lifetime. You will remember it. You will be surprised that you remember it in detail. After you awaken, when you are asked, you will be able to do the Morning Jig. It will be very easy. Now I want you to just rest and relax for a few minutes, because during these few minutes you will get extreme relaxation. These few minutes will be wonderful relaxation, even more relaxation than during a normal sleep. I will stop talking and in just a few minutes you will get very deep relaxation, so that after you awaken you will feel especially fine. You will feel better than before we started the session. Now you will have a few minutes of splendid relaxation, very comfortable, deep relaxation, so that after you awaken you will feel refreshed and new. I will talk to you again in a few minutes. . . .

[I let her rest for several minutes; then I awakened her.]

After Ruth awakened, I asked her whether she felt comfortable and relaxed. She assured us that she felt fine. But she still appeared to be a little drowsy, as though she had just been aroused from a deep sleep. Since I wanted her to be fully awake when I gave the post-hypnotic suggestion—the one about dancing the jig—I chatted casually for several minutes while the transition from lethargy to normality gradually took place.

Finally I suggested to Ruth that she stand up in the middle of the room and dance the jig for us. Her puzzled frown indicated that she might not have understood me. So I repeated the suggestion. But once again her dazed expression, like a bewildered child, made me feel that I had drawn a blank on this one.

I decided, though, to make one more effort before giving up. "Please, Ruth, stand up here," I said, indicating a place on the rug, "and perhaps some urge or sensation will suddenly strike you. Maybe you'll be able to do the jig for us."

She shrugged her shoulders, still apparently wondering what it was all about. Nevertheless, she got off the couch and moved toward the center of the room. For a few moments she stood there facing us, making a helpless, forlorn gesture with her hands. Then suddenly her whole expression changed; her body became vibrantly alive; her feet were flying in a cute little dance. There was a nimble jump, and then the dance seemingly ended with a routine which involved pressing her hand to her mouth.

I was intrigued with the ending. "What's this business with your hand on your mouth," I inquired.

"That's for a yawn!" she answered automatically.

I heard what she said, but I didn't comprehend its import. "For *what?*" I asked. But I might as well have saved my breath. Bridey Murphy and her jig were gone. In her place was a stunned Ruth Simmons, who not only couldn't answer my question but who was not even aware of the words she had just spoken.

While she sat down, still wondering what it was all about, I puzzled over the "yawn" matter. Then the pieces came together; it was the *Morning* Jig that had been referred to during her trance. Morning and yawn—it began to make sense. But logic was the only test we could apply at the time; since none of us there was a master of Irish jigs, the final check would have to await the search for Bridey Murphy in Ireland.

The third session marked the end, at least for a few months, of my experiments with Ruth Simmons. The company was sending me to New York to learn something about security analysis, the art of examining a stock or bond so microscopically that you can hope to forecast its future.

CHAPTER 13

Arriving in New York, where I enrolled in several courses in addition to the stock market study, I hardly had time to think about Bridey Murphy. But I did want to check certain points which I thought could be uncovered in New York. While MacIntosh's research books had yielded confirmation of several items—he had found, for instance, the Belfast *News-Letter*, Queen's University, the Cuchulain story, the *Sorrows of Deirdre*, and others—there was considerable information that couldn't be checked in Pueblo.

To take one example, Mac had been able to turn up nothing on the Irish town of Baylings Crossing. Bridey claimed to have passed through this place, but no atlas showed it. Either Bridey was wrong or there was some reason why this place failed to appear in any atlas Mac had studied.

So in Manhattan I tried to solve the mystery. First I telephoned the Irish consulate and asked whether they could tell me anything about a place in Ireland known as Baylings Crossing. But no, they had no record of any such place. They suggested that I try the

British Information Service. I did. The answer was the same: they couldn't find it, but why didn't I try the British and Irish Railways? I telephoned the British and Irish Railways, but it availed nothing. There just did not seem to be a Baylings Crossing.

It was not until several weeks later, while Hazel and I were spending a weekend with a friend on Long Island, that we finally had more encouraging news about the object of our search. Our host's neighbor, an enthusiastic gardener especially proud of her asparagus, stopped by to leave a generous sample.

During the ensuing conversation we learned that our visitor had spent a few years in Northern Ireland during World War II. Although I had no idea whether Baylings Crossing, if it actually existed, was in Northern Ireland, I took a shot in the dark: "Did you by any chance ever hear of a place called Baylings Crossing?" I asked.

"Certainly. I bicycled through it many times," came the prompt reply.

When I asked her why it wasn't on the map, she answered that no map would be large enough to list all such tiny Irish crossings.

A few weeks after that the incident above was practically duplicated. Talking to a woman about another matter, Hazel and I noticed that her speech was thick with the brogue of old Erin, and found out that she had been born there. Sure and she had been through Baylings Crossing many a time. And sure, she knew what she was talking about—of course it wouldn't be on any map.

So at least we now had unofficial confirmation of a place in Ireland that we could not find on any map or atlas. Yet Bridey Murphy had insisted that it was there.

Even St. Theresa's Church gave unexpected difficulty. The Irish consulate told me that they showed no such church in Belfast, nor was it listed in their Belfast telephone book. I was given the same information by a man who answered the telephone at the British Information Service. Before hanging up the receiver, however, he decided to check one more reference.

After several minutes he returned to the telephone. "Yes, there is a St. Theresa's in Belfast," he said. "It's a Roman Catholic Church." At the time, however, there was no way of knowing whether this was the right church or whether this was even the correct spelling.

During the early sessions Bridey, when asked for "Irish" words, had given us several expressions (such as "colleen" and "banshee") that almost any of us, without any intimate knowledge of language, would recognize. There were a few terms, however, with which I—and everyone else I asked—was entirely unfamiliar. For instance, the word that sounded, as it came from the tape recorder, like "brate." When MacIntosh couldn't dig it out of any of his source books I began to make inquiries among elderly Irishmen. But none could help me.

My luck didn't improve, moreover, when I resorted to the reference books in the New York Public Library. Nor did the English-Gaelic dictionaries solve the problem, and the closest thing I could find in them was the word "brait," which means expectation. This would seem to be stretching Bridey's definition, for she had contended that a "brate" was a little cup on which they made wishes and then drank from in the hope that the wish would materialize. "Very Irish, you know," Bridey had assured us.

I had almost forgotten my quest for the little "wishing" cup, when something turned up quite unexpectedly. I had been playing the tape recording for a well-known author, a woman of English descent, when Bridey referred to the cup. The author abruptly asked me to stop the recorder. Referring to her collection of antiques, she pointed out that she herself had one of these small cups, metal, with half handles extending from the top. She said, however, that she understood its correct name was "quait." Whatever its spelling, I finally had, it would seem, some evidence regarding the item that I had been tracking down in vain.

Another word that provided unexpected difficulty was "tup." Bridey had indicated that "tup" was a rather uncomplimentary reference to a male—a sort of "rounder," she had said. But the dictionary defined tup as a "ram." Further digging availed nothing —until I chanced to spot the word in Roget's Thesaurus. While doing some writing I had noticed that I was overworking the nouns "man," "fellow," and "chap," so I turned to the Thesaurus for synonyms. There, among a surprisingly long list of labels for the human male, was Bridey's "tup." Nothing indicated, however, the etymology of the word—nothing proved, in short, that it had been used in Ireland in the nineteenth century; that was still to be confirmed.

I had been in New York only one week when I came across an editor whom I had met several months before while investigating the Cayce story. Because of his actual experience with the Cayce readings, I had put him down on my list of businessmen to be interviewed.

He remembered me and promptly asked how I was faring with my psychic research.

"Well," I admitted, "it begins to look as though that fellow Cayce might have had something." Then I outlined for him what had taken place since I had last seen him, concluding my summary with the "uncovering" of Bridey Murphy.

He said he thought I might have material for a book there and suggested that I write out about ten thousand words and let him have a look at it.

I did.

Later we both decided that it would be a good idea to make a few more tapes with my subject before beginning a search for Bridey Murphy in Ireland.

At the end of the course in security analysis I returned home to Colorado. Arriving in Pueblo, I called Ruth and explained the need for a few more sessions just as soon as possible. She pointed out that it would not be possible to commence at once: the Pueblo baseball team was making its home stand, and she and Rex never missed a home game.

So I waited until the Pueblo Dodgers left for Kansas to do battle with the Wichita Indians. Even then it was not all smooth sailing. Rex was becoming somewhat concerned. "Look," he said, "I just want to sell insurance and be a regular guy; I don't want to be dubbed a crackpot or a screwball."

We eventually arranged for a session at Rye, a mountain resort where the Simmonses were vacationing for a few weeks. This fourth session, however, was cut short by a rather fantastic development.

Many times in the past I had instructed hypnotic subjects to open their eyes during a trance, but never in my experience had a subject opened his eyes unexpectedly. Nevertheless, that is exactly what happened during tape number four; it took place, moreover, in a manner that frightened everyone in the room, especially me, bringing the session to an abrupt and premature end. Here is the transcription of July 27, 1953 (after the preliminary age regression, which is omitted):

All right, now I want you to go back in your memory. I want
you to go back in your memory—on back, back—even before the
time you were born—even before the time you were born. Even
before the time you were born . . . drift on back in your memory
to a time before, to a time, any other time when you see yourself
in a scene which took place on earth . . . any other scene. And
just as soon as you see a scene that you'd like to tell me about,
you go ahead and tell me about it.

. . . I pulled . . . I pulled it off the roof with my brother.

You did what?

I pulled it off the roof with my brother.

What did you pull off the roof?

I pulled straw off.

Pulled straw off. I see.

Uh-huh.

All right. What is your brother's name?

My brother . . . he's Duncan.

Your brother's name is Duncan?

Uh-huh.

Do you see the house clearly, do you?

It's not the house I pulled it off.

What did you pull it off?

I pulled it off the barn.

The barn?

Uh-huh.

I see. Did you get a spanking?

Uh-*huh*.

Who gave you a spanking?

My mother.

Your mother?

She made me go . . . to my . . . chamber. And I had nothing
to eat.

What was your mother's name?

Kath . . . Kathleen.

Uh-huh. What else do you remember?

. . . Uh . . . I remember my . . . brother . . . came to the
door. He came over to the door, and he . . . talked to me, and
he . . . he was sorry. And he . . . *it was really his idea,* but I
didn't tell them.

Oh, I see. You took the spanking and you didn't tell them?

Well, he got spanked, too, but . . . they didn't . . . I didn't want to do it, but he said I should do it or he wouldn't play with me any more.

I see.

So I did it. But I didn't tell my mother that.

Was he younger than you?

No . . . he's bigger.

Is he older?

Uh-huh.

How much older?

He's . . . two years older than I am.

Uh-huh. And his name is what?

Duncan.

Who was he named after?

He was named after . . . my father and my grandfather.

That was their name too?

Uh-huh.

I see. How old were you when you pulled the straw off the roof?

. . . I . . . was . . . I think . . . I was about eight. [Irish brogue.]

About eight.

I think I was.

All right. Now see yourself getting a little older. See yourself getting a little older. See yourself growing up, watch yourself growing up. And pick any scene you want to and tell me about it. Just pick anything that you think would be interesting and tell me about it. Anything at all, and tell me about it.

. . . I . . . got a new sack comforter.

You got a new what?

Sack comforter.

Sack comforter?

Uh-huh.

What is that?

A coverlet for my . . . bed.

You did? What store did you get it from?

My mother sent . . . somewhere . . . some lady makes them. And she had it made for me.

Where did the lady live?

. . . She lives . . . she lives . . . Oh dear, I don't know where my mother sent exactly. She sent . . . to somewhere . . . to have it made . . . because I had . . . I had finished my school . . . and I had . . . I had done well . . . in school.

Did you?

Uh-huh.

How old are you?

I was . . . fifteen.

Fifteen?

Uh-huh.

What was the name of the school that you went to?

I went to . . . a day school.

Can you remember the name of it?

. . . Uh . . . uh.

Now relax and don't try hard . . . relax . . . relax . . . tell me the name of the school.

It was . . . Mrs. . . . Mrs. . . . Stray . . . Strayne's . . . Strayne's . . . Day School.

Do you know how you spell that?

Uh . . . yes, I remember it's S . . . S . . . S-t . . . S-t-r-a . . . I see the *sign* . . . it's a-y-n-e . . . uh-huh.

All right, is that what you see? S-t-r-a-y-n?

"E."

"E," all right. Mrs. Strayne, is that right?

Yes.

All right. And in what town is that?

That's in Cork.

All right. Now see yourself getting still older. Just relax . . . just relax. Now tell me for a moment . . . tell me . . . what is the state of your trance? Is it light, medium, deep, or very deep?

[From an article in the *Journal of Experimental Hypnosis*,[1] I learned that a hypnotic subject can be pretty well depended upon to gauge the depth of his—or her—own trance. Consequently, while hypnotizing Ruth for this session, I had explained that she would be able, while under hypnosis, to tell me at any time whether her trance was light, medium, deep, or very deep.]

Medium.

Medium? All right. Let's take just a moment to deepen the trance . . . take just a moment to deepen the trance. Now take a deep breath. I'm going to count to five. I'm going to count to five, and with each count you will notice automatically and strangely enough that your trance will become deeper and deeper. Number 1. Number 2. Number 3. Number 4. Number 5 . . . very deep . . . deep . . . deep, deep, deeper, and deeper. Now tell me, is your trance light, medium, deep, or very deep?

Deep.

[1] Vol. I, Number 2, April 1953.

Deep. All right. Now see yourself older. You last told me
about Mrs. Strayne's Day School. Now tell me . . . now tell
me . . . now tell me as you get older what scene you'd like to
tell me about. See some scene when you're somewhat older.
Tell me about any scene you like.
. . . Uh . . . My mother.
Yes?
My mother . . . she . . . made me a beautiful dress.
What for?
We were to have guests.
Remember who the guests were?
'Twas a friend of my father's . . . his family.
Uh-huh. What was their name?
It was MacCarthy.
How do you spell that name?
. . . It's M-a-c C-a-r-t-h-y.
M-a-c C-a-r-t-h-y?
Uh-huh.
All right. Now, how many MacCarthys were coming to visit
you?
   [Here she seemed to be counting while images were ap-
   parently appearing in her mind.]
One . . . two . . . two.
Who were they?
There was . . . a young man and his father. Young man and
his father.
The young man's last name was MacCarthy. What was his
first name?
His name . . . it started with a B.
Well, all right now, relax, relax. What was the father's name?
His father's name was John.
John MacCarthy?
Uh-huh.
And his son . . . what was his first name?
. . . Ah . . . it was Brian.
It was Brian?
It was Brian.
You're sure of that?
Yes . . . it was.
All right. Now see yourself getting a little older . . . see your-
self getting a little older. Now tell me how is your trance, is it
light, medium, deep, or very deep?
Deep.

All right. See yourself getting older . . . see yourself getting older. Can you see yourself, can you see yourself at the time of your marriage? Can you see yourself at the time of your marriage?

Yes.

All right. Are you in a church?

No.

You're not in a church?

No.

Where do you get married?

We were married in a cottage. . . . I couldn't be married in the church.

Couldn't be married in the church? Why not?

Because I just couldn't. Father . . . Father John said, "You can if you go over to the church," but I didn't want to go over to the church.

Oh, I see. All right, now you say Father John married you?

Father John.

Uh-huh. Father John. Now, what was Father John's last name?

Father John . . . Oh, it started with a G . . . started with a G . . .

Did you ever see it written? Did you ever see it printed? Must have been printed in the papers.

I saw it . . . I saw it on the papers . . . I saw a G . . . G . . . G . . . G-o, G-o-r, G-o-r-a-n . . . G-o-r-a-n.

Father John Goran?

Yes, Father John Goran.

Is that what it was?

Uh-huh.

Do you know what kind of priest he was?

He was a priest of St. Theresa's.

St. Theresa's Church?

Yes. Yes.

Uh-huh. On what street was St. Theresa's? What street was it?

It was on the main way.

What was the name of it?

. . . It was . . . it was . . . it was off Dooley Road.

It was off Dooley Road?

It was off Dooley Road on the main way.

Well, what was the name of this road, the one St. Theresa's was on?

. . . Brian used to say it's on the main way . . . I don't remember the road . . . or the way . . . off Dooley Road on the main way.

Off Dooley Road on the main way?

Yes.

Uh-huh. Was it on the same street that your house was on?

No.

It wasn't?

No.

Uh-huh. What was the name of the street that your house was on?

. . . We . . . lived . . . we had no road . . . we lived at the back of a house in a little cottage that . . . the big house was on Dooley Road.

The big house was on Dooley Road?

Yes. We used to walk to the main way. It wasn't very far to the . . .

About how far was St. Theresa's Church from that house?

Ah, it would take . . . Brian would just leave about five minutes before the bell. And he would be there in time.

Five minutes before the what? The bell?

The bells. He knew . . . every day.

He did, huh? All right, now just rest and relax and be perfectly comfortable and you'll find that you'll slip into a deeper and deeper trance. Deeper and deeper all the time. Deeper and deeper all the time. Deeper and deeper. Nothing will bother you, nothing will disturb you. Now you want to be completely relaxed and enjoy this, so that after you awaken you will feel even better than you do now. Now I'll ask you a few more questions. If you can remember, you just tell me the answers. If you can't remember, tell me that you do not remember. Now, how did Brian spell his name? How did Brian spell his name?

. . . 'Twas B-r-i-a-n.

B-r-*i*-a-n? It wasn't with a *y*?

No.

All right. Now what did Brian do? What kind of work?

He was a barrister.

And where did he work?

And he worked . . . with his father.

He did?

Yes.

Where at?

. . . He . . . worked part time at Belfast. He taught . . . at Queen's University . . . and he helped his father. He didn't actually work in his father's office, but his father would tell him people . . . in that country, that part, that he could . . . that he could help with. I didn't know too much, you know, he didn't want to tell me, but I know he . . . he just would write to his father. He would get a very small amount from him, but he worked hard.

I see. All right. Now, you realize that the kind of information we want, the kind of information we want is something in writing, something in writing, some way that we can prove that you lived that particular life. Now, can you think of anything that would be in writing or records that would prove that you were there?

[Tremendous sneeze from Bridey Murphy.]

[And this is the point where everybody in the room was petrified for a few appalling moments. Ruth, who had been in a reclining position, was brought to a sitting position by the force of her explosive sneeze; and now her eyes were wide open. Directing a subject to open her eyes during a trance, particularly a good subject like Ruth, is not uncommon. But I had never seen—or read about— a subject's spontaneously popping her eyes open as a result of sneezing. Consequently my first reaction was to suppose that she had been awakened by the violence of the sneeze. We were soon to realize, however, that Ruth was still very much in a trance; and when this fact dawned upon us, we were all scared stiff.]

Relax. Relax. Relax. How do you feel?

Could I have a *linen?*

A linen?

[Now confusion really broke loose. When she asked for a "linen," Rex stood up and stared at his wife; Hazel started hunting anxiously for a cover, as she misinterpreted Bridey's request for a "linen." The other witnesses were alarmed, too, as they instantly sensed that something was wrong. And while I finally deduced that what she wanted was a handkerchief, my composure was falling apart so rapidly that it was several moments before I finally took a handkerchief from my pocket and handed my subject her "linen."]

Now relax. Relax. How do you feel?

. . . I need a linen.

Yes, we're getting a linen . . . Close your eyes . . . relax . . . close your eyes . . . go back to sleep. Later I'll awaken you. In a few minutes I'll awaken you . . . All right, relax now, close your eyes. Relax and close your eyes. Relax and close your eyes. Now, do you hear my voice?

Yes.

All right, now we're coming back to the present time. We're coming back to the present time. We're coming back to the present time. Do you hear me?

Yes.

Do you hear me?

Uh-huh.

All right. Now, do you know where you are?

I'm in Cork.

You're Mrs. Ruth Simmons. You're coming back to the present time, and you're Mrs. Ruth Simmons. You're in Rye, Colorado. Do you hear me?

Uh-huh.

Do you hear me?

Uh-huh.

All right. Now, I'm going to count to five, and when I do, you'll awaken at the count of five and be Mrs. Ruth Simmons. You will be back at the present time and place. Do you hear me?

Uh-huh.

You understand what I'm saying?

Uh-huh.

All right. Number 1 . . . Number 2.

[Sneeze again.]

. . . Oh . . .

How do you feel? How do you feel? Are you awake?

. . . Brian said I had a chill.

[I can't deny that I was badly frightened by now. No use trying to deny it, because the tape recorder at this point plainly indicates that my voice was cracking. It seemed as though she was going to insist upon retaining her identity as Bridey. Had I kept my presence of mind at this stage, I could have continued with the questioning. I was less than half finished, and this might have been an especially opportune time to quiz her. But now there was only one thing on my mind—getting my subject out of that trance and back to the present time and place.]

You're going to forget about Brian! You're going to forget about Brian. By the time I reach the count of five you will awaken and you'll be Mrs. Ruth Simmons. Do you hear me? Do you hear me?

Uh-huh.

Number 1. Number 2. Number 3. Number 4. Number 5. You will awaken and you're Mrs. Ruth Simmons. You will awaken and you're Mrs. Ruth Simmons. Ruth, how do you feel? Ruth? How do you feel? How do you feel, Ruth? Do you feel all right?

Uh-huh.

[As Ruth was visibly once more herself, my sigh of relief could be heard all over the room.]

CHAPTER 14

"Bridey" sneezed again during the fifth session. But this time we had a "linen" ready for her, so it didn't disrupt the making of the tape recording. This session, which took place August 29, 1953, proved to be one of the best. Ruth seemed to fade away, and in her place was a saucy, rather flippant Irish girl named Bridey, who manifested a distinct personality, talked back, registered moods ranging from suspicion to gaiety, and in general appeared to thoroughly enjoy the whole thing. As usual, the session took place in the presence of half a dozen witnesses.

I want you to go back, back, and back to your last lifetime on earth. I want you to go back to the end of that lifetime. You've already told us about that lifetime . . . that lifetime in Ireland . . . You've already told us about that. I want you to go back to the end of it—after, just after they had ditched your body. Do you remember that? Can you remember? Can you remember that scene? Can you drift on back to that scene? When they were ditching your body?

Um-hmm. Um-hmm.

Do you see it all right now, do you?

Um-hmm.

All right. Is Father John there?

Um-hmm.

Father John is there?

Um-hmm.

Who else is there?

Brian . . . 'n' Mary Catherine, 'n' the man who played the pipes.

The man who played the pipes?
Uh-huh . . . the Uilleann pipes.
The what pipes?
The Uilleann.
Oh, I see. Who else was there?
Uh . . . uh . . . uh . . . Mary Catherine's husband . . . 'n' . . .
You told us his name was Kevin. You told us his name was Kevin. Is that right?
Kevin Moore.
Kevin Moore?
Yes.
All right. Now, as to Father John, you say he was there?
Uh-huh.
What was Father John's last name?
Oh . . . 'twas . . . G . . . Father John . . . Joseph . . .
John Joseph?
John Joseph. He spelled it once . . . G . . . G . . . o . . . G. 'Twas G-o or G-a . . . r . . . m . . . m-a-n . . .
Could it have been Gorman?
Yes.
Gorman? G-o-r-m-a-n?
Yes. It was G-o-r-m . . . o or a-n.
All right. That's all right. Now, where they're ditching you . . . Can you read that tombstone and see what it says? Your tombstone . . . where they're ditching you there. Can you read it and tell me what it says?
It's . . . uh . . . Bridget . . . Kathleen . . . M. . . . MacCarthy.
What does the *M* stand for?
For Murphy.
For Murphy. All right. What about . . . what about anything else on the tombstone? Are there any numbers on the tombstone?
. . . One . . . seven . . . and I think it's a nine . . . and an eight . . . And there's a line.

[When she referred to the line that separates the two sets of numbers—"And there's a line"—she made a motion with her finger, indicating the drawing of a line.]

There's a line. All right.
And . . . a one again.
One again?
Yes. And an eight.
Um-hmm.

And there's a . . . let's see . . . a six . . . there's . . . And . . .
Brian said you didn't do it very plain. It's a four, though.

[When she came to the last number, the four, she seemed
to be remembering a scene during which Brian had complained—after Bridey's death and the making of the tombstone—that the last number was not sufficiently clear. "It's
a four, though," Bridey assured us.]

Brian said they didn't do it very plain?

. . . He was upset about it.

He was?

It was a four, though.

All right, now rest and relax. You're going to feel very comfortable. You're going to enjoy this session more than any previously. You're going to enjoy this session very much. Because it's
going to be comfortable, and it's actually going to be fun remembering all those things. And your memory will be sharper and
clearer tonight. Your memory will come back very, very sharp.
And after you awaken, you're going to feel fine . . . you're
going to feel just fine . . . you're going to feel very relaxed and
refreshed. Now, at the time that they ditched you . . . at the
time of your death . . . did they make out a death certificate?
Did they make out any kind of death certificate or publish anything in the newspaper?

Oh, why don't you ask Father John?

[She asked this plaintively, almost painfully. It was as
though she could not understand why I bothered her with
the matters of official records when Father John was the
obvious person to approach in such cases.

Many who have listened to this line on the tape recorder have asked why I did not further pursue the point
by rebounding with a question such as, "Where can I find
Father John?" But such a query might have resulted—although I don't know for sure—in undue confusion or uneasiness, which I had assured Rex I would always try to
avoid.]

All right, now relax. Relax. Now, relax. What did you say your
husband's name was?

Brian.

Do you remember the name of Brian's mother?

. . . I . . . would have to look in the Bible. . . . I don't remember.

All right. Do you remember the name of Brian's father?

. . . Brian's father was John.

177

All right. How about Brian's uncle?

[Here Bridey did something which she repeated at various stages throughout all the tapes. Instead of directly replying only to the question, the nature of the query sometimes prompted her to think of something additional which pertained to the same general subject. This time, for instance, the mention of Brian's uncle did more than effect the recollection of his name; it spurred Bridey to remember something else, an incident involving the uncle's marriage.]

. . . His father was upset but he married an Orange. But he wasn't upset when he married *me!* Let's see . . . you mean his uncle that married the Orange?

Married what?

The Orange.

Married the Orange?

Mm-hm.

Yes. What was his name?

His name was Plazz. Plazz.

How do you spell that?

. . . P-l-a-z . . .

All right.

Z.

Two *z*'s?

Two *z*'s.

All right. Now, does Brian have any brothers or sisters?

No, his—— That's it! . . . His mother, his mother . . . his mother died. He had a brother . . . he had a brother. . . . It was a still child, and his mother died. He went then with his grandmother. . . . It was a still child.

Well, was this still child born before Brian or after Brian?

Oh, *after!*

Oh, I see. Then Brian would have been the oldest?

Brian wouldn't have been born if his mother had died!

[Chuckling.] All right, all right . . . Brian would have been the older. Yes, that's right. . . . All right, now you told us before that Brian taught at Queen's University.

Um-hmm.

Well, now Queen's University . . . Queen's University was a Protestant school . . . and Brian, Brian was a Roman Catholic.

I know.

Well?

I know. He taught *law.* He didn't teach *religion.*

And they had some . . . they had some Roman Catholics teaching there, did they?

Yes. Several.

Several, hmm?

That I knew.

Several that you knew?

Yes.

Can you name just one?

Um-hmm.

Who?

There was a fellow there. His name was William McGlone.

William McGlone?

Um-hmm. McGlone.

McGlone.

Do you want me to spell that?

Yes.

M-c . . . G . . . That's a large *G*.

Yes?

L-o-n-e.

Uh-huh. Do you remember anybody else at Queen's University there? Anybody . . . either Catholics or Protestants?

Well . . . hmmm . . . I think it was, it was Fitzhugh or Fitzmaurice. There was a Fitzhugh *and* a Fitzmaurice.

All right.

Mm-hm . . . Fitzhugh . . . Fitzmaurice.

All right. All right, tell me something else. Queen's University was called Queen's University after about 1847, which means that Brian was about fifty or maybe even a little older.

Mm-hmm. He worked with his father, you know. And that was what he had to do . . . had to let down, you know . . .

Well, didn't he . . . ?

He wrote, too.

He wrote, too?

Mm-hm. He wrote for the *News-Letter*.

He wrote for the Belfast *News-Letter*?

Yes, he did.

Well, you told me before that Brian had several articles in the Belfast *News-Letter*. Did you mean they were about Brian, or were they . . . ?

Oh *no*. He wrote about . . . just different cases, and you know . . . the things . . . that the . . . oh, that were recorded in different . . .

Oh, he just wrote *about* them?

Oh yes.

Did he ever sign his name to them?

Oh, I'm sure he would.

Did you read any of them?

. . . Oh, they were above me.

They were above you?

Mm-hm.

I see. Did you ever read the Belfast *News-Letter?*

Mmmmmmmm . . . Oh, a bit.

Now, what about . . . what about . . . what about these articles by Brian when he wrote for the Belfast *News-Letter?* About how old was he at the time he wrote for the Belfast *News-Letter?*

. . . Mmmmmmm . . .

In other words, it's very important that we find the year or about the year that he wrote those articles for the Belfast *News-Letter.* Do you think you can give us that year? Go ahead and think out loud, if you want. While you're thinking about it, you can think out loud.

. . . Ah . . . it was . . . it was after we were married and had our . . . let's see now . . . we had been married for . . . hm . . .

[Big sneeze from Bridey.]

Relax. Relax, relax. Relax completely. Now, when you were back . . . You'll be very comfortable now. You'll be very comfortable. Do you feel comfortable now?

Mm-hmm.

That's good. Now after you awaken, you'll feel still more comfortable. You'll feel fine after you awaken. You'll feel fine after you awaken. You'll feel fine. Now, when you were in Belfast, when you were in Belfast——

Twenty-five years . . .

[At first I didn't realize that she was still answering the same question that I had asked her before she sneezed. The sneeze had thrown me slightly off the track, as I was a little concerned about it—but not nearly so scared as I had been during the fourth session. And I was not the only one who was concerned. Immediately after the sneeze, Rex came forth with a handkerchief; he was making certain that his wife would not this time be forced to wait for a "linen."

In any event, it was a few moments before I realized

that Bridey had picked up the question just where she
had left off before the sneeze.]
Hmm?
You asked me when he wrote.
Oh. You're still answering that. All right. You say . . . What
was twenty-five years?
We were married. That's . . .
You mean you were married about twenty-five years when
he started writing for the Belfast *News-Letter?*
Yes.
Is that right?
Yes.
All right.
More, maybe more. But 'twas after we were married that long.
All right.
Mm-hm.
Now, when you were in Belfast, when you were in Belfast
. . . did you do your own shopping?
. . . I . . . did some of it.
Did some of it?
You see . . . I . . . Brian wouldn't let me do it all. But I did
some of it. Uh . . .
Can you name some of the things you bought and some of the
places you bought them at? Some of the things you bought and
some of the names of the stores that you traded . . . where you
traded? Some of the names of the stores where you traded?
Uh. . .uh. . . I went to Farr's. [Broadly Irish here.]
To where?
Farr's.
How do you spell it?
. . . Uh . . . F-a-r-r. F-a-r-r.
F . . . a-r-r?
Um-hm.
What did they sell?
Oh, they sold the foodstuffs.
Food stuff?
Foodstuff.
Do you know what firkin butter is? F-i-r-k-i-n? Firkin butter?
Firkin butter . . . ?
Do you know what it is?
Firkin butter . . . It's a spread.
You know what caper sauce is?
Yes.

What's caper sauce?

It's a sauce with . . . It has the small capers in it. . . . They're little, tiny black. . . . They look like a . . . clove . . . are capers . . . And you put them on fish. . . .

I see.

Capers . . .

Did you ever buy any camisoles?

Um-hmm.

[The whole point of this question was to lead her to mention the denominations of the money she used at that time. Realizing that the currency would be different from ours, we were anxious to see what Bridey would have to say on this topic. But we had decided to approach the matter obliquely. Rather than ask for the currency denominations point-blank, the question was designed so as to ask her about some item she had purchased—and then inquire as to how much money she had paid for that item. Knowing she had purchased camisoles—she had told us this previously—we employed this tack.]

Where did you buy your camisoles?

. . . Oh . . . I . . . ah . . . hmmm . . . I went there two times. That's a—*ladies'* thing. You know, that's a . . .

Um-hm.

I know . . . that . . . place. Oh . . .

What's the name of it?

. . . Hm . . . I tried . . .

Your memory will get clearer and clearer, your memory will get clear and sharp, and you'll be able to tell me.

. . . Oh dear. I know it.

You told us the name was Cadenns House. Is that right?

That's it!

Is that right?

[With wonderment.] How did you know? That's a ladies' place, you know.

Yes. But you told me once before.

Cadenns House is it.

Uh-huh. About how much money did you pay for a camisole?

. . . Ah . . . It . . . it was . . . tch [clucking tongue against teeth] . . . Oh, it was . . . Oh, it was less than . . . Oh, I don't . . . It wasn't . . . It was over a pound.

It was over a pound?

Oh . . . I can't . . .

A pound and how much?

You see, we had a . . . a . . . an arrangement where Brian, he handled things for them, and it was not the same for anything he got. That's why he did the shopping. . . . He had places there where he had to buy the things because he had an arrangement with the proprietors.

I understand.

You know, and I can't remember . . .

A pound and about how much?

Hm . . . tch . . . hmmm . . . tch . . . I'd say . . .

Just about how much?

Hmm . . . sixpence. 'Twas over a pound, and I'm not . . .

About a pound and sixpence?

About . . . Maybe. I wouldn't want you to tell them that I said they . . . that I paid that much, though.

All right. All right, we'll forget about that. Now, let's just talk about money in general. What were some of the . . . What kind of money do you have? Did you have any paper money?

I didn't have very much. I——

Then what were some of the coins? What were some of the coins named?

Uh . . . there was a tuppence.

Tuppence?

Tuppence. 'N' . . . there was a half . . . a copper—half . . . penny. And there was a sixpence, and there was a . . . a . . . tch . . . You know I'm not supposed to know about the money things.

You're not supposed to know . . .

Don't have the money 'n' the . . .

Um-hmm.

Because it's not my place.

I see.

. . . About the money . . . there was pounds. But don't you say that to . . .

All right. All right, now did you have any favorite hiding places where you would hide . . . oh, some of your own personal possessions . . . maybe some money or some letters or anything else? Did you have any favorite hiding place?

Why do you want to know?

[These six short words have to be heard on the tape recorder in order to be fully appreciated. The sly suspicion with which this sentence was charged has never failed to evoke a burst of laughter from every audience who has listened to the recording.]

183

Well, I would like to know where we can find some written evidence, where we can find some written evidence, some records that will prove that you lived in Ireland.

. . . Um . . . tch . . .

You don't have to tell us about a hiding place. But perhaps you can tell us about some written records that would prove that Bridget Murphy MacCarthy lived that life in Ireland. Can you think of anything that would prove that?

. . . Mmmm . . . oh, I think you could go to the church or go to the town. . . .

Would the church have some records?

Oh, I'm sure they would.

What kind of records would . . . ?

We had to give a tithing.

Tithing?

We had to be . . . obligated. I had to sign. And I wanted to do it, but Brian was very certain we must!

Um-hmm.

And then . . . And do you know that when we had . . . that when we were married, they had to put it on the church board?

Put it on the church board?

And they would have put there *all* about us . . . where we were from . . . how much we . . . how much money we had . . . Oh, everything. Everybody in the family that ever got hung. You know.

And that was at St. Theresa's, was it? St. Theresa's Church?

Yes. That was in Belfast.

Did you ever go to Communion and Confession?

Oh *no*. 'Twasn't allowed. You can't . . . But Brian did.

He did?

You want to know about that, you'd have to ask Brian about that.

I see.

Um-hmm.

Now, after you awaken, after you awaken, I'm going to ask you to draw a little sketch, a little sketch. I'll give you a pencil and a paper, and you'll draw a little sketch. You'll draw a little sketch showing where the place was that you lived in relation to St. Theresa's Church—in relation to St. Theresa's Church. In other words, you can just draw some squares.

[Another sneeze from Bridey.]

Now relax, relax and just go deeper and deeper asleep. Now, after you awaken, you'll be able to draw us a rough little sketch showing how your grandmother's . . . how Brian's grandmother's house was located in regard to St. Theresa's Church. Can you see that in your mind? Can you see where Brian's grandmother's house is?

Uh-huh.

And can you see where St. Theresa's Church is?

Uh-huh.

And you can see that Brian's grandmother's house, as you told us, was on Dooley Road?

Dooley Road.

Uh-huh.

I don't want to disappoint you. I can't draw.

You won't have to draw. You won't have to draw. You just draw lines, just draw lines to show us how many blocks and so forth. Can you see that?

Uh-huh . . . Yes . . . I . . .

See, just lines like a map to show how many . . . how many blocks and about where it's located. You can do that, can't you?

I will try.

All right. Now, rest and relax. Rest and relax. Can you tell me, can you tell me what your favorite song was? What was your favorite song?

Uh . . . I liked the . . . "Londonderry Air."

What else?

I liked . . . "Sean" . . . "Sean."

What was it?

"Sean." 'Twas a song about a young boy.

"Sean?"

"Sean."

Uh-huh. Give me one more favorite song.

. . . Um . . .

One more favorite song.

. . . Ohhh . . . tch . . . uh . . . uh . . . eh . . . "The Minstrels' March."

"The Minstrels' March?"

Yes. I . . . There's no words, but I just liked the march.

Uh-huh. How about your favorite poem? What was your favorite poem?

. . . Uhh . . . tch . . . my favorite poem . . . I don't recall my favorite poem. I just liked it. . . . I liked to read.

You liked to read?

Yes, I did.

What was your favorite book?

Oh . . . mmm . . . I liked the s——

What was your favorite book?

[Rather shyly.] You'll laugh. I liked the weird stories, and I liked the stories of things beyond, and I liked the dreamy stories about Cuchulain my mother used to read.

Uh-huh. Do you remember any author, anybody who wrote . . . any of those books? The name of any man who wrote any of those books?

I remember . . . man named . . . I read about a man . . . Keats. I read things by a man named Keats.

What did he write? What kind of stuff?

He . . . he was a Britisher. [Defiantly.] But I read it! . . . hmm . . . He wrote fine things. He wrote some poetry too.

Did you ever . . . Can you remember any one book? Give us the name of any one book you read and the name of the man who wrote it. . . . Any book, any book at all.

Umm . . . Remember the name of the book. . . . Can you . . . You could see who. You go to the *lender*, and he'll tell you who wrote it. *The Green Bay*.

> [In other words, she was telling me the name of the book. But as to the author—well, I would have to go to the "lender" (apparently something equivalent to our libraries), and the "lender" would tell me who wrote it.]

The Green Bay?

The Green Bay.

All right. That's good. That's good. Now . . . now, did you ever hear of Blarney Castle?

I heard of *blarney*.

What about blarney? Tell me about blarney?

Oh . . . blarney, that's . . . There's a place where you go, and you know, you put your feet above your head, and you . . . It's a myth. Brian says that Father John would tell you the truth about *that*, too! You have to . . . Believe you put your lips to it, and then you get the tongue . . . the gift of the tongue.

I see. Now, when you were in Cork, when you were in Cork, did you know about blarney then?

Oh, just . . . My mother would say, "You're full of the blarney."

But you'd never been to Blarney. You'd never been to the stone you were talking about?

I don't recall.

Now, you told us before when you were in Cork. You told us

186

before when you were in Cork that you made wishes, that you made wishes on a little cup.

Um-hmm.

Called something like a "brate."

That's a brate.

How do you spell it? Did you ever see it spelled?

Oh dear . . . I saw the cup.

You never saw the word spelled?

Uh . . . You . . . you wish on it. I . . . I don't know how to spell all the words, you know.

All right. That's all right. But it was a little cup, and it sounds like "brate"?

Sounds like a "brate."

All right . . .

And you wish on it, and your wishes all materialize. . . .

All right.

Um-hmm.

Now, where did you go to dance? Where did you go to dance?

Mrs. . . . Strayne's. Had a hall.

Well, what instruments, what instruments were used?

There was a . . . lyre, and there was a . . . the pipes. Now I told you about the pipes, but don't ask me how to spell 'em!

[This sudden declaration was expressed with such emphasis that the witnesses—at the hypnotic session—could not help breaking into laughter.]

[Laughing.] All right. All right. Now, what was your favorite dance?

Oh, I . . . I just liked to dance. I liked some jigs . . . different jigs I liked.

What jigs?

Umm . . . There was the Sorcerer's Jig. . . . That was a fast one.

What kind of jig?

Sorcerer's Jig.

All right. The Sorcerer's Jig. All right.

And the . . . There was the . . . Oh! My foot. My foot! [Gasp.]

[Even though the tape recorder plays back these words very clearly, I missed this first reference to her foot. The microphones, you see, were placed very close to her mouth and ordinarily, therefore, did an excellent job of picking up all of Bridey's utterances. On the other hand, when I leaned away from my subject in order to look at my notes —which I had begun to prepare since the second session

—I sometimes missed a few words here and there; in this case I did not hear the remark about her foot.]

What was the name of the place where you went to dance? The name of that . . . Did you say it was a hall?

Mrs. Strayne's hall. She was . . .

Was that the same place you told us about before? Where you went to school?

She had a hall. [Testily.] I didn't go to school in the hall!

All right. All right, now, now get the . . . Think about the time that Father John married you. Think about the time that Father John married you.

He didn't marry me. He didn't ever get married.

[Once again these words must be heard in order that the feeling be conveyed. Bridey seems very sad here, almost in tears.]

I'm talking about the time that Father John performed the marriage ceremony for you and Brian.

Oh . . . uh . . . Yes, he did.

All right. Now I want you to think, and think out loud if you want to. Try to . . . try to remember what year that was. See if you can . . . see if you can think out loud and find out what year that was.

. . . Uh . . . uh . . . hmph. . . . You see, I was . . . I was . . . uh . . . I was sixteen in 18 and 14. It was . . . 18 . . . and . . . 18. 18 and 18.

How old were you? And we can figure it out for you. How old were you when you got married?

Well, I was twenty when I got married. [Indignantly.] I figured it out *myself*.

Oh, then it was 18— Oh yes. I see. I see. All right. All right now . . . Now, let's talk again about that lifetime in Cork. Now, when you traveled from Cork to Belfast . . . when you traveled from Cork to Belfast, how did you travel from Cork to Belfast?

I traveled in the livery.

All right. Now I want you to name . . . I want you to name some of the towns, some of the places you went through from Cork to Belfast. . . .

From Cork—to go to Belfast . . . Hmmm . . . hm . . .

Go ahead and think out loud. Think out loud and tell us what you're thinking. What places between Cork and Belfast?

[Here is another example of a question's reminding Bridey of some associated episode. There was a pause while she seemed to be contemplating something; and then she finally spoke—to explain that she had been thinking of something other than my question.]

. . . Forgive me. I wasn't thinking about that.

What were you thinking about?

I was thinking that my father was so unhappy. You know, we took the horse, 'n' he was a very worried man. And he felt he'd lost so much. . . . I was going so far away. He went . . . he went to the bed over it.

Is that right?

Oh, he was so upset. And I—I was unhappy to go then.

And what. . . And you took the horse and you left?

[When I interrupted Bridey here, all the witnesses in the room would have liked to pull me away. In short, they would have preferred to hear more of the personal "life and times of Bridey Murphy." But our real job was to dig for the solid, evidential checking points, and I could not see how her father's sentiment could help us in this direction. So I steered her back to the original question.]

Um-hmm.

Oh.

Um-hmm. He was . . . oh . . . he was unhappy with me, and [rueful little laugh] . . . I . . .

All right. Now think about that trip, think about that trip with the horse and the carriage. Tell me about some of the places you went through. Tell me about some of the places . . . the names of some of the places. You told us before. . . .

Well . . .

You told us before, for instance, Carlingford.

Well, yes, I've . . . You want to know the names of the places?

Yes, the names of the places, tell me.

That's the name of the lough, you know, and the . . . the lough was there first, and then there was the . . . place. It was . . . Let's see.

Yes. What else?

And we went through . . . mm . . . mm . . . Munster. We went through a little . . . place. We stopped for potato cakes. . . . Oh . . . potato cakes.

What's the name of the place?

. . . 'Twas . . . umm . . . Starts with a D. I could see a D and an o . . . and a . . . b . . . D-o-b . . . and a y.

All right.

Do-by.

All right. Now I want you to think about this for a moment. [Whisper.] Doby.

I want you to think about this. You told us before there was a place by the name of Baylings Crossing.

Ah, it's just a *spot,* you know. [Little chuckle.]

Well, where was it? Was it close to Belfast, or was it close to Cork?

It was closer to Belfast.

Closer to Belfast. All right, now what about Mourne? You told us about Mourne. Where was Mourne, closer to . . .

Mourne is near Carlingford.

Mourne is near Carlingford?

Yes. Mourne . . . near . . .

All right. Now can you see yourself in your mind, can you see yourself in your mind doing the Sorcerer's Jig? Can you remember yourself doing the Sorcerer's Jig? Can you see yourself?

Oh, I'd do it with Brian. . . .

Uh-huh. Can you do the Sorcerer's Jig by yourself without a partner?

[Little snort of laughter.] I don't believe so.

All right. . . .

You have to do . . . You go round in a circle, you know, and hold hands.

Uh-huh. All right. Now relax, relax. You're going to feel fine after you awaken. You're going to feel fine after you awaken. You're going to feel even better than you do now. This is going to be very, very pleasant. Now, did you play a musical instrument yourself? Did you play a musical instrument?

Hmph . . . hmph . . .

> [Once again it seemed as though she were thinking of some scene to which the question had deflected her memory. The indignant, staccato-like "Hmph," which she repeated, indicated that, instead of directly replying to the question, she was reflecting on some other incident.]

Did you ever play the lyre?

Oh, I don't . . . I played *at* it. You don't want to say I *played* it.

Uh-huh . . .

My . . .

Can you remember any tunes that you played on the lyre when you were "playing at it"?

. . . Hm . . . Played just beginner's pieces. I wasn't enough . . .

Do you remember any of the pieces you tried to play?

I played . . . ah, I played . . . "Fairies' Dance". . . . I played "The Morning Jig". . . . I played . . .

You played "The Morning Jig"?

[Jauntily.] *Mm*-hmm! Played "The Morning Jig."

All right, now one thing about your father . . . one thing about your father. What did you say your father's name was?

. . . My father?

Yes.

. . . Was Duncan.

Are you sure that Duncan, Duncan Murphy . . . Are you sure that Duncan Murphy was a barrister?

[This query was injected for a number of reasons. In the first place, even though it is quite possible that the daughter of a barrister might have married the son of another barrister—this may even have had something to do with their meeting in the first place—still I wondered whether they were all really barristers. Or could it have been that Bridey, because she married a barrister's son, was upgrading her social status a bit when she told us that her own father, too, was a barrister?

Furthermore, she had told us that she lived in the Meadows, which she said was a district outside of town. I wondered, then, whether a barrister would have lived in the country.]

That's what he told my mother and me.

You think he was a barrister?

Yes.

Did he do any other kind of work?

He did some . . . cropping.

Some what?

[Impatiently.] Cropping.

What's that?

[Quite annoyed.] Cropping! It's to *grow* things.

Oh, I see. I see. All right. All right.

[With some distress.] My foot.

What did you say?

My *foot.*

What about your foot?

. . . Hmm . . . it's . . .

[This time I clearly heard the complaint about her foot;

191

and as I could not perceive what the trouble was, I decided to awaken her. Witnesses at the session, and many who have listened to the recording, have pointed out that the complaint regarding her foot, in both instances, developed shortly after the references to her dancing the jig.]

All right. I want you to rest and relax. I want you to rest and relax. I want you to rest and relax. I want you to rest and relax. You're coming back to the present time and place. You're going to forget about that lifetime in Ireland. And now you're going to think about your lifetime in the United States. Now, I'm going to count to five. I'm going to count to five. And at the count of five, you'll awaken and you'll feel fine. You'll be Ruth Simmons, and you'll feel even better than you do now. You'll feel just fine in every respect. And your foot will feel fine, your feet will feel fine, your legs will feel fine, your body will feel fine. Your head will be clear. . . . Your head will be clear. Your nose will be clear. . . . All will be clear. And in the future . . . in the future you will be free from allergies. After you awaken tonight, you will be free from allergies. You will no longer be bothered by allergies.

[Still in the Bridey voice.] I don't have allergies. I have a *chill.*

All right, now you won't have a chill. After you awaken, you'll feel fine. You won't be bothered in any respect.

All right.

Number 1. Number 1 . . . Number 1, you're coming back to the present time and place. Number 2, number 2. When I reach the count of five, when I reach the count of five, you'll be Ruth Simmons and feel fine. Number 3, number 3. Coming back to the present time and place. Number 4 . . . number 4. When I reach the count of five, when I reach the count of five, you'll be Ruth Simmons, and you'll be at the present time and place, and you'll feel fine, you'll feel fine in every respect, and you'll breathe clearly, and your head will feel fine. You'll feel fine all over. Number five, number five. Completely relaxed and you feel fine. Now you can awaken, and you'll feel fine. Number five . . . You feel fine, you feel just fine . . . you feel fine. . . .

CHAPTER 15

Before finishing the book, I wanted to make one more tape. There were still questions left unanswered. Where had she been buried (or "ditched," as Bridey would have termed it)? What was Brian's full name—that is, did he have a middle name? If she had been married in Belfast, would her parents have permitted her to travel with Brian prior to the marriage? Did she remember any songs that she could sing now?

And we wanted to have her dance the Morning Jig again, just as she did during the third session in response to a post-hypnotic suggestion. But this time we planned to take motion pictures of the flying feet of Ruth (or of Bridey, depending upon your point of view). So we invited a cameraman replete with equipment.

The sixth tape, therefore, was made on October 1, 1953. After the regular age regression, Bridey came forth with a question that took me by surprise. "Who are you?" she suddenly wanted to know. It was the first time during all the experiments that she had asked such a question. Here is the transcription:

Now I want you to drift on back, even before that. I want you to go back to the time before you were born, even back before you were born into this lifetime. You told us once before that you remembered yourself in a place of waiting . . . that you were in a place of waiting. Do you see yourself in that place of waiting? . . . Do you see yourself in that place of waiting? All right. Now rest and relax. Be very comfortable. Be very, very comfortable. You're going to enjoy this very much. It's going to be a lot of fun. Now I want you to go back to that life experience in Ireland when you were Bridey Murphy. Now, can you remember that lifetime in Ireland, when you were Bridey Murphy? Can you remember that?

. . . Mm . . . Umm-hmm.

All right. Now I want you to go back to the time of your marriage. Can you remember when you were married? When Bridey Murphy was married? Can you remember that? When you were married?

. . . Who are you?

[This was the first time, during all these sessions, that she asked such a question; it may, furthermore, support the contention of those students of hypnosis who suggest that the hypnotist should personally project himself into the total situation, assuming some identity and thus reducing possible confusion for the subject.

As it was, I was taken by surprise and gave a well-hedged answer.]

I am your friend. I'm your friend.

We have traveled before.

Tra——? We have traveled before?

Um-hmm.

[Again I was taken by surprise; this sort of thing had never previously popped up. I didn't even know what she meant by the remark that we had traveled before. And I was not inclined to pursue the topic.]

That's good. Now, can you see that . . . can you see that time that you were married? Can you see that time?

Um-hm.

All right. Now tell me what was the name of the man you married?

Brian.

Was Brian his middle name or his first name?

. . . Uh . . . They called him . . . Brian . . . his father's name . . . You want to know about who I married?

Yes. What was his whole name? What was Brian's whole name? His full name? Brian's full name. Was that . . . did he only have the one first name or did he have a middle name?

Oh, he had several names, you know.

Oh well, then tell me all his names. If you can remember them.

He had . . . Sean. [Pronouncing it "See-an" rather than the Gaelic "Shawn"] Sean. S . . . Do you want me to spell it for you?

Yes.

S-e-a-n.

All right.

And he had Joseph for the Church.

Yes.

And he had Brian.

Sean [pronouncing it "Shawn"] Joseph Brian?

[You will recall that, in referring to the name of a song during the previous session, she used the pronunciation "Shawn." But here, alluding to the name of her husband, she pronounced the name as "See-an." Her explanation follows.]

See-an.

See-an?

It's "Shawn" too. But "See-an" is the right way.

All right.

Mm-hm.

Any other names? And did Brian come before the Sean Joseph? Or was it Sean Joseph Brian? Was it Sean Joseph Brian?

No. Sean Brian Joseph.

Sean Brian Joseph. And the last name?

MacCarthy.

Fine. Now, relax comfortably. You're going to enjoy this. Relax and let's enjoy it completely. Just relax completely. Be very comfortable. Now, where did you get married? Did you get married in Cork or at Belfast?

I . . . got married at Cork.

You got married in Cork?

I got married . . . in Cork. But I didn't tell my folks I got married again in Belfast too.

Oh, I see. You first got married in Cork, and then you were married again in Belfast?

Don't you repeat that.

No, no, that's . . .

You repeat things.

[Laughs.] No, I won't repeat those things.

[I now have the subject's permission to "repeat those things."]

Um-hm. But I didn't get married in the church. I just did it . . . to make Brian happy.

I see. Then you got married first in Cork and then in Belfast?

I got married so that my folks could see me, 'n' . . . They were unhappy about it, you know. I mean, they . . . felt that I was . . . that they were losing me. My father was very upset.

I see, and you . . . and you went to Belfast in a livery, you told us.

Yes.

Well, you used your father's horse. You told me that you used your father's horse. But where did you——

[A little indignantly.] That's all right.

I know. But where did you get the livery?

Well, the livery . . . it belonged to . . . it was a stable . . .

Mrs. Strayne's . . . husband had a stable.

Oh, I see. All right, now rest and relax. Be very comfortable. Rest and relax. Rest and relax. Now, when you finally got married in the church, did you become a Catholic?

No. I told you that I didn't. I don't . . . I didn't accept it. I didn't get married in the church. I got married at Father John's . . . room.

Father John's room?

Um-hm.

I see.

He did it as a favor.

Uh-huh.

But it was . . . just so it would be recorded for . . . the Church. For the children we didn't have. . . .

I understand. Now, rest and relax. Rest and relax and be very comfortable. Enjoy this. In other words, you couldn't attend Confession and Communion because you weren't really married in the church?

I didn't want to.

You didn't want to attend Confession and Communion?

I'd been taught all my life. Why should I want to do that?

I see. All right.

I didn't condemn him.

What did you say?

I didn't condemn Brian. That was the way he was brought up. But he didn't condemn me.

I see.

If we had children, I promised that they would be what he wanted them.

I see. Now, what was the name of Brian's grandmother? Brian's grandmother who lived there very near you. What was her name?

You mean her first name?

Yes. Was her last name MacCarthy?

Oh yes.

What was her first name?

Mmm . . . They called her . . . oh . . . They called her . . . Oh, how would you say it? They called her . . . Delilinan.

Devinan?

De*lil*inan.

I see. All right.

Delilinan.

All right. Now, there in Belfast, when you lived in Belfast . . .

Uh-huh . . .

When you lived in Belfast, did you do your own cooking?

And who would do it if I didn't?

[Chuckle.] You didn't have a maid?

Oh no.

I see. What was your favorite dish?

Um . . . I . . . I liked . . . uh . . . platters . . . or flats of potato cake . . . But I certainly had my fill of potato cake.

Did you like anything else?

I liked . . . Oh, I liked . . . um . . . I liked beef, and I liked . . . there's a root they cook . . . and I liked radish root with beef . . . and I like . . . um . . . stew . . . stews. . . . Oh, I like . . . I like all the dishes that are made in the . . . flats.

All right. Where did you buy your foodstuffs? Where did you buy your foodstuffs?

I bought . . . Brian bought it at the greengrocer's.

What was the greengrocer's name?

Oh . . . tch . . . John . . .

Your memory will be clear. Your memory will be clear. . . .
. . . John . . . John . . . They called him John. . . . It started with a C. . . .

All right. Spell it for us . . . for me.

There was a . . . C . . . a . . . r . . . two r's.

Carr?

[Going right on with the spelling.] i . . . g . . . I'm not much at spelling.

I know, but we can get this. C-a-r-r-i, you said. C-a-r-r-i.

G . . . It was g-a-n or e-n, or . . . Carri . . . Carri . . .

C-a-r-r-i-g?

. . . A-n . . . Just . . .

Carrigan?

Yes, that's it.

C-a-r-r-i-g-a-n?

C-a-r-r-i-g-a-n.

You think that's it?

I think so.

All right. . . .

Maybe not the right spelling, but that's his name.

All right. Now, where did you buy your shoes? Do you remember where you bought your shoes?

Uh . . . mmm . . . I bought 'em . . . I didn't do much of the buying.

Well, do you remember the name?

I . . . It started with a . . . [Giving up.] Oh, all this spelling
is wearing me out.

Well, all right, if it's bothering you, do not spell it.

It's a . . . It's a house . . . or something . . . Cadenns . . .

You told us Cadenns House before. Is that right?

That's the place.

All right.

Cadenns House. I don't know how to spell it.

All right. All right. Now rest and relax. Rest and relax. And
enjoy this. Enjoy this. We can have some fun. We can enjoy this.
Be comfortable.

If we ever get through spelling, we can.

[Laughs.] All right. We'll try not to bother you with spelling
any more.

Um.

We'll try not to bother you with spelling any more.

Yes.

Uh. How were the streets lighted? How were the streets
lighted there in Belfast?

. . . Oh dear [Sigh]. . . . They were just . . . I don't know
. . . You'd have to ask Brian about those things. . . . That's not
for a woman. They were just poles with lights on 'em.

Poles with lights.

Um . . . They weren't . . . They were burning . . . burning
some way. I don't know about that. I'll . . . I'll ask.

[Whom she would ask and how she would ask, I don't
know. This, as already explained, was one of those things
that I hesitated to probe for fear that it might precipitate
undue confusion, which I had vowed to avoid.]

Now how about . . . Did you ever write anyone any letters?
Or did you ever get any letters from anyone?

. . . Oh . . . I . . . I'd get letters from home.

From Cork, you mean?

Uh-huh.

Did you save any of those letters?

Oh, I did. I saved them.

Would you tell me where you kept them, so perhaps we
could find them?

I had them in the hut.

In the hut?

In the house.

Any particular place?

Oh, I had them . . . You know where the . . . you know

where the . . . There's a . . . a pewter dish, and it's . . . a funny brown color, and it's on the second shelf.

On the second shelf?

And I had a little tiny . . . portfolio, and I had it up there. And I had some ribbons, and I had some . . . letters. And I had some . . . mm . . . just . . . I had some tiny little sacks of rice. And I had . . . they were sewed to my . . . hm . . . There is an elastic band that my mother gave me to put around . . . my leg . . . And you'd snap the little rice bags on it. And it's a sign of . . . purity. And she wanted me to wear it. And I kept it when I went away.

All right. All right, now I'm going to name some names. Maybe you will recognize one or more of these names. I'll just name some names. If you recognize any, you'll tell me. Now I'll just start naming some names. And if you recognize any of these, you tell me.

[On my way home to Colorado—just prior to these last three sessions—I had stopped in Washington on business. While there, I went to the Congressional Library and asked whether they had any old copies of the Belfast *News-Letter*. They had one copy, dated 1847, and I copied these names from that issue. I was hoping that one of these names might have some special meaning for Bridey. But nothing developed.]

Um-hm.

R. Percival Maxwell.

What a name. Tch. Who'd recognize a name like that?

[Laugh.] John Lawe's Timber Yard.

John what?

John Lawe. John Lawe's Timber Yard.

John Lawe's Timber Yard . . . That's a man's name?

Yes. Do you recognize it at all? Does it mean anything to you? John Lawe's Timber Yard on 13 James Street?

Uh . . .

All right. Langtrees and Herdman . . . Langtrees and Herdman . . . Langtrees and Herdman. Does that mean anything?

What was that other one?

John Lawe's Timber Yard, you mean?

[Whispers.] John Lawe's Timber Yard . . . timber . . .

On James Street.

It's at 13 James Street?

Yes. Do you remember where 13 James Street was?

Oh, I should. There's something about that . . . Timber Yard . . .

All right, let's——

Did he . . . did he . . . did he need a . . . did he need a——

Did he know Brian?

I don't know.

I think that he . . . I believe he knew . . . oh . . . oh, something about him. You just bear with me. About him. . . . He's a . . . Oh, I know something about him . . . John Lawe's Timber Yard . . . He's . . . oh . . . You go on. I'm going to think about it.

All right.

John Lawe . . .

Now how about the Forster Greene and Company? Forster Greene and Company? . . . Do you remember the Robert Williamson triplets?

. . . I don't remember that.

How about the name John Craig? John Craig? Remember that name? . . . John Craig . . .

Uh . . .

Hardware?

Hardware? John Craig Hardware?

Um-hm.

Are these places in Belfast?

Yes. Yes, that's in Belfast.

That's in Belfast. I . . . Have you been looking at Brian's books?

No.

Where did you get the names?

I got that name from the Belfast *News-Letter*.

[Murmurs.] Ah, yes.

Now, how about—— What did you say?

I believe some of those names are in Brian's books.

Well, they might be. Now you don't . . . Just . . . just listen to the names, and if any one name means anything in particular, you tell me about it. Now, here's some more names. Thomas Edward . . . Cliff Leslie . . . William Nielson Hancock . . .

Oh . . .

James Gibson . . . Richard Homer Mills . . .

Oh . . .

Ecklin Molyneaux, Molyneaux . . . Ecklin Molyneaux? And then in Cork maybe you knew Michael Barrie or Sir Robert Kane . . .

No . . .

Now in Belfast, you know the name of the large tobacco company in Belfast?

[She herself had told us on an earlier tape that there was a tobacco company and a rope company that she remembered, although she could not recall their names; I hoped that she might now be able to remember the names.]

The tobacco company?

Mm-hm.

I know there's a big tobacco company, and there's a big rope company because they . . . Brian has them in his books too. But I don't remember the names.

Don't remember the names. All right.

There's a tobacco house, and there's a rope place. They make rope.

All right. Now, now, let's go on back to Cork. Let's drift on back to Cork. Let's drift on back to Cork. Now, you had a good time in Cork. You enjoyed your life in Cork. Now, we'll enjoy talking about it tonight. We'll enjoy talking about it. Now think about your brother in Cork. Think about your brother. You told us his name was Duncan.

Mm-hmm.

Now, what's his whole name? His full name?

. . . Duncan . . . Duncan . . .

Did he have any other names?

I had a few for him.

You had a few, yes. Did *he* have any?

. . . Duncan . . .

Was it just Duncan? Or did he have any other name?

He had . . . yes . . . On his . . . record in the Bible . . . Duncan . . . Blaine . . . Murphy.

Duncan Blaine Murphy?

Duncan Blaine Murphy.

Did Duncan ever get married?

Duncan . . . Yes, he did.

Did he have any children?

. . . I—yes, he did.

Did he write you about this when you were in Belfast? Did he write to you about it? Did he write you about . . . Or did he . . .

He married. He married Mrs. Strayne's daughter.

He did?

. . . She was a beautiful girl.

What was her name?

Amy.

The daughter's name was Amy?

Amy.

All right.

A-i-m-e-e.

A-i-m-e-e?

E-e.

Mm-hm. All right. Was Duncan a cropper? Like his father? [This question was purposely slanted to explore further Duncan's occupation. It is to be noted that here Bridey made no reference to her former allegation that Duncan was also a barrister.]

Yes . . . He was . . . he was supposed to be. That's the way it went.

All right. Now, what kind of crops?

Well, there was . . . oh . . . it was divided off. There was . . . flax . . . and there was hay . . . and there was . . . some . . . Way in the back, there was some tobacco. And there was . . . hmm . . . corn . . . and . . . Did I say flax?

All right. How did you take up those crops? How did you harvest them? What kinds of implements or tools?

I didn't do it.

No. I mean how did they do it?

They cut them down. They had a . . . long . . . I don't know what they called it.

All right.

Long handle, and it had a . . . funny blade.

All right. Do you remember your address in Cork? Do you know your address in Cork?

. . . Just the Meadows.

Now how about . . . how about the Morning Jig that you told us you danced before? Can you see yourself doing the Morning Jig? . . . Can you watch yourself in your mind doing the Morning Jig?

Mm-hmm.

Can you see yourself?

Yes.

All right. Now watch yourself carefully doing that Morning Jig. Watch yourself doing the Morning Jig. Watch yourself doing that Morning Jig . . . in your mind. See yourself.

Mm-hm.

After you awaken, I'll ask you to do the Morning Jig. I'll ask you to get up and do the Morning Jig. And you will want to do it. You enjoyed it so much, you will enjoy dancing it again.

Mm-hm.

And tonight, after you awaken you will do the Morning Jig twice. You will go through the Morning Jig twice. After you awaken. After you awaken. I'll ask you to get up and show you where to dance the Morning Jig. And you will be glad to do it. You will enjoy doing it.

Mm-hm.

All right. Now do you remember your little brother? Do you remember your little brother, the one that died? The one that you told us died when he was very young? Your little brother.

I don't remember very much.

Do you remember what he died from?

[No answer.]

. . . Some kind of . . . black-something.

All right.

Or something . . .

All right. Now tell me, can you sing? Can you sing?

Mm-hmm.

What song do you like? What Irish song do you like?

Mm . . . mm . . . I like "The Londonderry Air."

Can you sing "The Londonderry Air?"

. . . I'd rather not. I don't like to sing very well.

Is there any other song, any other real short song that you would like to sing? . . . Just some little short song . . . Perhaps some gay little song that you liked.

Mmm . . . [Sings]   Father's girl's a dancing doll.

                  Father's girl's a dancing doll.

                  Sing around and swing around.

                  Father's girl's a dancing doll.

Very good. And did you sing that in Ireland? Did you sing that at Cork?

Uh-huh.

All right. What was the date of your birthday? That is, the month and the day. The month and the day of your birthday?

. . . Mph . . . I was . . . mm . . . 'twas in the holidays. 'Twas in the holidays.

Do you remember the month?

'Twas the twelfth month.

Twelfth month?

Uh-huh.

What about the day?

It was the . . . twentieth day.

Twentieth day of the twelfth month?

Uh-huh.

[This does not correspond in any way to Ruth Simmons'
birthday—neither the month nor the day.]

All right. I want you to take any one day in Cork . . . any
one day that was very pleasant. Recall any one day that you
particularly liked. Recall it to your mind, and tell me about that
whole day. Just tell me about that day, what you did that day
from the time you got up till the time you went to bed. Tell me
about that day.

. . . Mm . . . Got up for a fitting. And I . . . had . . .
one, two, three . . . new . . . slips. And they had wide
sashes. And . . . my mother spent the whole morning . . . making me . . . three pretty slips with sashes. And I had . . . slippers. . . . They were sent to me. White slippers. And I went
to . . . Mrs. Strayne's . . . for a . . . tea and cakes . . . for . . .
Genevieve. Tea and cakes for Genevieve, and I wore my white
slips with the . . . green sash . . . and my new shoes. And they
said . . . "You're . . . a . . . ve-ry pretty little girl." . . . But she
was with her hand out for what I brought her, too.

[Chuckle.] All right, what else?

And I had tea and cakes, and I spilled . . . And I . . . I had
to . . . take the slip off, and I had to stay back in the back parlor
till it dried.

All right. Did anything else happen that day?

That was a pleasant day. The party. Tea and cakes, and three
new—slips.

Did you do anything else that day?

[No answer.]

And what was the fitting for? Why was there a fitting?

For my three new slips. I had to have the one done for
Genevieve's tea and cakes, and . . . my mother said, "We will
just make three while we've got you on the board."

All right.

. . . A little girl likes pretty things.

Now can you tell me . . . what was your word for ghosts?
What's your word for ghosts?

A banshee.

Is there any other word for ghost?

. . . If you want to know the Gaelic words, you'll have to ask
somebody else.

All right.

A banshee . . . or a . . . a . . . ghost is a spirit, or a . . .

All right. Now while you were there in Cork, while you lived at that house in Cork, did you say any prayers or blessings before you ate? Did you say any prayers or blessings before you ate?

Yes.

Can you say one now?

We said . . . Bless . . . bless this . . . mm . . . this . . . Bless this food . . . Umm . . . Bless this . . . Keep us happy, bright, and good. . . . Bless this . . . bless this . . .

[It is interesting to note that on the very first tape Bridey delivered this blessing without any hesitation. But here she stumbles and is unable to recall all the words. This is possibly an indication that a deeper trance was achieved during the first session. In regard to the recall type of ordinary hypnotic age regression, Le Cron wrote (in *Experimental Hypnosis*): "Such memory recall may be only partial and rather vague; at other times it may be clear and remarkably redundant."]

You said that prayer for me once before. You said that for me once before. Are you having trouble remembering it now?

Bless . . . I know it. Bless this house. . . . Bless the food. There's more. Bless . . . Keep us happy, bright, and . . . good. But there's some more.

All right. Don't worry about that. Did you ever hear of Killarney? Did you ever hear of Limerick, or Galway, or Clare?

Limerick. There's a County Limerick.

Limerick was a county?

There's a county, Limerick.

All right.

And there's a . . . Galway. Galway.

What is Galway?

'Tis a port.

A port?

A port.

All right. Now, let's for just a minute . . . let's for just a minute drift back to Belfast. Drift back to Belfast. Now, tell me, on the street in front of St. Theresa's Church, in front of St. Theresa's Church . . . what was the road made of? Was it a dirt road or a brick road? What was it?

[During the fifth session, you may recall, Bridey was directed to draw, as a post-hypnotic suggestion, a simple sketch showing the respective locations of her house and St. Theresa's Church. At the end of the session she responded to the post-hypnotic direction and made the drawing.

Several days later, however, Hazel looked over the "map" and noticed dozens of tiny circles that our subject had sketched in what was supposed to be the street. "I'll bet she meant these little circles to be cobblestones," Hazel suggested. So I decided, without saying anything to the subject, to find out whether these could have been cobblestones. Hence the question above. And it should be observed that I did not refer to a "stone" road; I asked whether the road was dirt or brick.]

'Twas a stone road.

Stone road? What did they call those stones?

Cobbles.

All right. Now did you ever receive the last rites or the Extreme Unction before your death in that lifetime? Did you ever receive the last rites or Extreme Unction?

[Positively.] No!

But they ditched you in the . . . in the . . . They ditched your body in the . . . St. Theresa's churchyard?

[Suddenly.] Are you a Catholic?

No. No, I'm not.

. . . They ditched me. . . . I wasn't on the *hallowed* ground.

Oh, you . . . you weren't on the hallowed ground. I see. All right. All right, now rest and relax. Be perfectly comfortable . . . perfectly comfortable. Be very, very comfortable. Now, what was the name of your family . . . there in Belfast—what was the name of your family surgeon?

. . . I don't know what you mean.

Chirurgeon?[1]

Ch . . . ?

The man who took care of you when you were ill?

Yes.

What was his name?

I *was* ill. I caught a ter-rific chill.

[The reference to the "chill" will probably lead the mind of the reader to flash back to earlier sessions, when she had also complained of a bad chill experienced during the

[1] Archaic form of "surgeon."

206

Bridey Murphy lifetime. Since many researchers in this field contend that some current afflictions have their origin in past-life experiences, several of the people working with me on this matter wondered whether Bridey's "chill" could in any sense be germane to Ruth's present allergies.

There was never sufficient time, though, adequately to look into this possibility. Nor did the following direct suggestion result in any substantial improvement.]

Now, you'll never have that chill again. That chill will never bother you again. That chill will disappear. In the future you will be free from all the effects of that chill. That chill will never bother you. That chill will disappear, it will vanish, it will leave you. The chill will leave you. Now and forevermore, the chill will not bother you. The chill will go away. The chill will leave you. And after you awaken, you will be free from the effects of the chill. The chill will never again bother you. You will be free after you awaken. And now your body is becoming warmer and pleasantly comfortable. Your body will become warm and pleasantly comfortable. You're feeling fine . . . feeling just fine. And your head will be clear, and your nose will be clear. And you'll feel fine after you awaken. You'll feel fine after you awaken. Now relax. Relax, because you're going to awaken. In a little while you're going to awaken. In just a few moments you're going to awaken. After you awaken, you will want to dance the Morning Jig. After you awaken, you will want to dance the Morning Jig after you awaken. After you awaken, soon after you awaken, I will ask you . . . I will ask you to take a spot on the floor and do the Morning Jig. And you will do it twice, and you will feel fine. Now, I'm going to count to five. I'm going to count to five. I'm going to count to five, and you'll awaken at the count of five. You'll be back at the present time and place. You'll be back at the present time and place. You'll be Mrs. Ruth Simmons. You'll be in Colorado, and you'll feel fine. You will feel comfortable and warm. And the chill will never again bother you. You will never again be disturbed by the chill. Nor will you be disturbed by any allergies, if the chill caused the allergies. You will never again be disturbed by them. You will be free from them. And you're feeling more and more comfortable all the time as I begin to count. Number 1. Number 2. Number 3. Number 4. You'll awaken gradually. When I reach the count of five you'll be at the present time and place, and you'll feel fine. Number 5. Now, you're going to awaken and feel fine. You'll open your eyes gradually. Open your eyes gradually to get adjusted to the light. And you'll feel fine and very, very comfortable. You'll feel just fine. Now . . . the lights too bright? Lights too bright?

Ooh.

How do you feel, Ruth?

CHAPTER 16

In asking people to listen to the tape recordings, I had particularly sought out keen thinkers whose incisive analyses would probe all possible explanations of the Bridey Murphy phenomenon. And I was especially interested in drawing out a conclusion from one listener whose brilliance and penetrating logic had won him national prominence. Consequently I called on him several months after he had listened to the recordings.

"You've heard the Bridey tapes," I said, "and you've had time to think about them. Now what's your opinion of the whole thing?"

"I've given those tapes considerable thought," he answered. "At this point I'd be unwilling to state a definite conclusion. But I don't mind listing some general observations.

"In thinking over the Bridey matter, for instance, I was reminded that philosopher Hume said that no testimony is sufficient to establish a miracle unless the testimony be of such a kind that its falsehood would be more miraculous than the fact which it endeavors to establish. And in the Bridey Murphy case I admit that alternative explanations are more fantastic than the rebirth explanation she gives while under hypnosis. Her explanation, in fact, is the only one which seems to fit all the facts.

"For example, an alternative theory which will probably be suggested by some is that your subject has read or heard a story which she has adopted as her own. But this idea has too many shortcomings. Hearing or reading a story would not account for her subtle Irish brogue while under hypnosis; it would not account for her ability to dance the Morning Jig. Furthermore, Bridey's life is too drab and unromantic to have been the theme of any story. And if there is such a story, where is it?

"If she had read or heard all this, your subject could easily explain that fact under hypnosis. But she insists that she actually lived through those experiences. And I believe I'm safe in saying that anyone who has *listened* to your tapes will promptly agree that the spontaneity and character of her responses—and her association of thoughts—indicate that this is a person who is actually relating her own experiences and not merely repeating a tale.

"On top of all this, it is very unlikely that any story would have included the after-death episode that Bridey describes."

"What about the possibility that the whole thing might have been produced by fraud?" I asked him.

"That's even less tenable than the story theory," he replied, "for some of the reasons I just mentioned. Moreover, if there was trickery or deception, it means that your subject was acting. And if what I heard was a histrionic performance, then Ruth Simmons is a greater actress than Sarah Bernhardt.

"Besides, much of the information she disclosed while in trance simply was not available to either you or her. Some facts were not even available on this side of the Atlantic. No, fraud is not the answer.

"Any alternative explanation, it seems, would have to include the fantastic combination of ingenious and costly research, histrionic perfection, astonishing coincidence, plus fraud and collusion. The probability of such a combination fades to the point of impossibility.

"But despite these observations, we still know far too little about the mind to conclude safely that the Bridey Murphy case proves the reincarnation principle. About all I can say—and perhaps all you should say—is that it is an interesting piece of evidence and might point the way to further exploration."

Yes, I admitted to myself, that was about the size of it.

Later, when I was about to leave, he added one more observation: "There is another hopeful aspect of the Bridey case. For years men have been trying to learn whether man's consciousness survives the death of his physical body. Almost invariably investigations in this area have gone in only one direction—the attempt to establish some sort of communication *after death* of the physical body.

"The Bridey type of experiment at least suggests the possibility of *reversing* the direction of these investigations—of establishing evidence, that is, of individual consciousness *before birth.*"[1]

His point was clear. To prove the survival of consciousness after death is a task fraught with extreme difficulty. By reversing the direction, however, we are at least provided with a solid launching platform—a living, conscious being.

CHAPTER 17

As I played the tape recordings for various groups in both Colorado and New York—groups which included hardened skeptics from the ranks of doctors, lawyers, clergymen, and Wall Streeters—I was naturally bombarded with questions. Some of these queries were repeated so frequently that it might be well to touch on them at this point.

Naturally, most listeners wanted to know about Ruth Simmons' reaction. How does a normal twentieth-century woman—a youthful matron primarily interested in her family and a well-maintained home—react to hearing her own recorded words describe a previous lifetime in nineteenth-century Ireland? To be sure, Ruth, who had never before given a thought to the reincarnation concept, was stunned by the impact of the first disclosure of Bridey; she gasped again and again as the Bridey story unfolded.

On the other hand, her interest subsided quickly as she returned to her normal duties as a housewife. Even playing bridge or watching the local baseball club took definite priority over another "Bridey session." She now took for granted that in her last lifetime her name had been Bridey Murphy, and that was that. As a matter of fact, she said, "I know there has got to be something to Bridey Murphy, but it has in no way affected my outlook in this lifetime."

The attitude of her husband can perhaps be best summarized by his reply to a group who had sought him out to learn whether he accepted the rebirth idea. "What choice do I have?" he asked. "I know my wife and I know all that information could not be

[1] A New York psychiatrist has already been quoted as follows: "Prenatal psychology may shatter the last fetters with which scientific materialism has bound our minds."

pouring out of Ruth." He added that they owned no encyclopedia or reference books, nor did they even have a library card.

One problem which particularly disturbed thoughtful listeners was bluntly expressed by a newspaper editor who asked, "If this Bridey Murphy business, with all that it implies, is true, then why am I hearing about it for the first time from a businessman? How can it be possible that some psychiatrists are not running into the same thing?"

In the first place, it should be made clear that some psychiatrists *have* been "running into the same thing" for years. Brief reference has already been made to the British psychiatrist, Dr. Sir Alexander Cannon, who long ago encountered the principle of reincarnation. This knighted scientist, the holder of an imposing list of degrees, wrote as follows:

> For years the theory of reincarnation was a nightmare to me, and I did my best to disprove it and even argued with my trance subjects to the effect that they were talking nonsense, and yet as the years went by one subject after another told me the same story in spite of different and varied conscious beliefs, in effect until now, well over a thousand cases have been so investigated I have to admit that there is such a thing as reincarnation.[1]

Nor does this man stand alone. There are, indeed, a number of scientists whose experiments have led them to the same conclusion. The first part of the answer, then, is that some specialists *do* know about this other dimension and have been publicizing their findings. For some reason, however, their reports have never been circulated as extensively as they might have been.

The other part of the answer concerns those scientific workers who know considerably more than they admit. But for this they can hardly be blamed; it is the code of the sophisticated. One young person, explaining her silence after she discovered evidence of rebirth, summarized her position with these words: "All this experience I kept to myself as a profound secret, for, young as I was, I realized what judgment the world would pass upon the narrator of such a story."

Kipling, too, had given some thought to this same problem: "I

[1] Dr. Sir Alexander Cannon in *The Power Within.*

211

saw with sorrow that men would mutilate and garble the story; that rival creeds would turn it upside down till, at last, the western world which clings to the dread of death more closely than the hope of life, would set it aside as an interesting superstition. . . ."[2]

It is not surprising, then, that we do not hear more from professional quarters. Many well-established specialists likely conclude that they would have more to lose than to gain by evincing an active interest in this subject.

A businessman, on the other hand, need show no such reticence in disclosing the results of his experiments. It is doubtful, in other words, that the tonnage of steel products distributed by my company will decline as a consequence of my experimentation.

In any event, there is good reason to believe that at last—during the next decade—we will be hearing a good deal more about these investigations from all quarters.

Another question that inevitably pops up is: If we have all had previous lifetime experiences, then why is it that we have no memory of them? Obviously I am not qualified to solve this problem. I can, however, at least point out what other researchers have theorized; and these hypotheses range from Conan Doyle's comment that "such remembrance would enormously complicate our present life," to the theory of another student, who contends that perhaps we might remember something of our past but that our training and conditioning, particularly in the Western world, has "washed our brains," obliterating these memories.

The latter observer believes, in short, that many children carry memories of their prenatal past, but that these memories are gradually washed away by the repeated suggestion, both directly and indirectly, that all children are original creations at birth. (The power of conditioning by "brain washing" has been dramatically exploited, although for entirely different purposes, by the Communists who "re-educated" GI prisoners in Korea. The captives were at first inclined to laugh at the Red efforts, but the persistent, organized conditioning—hypnosis in slow motion—finally eroded away ideas and beliefs of some of our servicemen with a success that shocked the Western world.)

Even so, it seems that some persons do retain memories of a previous life. The example of the Indian girl, cited on page 103,

[2] *Finest Story in the World.*

while more sensational than most cases, is not a rarity in oriental countries. In any event, our memory is not a true measure of whether we have had a prior existence. As one author wrote, "Doubtless the butterfly has no recollection of its previous life as a worm; but this defect in its memory does not change the facts, nor affect its identity."[3]

The reason why we cannot remember our past should not, according to Rudolf Steiner, be our primary concern. "Not this we should ask," he wrote, "but rather: 'How may we attain such knowledge?'"

It must be conceded that science does not yet know how memory works. Meanwhile, few of us can remember even those events that occurred before the age of three. So how can we *normally* expect to recall memories of a prior existence? In this respect it is interesting to note that hypnosis often brings back the forgotten memories of infancy. (And victims of general amnesia, who seldom recall *any* prior events, often respond to hypnosis.)

The consensus of opinion on this topic would seem to be that, although we do not remember specific incidents of previous life episodes, we still carry over impressions, tendencies, capacities,[4] and dispositions—subconscious checks and balances—which restrain us from repeating past mistakes and guide us in the eternal process of evolution.

Many times during discussions of this issue the charge has been made that the reincarnation principle was "unfair"—that to plod forward without a conscious record of our past is altogether unjustifiable. Whether we like or dislike the theory, however, is hardly the central issue. Our first job is to establish whether it is a fact.

In every group who listened to the Bridey Murphy regression, there was always at least one imaginative person who promptly perceived another possibility: "If you can regress her into the past, then what about taking her into the *future?* In short, what about age *progression?*"

For obvious reasons I have never tried to take a hypnotic subject into the future. Even if the subject's "prophecies" turned out to be sheer nonsense, considerable anxiety might be aroused

---

[3] *Eternalism*, by O. J. Smith (Houghton Mifflin Co.).
[4] This might, for example, have a bearing on the child prodigy enigma.

while she awaited the outcome of events. If, for instance, she "sees" at some particular time in her future a hospital, sickness, injury—or worse—then she, and any friend or relative who hears about it, is likely to suffer nervous apprehension until the designated date has been safely passed.

There are, however, scholarly journals of hypnotism[5] which include reports on age-progression experiments. This is one more exciting field in hypnosis from which interesting developments are expected.

The subject of heredity, too, usually arises during the quiz period. To begin with, we should be ready to concede that the known principles of heredity include a great many more mysteries than solutions. Who among us has not been baffled by the ever-present anomalies of brothers who differ radically, by the genius who springs from a background of mediocrity, by the criminal who descends from eminent ancestry? Children of a genius, with few exceptions, rarely attain the stature of the parent; the antics of child prodigies are fantastic; and the extreme physical and mental differences within a single family are inscrutable.

To be sure, the doctrines of heredity, no matter how they are stretched or twisted, are strained in any attempt to account for these enigmas. On the other hand, the reincarnation principle fits the picture rather neatly: The reincarnating entity, having already molded these capacities, characteristics, and tendencies in previous experiences, could carry them forward into the present life.

What about the other side of the argument—the similarities found within a family? Here, let us borrow a quotation from Dr. John McTaggart:[6]

> The man whose nature had certain characteristics when he was about to be reborn, would be reborn in a body descended from ancestors of a similar character. It would be the character of his ancestors and its similarity to his character which would determine the fact that he was reborn in that particular body rather than in another. The shape of the head does not determine the shape of the hat, but it *does* determine the selection of this particular hat for this particular head. . . .

In short, the argument against heredity as the *whole* story in

---

[5] *Journal of Clinical and Experimental Hypnosis* and *British Journal of Medical Hypnotism.*
[6] *Human Immortality and Pre-existence,* by Dr. John McTaggart.

explaining character and ability is a compelling one. In the words of the New Testament, "That which is born of the flesh is flesh; that which is born of the Spirit is spirit."[7] And it is interesting to note that this statement follows almost immediately after the counsel to Nicodemus that, "Except a man be born again, he cannot see the kingdom of God."

Can the Bridey Murphy type of experiment be repeated with everyone? This question is asked by a surprising number of persons eager to explore their own past. And it is a curious fact that a preponderant majority of those who volunteer as subjects are women. Why women are especially interested in prenatal regressions I don't know, but their interest is definitely keener than that of men.

Someday—and perhaps that day is not so far distant—it may be a simple matter to probe the depths of the psyche of almost any subject. At the moment, however, it must be recognized that Ruth Simmons is an uncommonly good hypnotic subject, and this capacity, as has been already explained, simply is not present in everyone. Consequently, "Bridey Murphys" are not likely to be unveiled every day of the week. Even so, now that many investigators are beginning to delve into this field, there will undoubtedly be forthcoming, from time to time, experiments which will make the Bridey effort seem amateurish.[8]

I have no idea, furthermore, how much can be accomplished with the assistance of drugs. If sodium amytal or sodium pentothal, for instance, were to be used in conjunction with these experiments, it would be interesting to learn what could be achieved with otherwise poor subjects. I am hoping that doctors will investigate this phase.

How about the population problem, the vast increase in the population of the earth? Here a moment's reflection discloses at least two basic considerations. In the first place, the *total* number of entities both in this and the astral world can remain the same while the balance shifts between the number of entities on earth

[7] John 3: 6.
[8] On the other hand, we might also expect at least two consequences of a different sort. For one thing, there may be a rash of spurious regressions. Then, too, there will be the inevitable charges that hypnotic prenatal regressions are absolutely impossible. And such charges will likely originate, as usual, from within the very ranks of those most concerned with the subject— in this case, from hypnotists and psychologists.

and the number in the unseen world. As the population on earth increases, the number of individual entities in the unseen world might be decreasing.

Then, too, the history of modern man goes back only a few *thousand* years. But geologists assure us that our earth is a few *billion* years old. Archaeological discoveries in the Orient, Egypt, Cambodia, and Mexico establish the fact that great civilizations once existed where there is now scarcely more than wasteland. So it is even possible that there was at one time a larger population than we supposed.

Does a previous existence account for our sometimes finding ourselves in a scene or circumstance which seems oddly familiar? Nobody can answer this with certainty; the reincarnation hypothesis is merely one possibility. The French have a term for this: *déjà vu.*

And Sir Walter Scott had something to say about it too:

How often do we find ourselves in society which we have never met, and yet feel impressed with a mysterious and ill-defined consciousness that neither the scene nor the speakers nor the subject are entirely new; nay, feel as if we could anticipate that part of the conversation which has not yet taken place.

What happens to the race, nationality, and sex of a person during this evolution through lifetimes? Obviously the nationality must change at times. As to sex, my own experiments—and I have had a total of only three subjects in prenatal regressions—have not disclosed any change of gender experienced by subjects recalling prior lives on earth. Besides Bridey Murphy, I had a female subject who claimed to have been a spinster schoolteacher in nineteenth century America, and a male subject who (under hypnosis, of course) related an interesting previous experience in which his sex had not changed.

Other investigators, however, report that they have encountered changes of sex from one incarnation to another. They contend, moreover, that there have been racial changes as well. (These findings, incidentally, are supported by the readings of Edgar Cayce, who maintained that race, nationality, or sex might alter from one life experience to the next.)

Naturally there have been plenty of questions put to me that I am far from qualified to answer: At what point does the "high-frequency electromagnetic charge" (or psyche) enter the human embryo? Is there any observable pattern in the lapses of time between one lifetime and the next? What determines whether the psyche reincarnates again quickly (as claimed in the case of Shanti Devi, the Indian girl) or delays the process for a half century or more? What are the mechanics of reincarnation—just how does the psyche become infused into the embryo? And, as I asked Bridey Murphy, "Who takes care of all the details?"

While admitting my own ignorance, I must comment that those studying reincarnation, including scholars with minds much more perspicacious than my own, have attacked all these issues, and more, head-on. Their conclusions are plausible and appear, what's more, to fit all the facts. There are a surprising number of volumes[9] dealing with these topics, and I am reliably informed that there are even now several more being written, soon to be published.

Naturally I have made many mistakes as I have stumbled along. As I look back now, I can think of a good many things that should have been done, of questions that should have been asked. But I am not a professional at this business. Then, too, my experience in this field has all come so suddenly.

Besides, I had nothing to steer me, not even a textbook. In almost any other sphere, some guidance would be available. On hypnotic age regressions, for instance, there are "how-to" books, complete with suggested techniques, some even quoting entire sessions verbatim. But what is the best method, after regressing the subject to infancy, of going on back "over the hump"? There were no printed instructions on this phase, and so I simply had to plunge in as best I could.

As to questioning a subject, my first session presented a really perplexing problem. How does one interrogate a young woman who abruptly announces that she spent the previous century in Ireland? Perhaps she knew where *she* was, but I was lost!

And subsequent meetings were no easy matter, either. I had the help of some keen thinkers, including lawyers, in framing questions, but we were all beginners at this sort of thing. One attorney told me that he had called in his whole office staff and

[9] See *The Imprisoned Splendour*, by Dr. R. C. Johnson; *Problem of Rebirth*, by Honorable Ralph Shirley; *Many Mansions*, by Gina Cerminara; *There Is a River*, by Thomas Sugrue; *Ring of Return*, by Eva Martin.

posed the problem for them: "If a woman walked in here today and claimed that she had lived in Ireland from 1798 until 1864, what questions would you ask her in order to prove conclusively that her statement was either true or false?" They were stumped.

The interrogation of Ruth Simmons was also encumbered by other limitations. The whole experiment would have collapsed without the co-operation of Rex Simmons, and so his recommendations—he never issued commands—had to be scrupulously observed. After the first time he asked, in order to make certain that Ruth would not be unduly fatigued, that no session take longer than one hour. Since this included the time required for the hypnosis and the ordinary age regression, there was not too long a period left for the interrogation of Bridey Murphy.

Rex had other concerns too. He reminded me that every time the New Amsterdam episode had been mentioned during a trance his wife had been noticeably seized with pain. So after that I avoided the subject of New Amsterdam. Moreover, I tried to avoid any type of question that might possibly result in his wife's anxiety or discomfort.

There was also another brand of questioning that had to be deleted. Anything of a very personal or intimate nature was avoided. While it could be especially interesting—and might possibly even develop significant factual material—still it might result in disclosing incidents of an embarrassing nature.

And everything happened so quickly! I finished chasing down the Cayce story in October, recorded the first tape in November, the third tape in January, and then left for New York four days later. I had been in New York less than one week when an editor suggested that I start putting it all down on paper.

CHAPTER 18

The search for Bridey Murphy, the editor decided, should be conducted by independent investigators on the spot in Ireland. The editor took note of the fact that neither I nor my subject had ever at any time been abroad, and it was deemed best that this status be maintained until after the final manuscript had been turned in. Consequently, the matter of the search was put into the hands of an Irish legal firm, various librarians, and other investigators whose names were not even revealed to me at the time. In this way I could in no manner influence the investigators, nor could I even communicate with them. It was to be, in short, a wholly independent project.

It early became clear that the search for Bridey would be far from the simple matter that we had at first presumed. It soon became evident, in fact, that the search would easily be a major research project in itself. A Cork librarian reported, "Ordinarily, no registers of births, marriages, or deaths were kept before 1864." The representative of a London newspaper, which had become independently interested in making its own search, wrote, "Apparently the records for that period are extremely rare."

Another expert on such matters reported, "In my opinion you will find no immediate nor easy solution to the problems set out." He added, "You have a lengthy search ahead of you." And he took pains both to underscore and double-space the word "lengthy." The problem was further complicated by the fact that Murphy was the most frequent surname in Ireland.

It became obvious, therefore, that a full-scale search for Bridey would be a truly formidable undertaking. It might actually necessitate my going to Ireland, running down every possible lead, interviewing anyone who might have information, and even advertising in Cork and Belfast newspapers in the hope of finding significant facts. Indeed, it looked as though this were a job for a detective agency.

But all this would take considerable time, and the final manuscript had to be turned in five months before date of publication, which was already scheduled for late fall 1955. Accordingly, it was decided to publish those findings which had developed by the spring of 1955. Several points of interest had been uncovered, and some of the facts were especially interesting.

In regard to Bridey's father-in-law, the barrister, an Irish solicitor made the following report: "We have heard from the Registrar of Kings Inn regarding the barristers in Cork, 1830, and we understand that there was a John McCarthy. . . . He was from Cork and was educated at Clongowes School. He would therefore be a Roman Catholic." The facts as reported would fit Bridey's allegations, and at that time there was only one barrister of that name.

On one tape Bridey told us that Brian had bought "foodstuffs" from a greengrocer whose name, she said, was John Carrigan. She gave us both his first and last name, and even spelled the last name. A statement from a Belfast librarian discloses that, indeed, there had been a John Carrigan who carried on a business as a grocer at 90 Northumberland Street. And since there was only one such John Carrigan in that business in Belfast at that time, this fact would seem to be noteworthy.

On another tape Bridey had told us that she had purchased "foodstuffs" at Farr's. She did not give us the first name, but she spelled the last name. Research in Belfast brought confirmation. William Farr, the report said, was a grocer at 59–61 Mustard Street, which lay between Donegall Street and North Street. Here again there appears to have been no other Farr in that business at that time in Belfast.

An Irish commission on folklore was asked whether there had been, as Bridey described, an Irish custom of having a dance when a couple was married ". . . just an Irish jig thing; you dance and they put money in your pockets . . ." The commission answered, "Holding of a dance on the occasion of a wedding was common practice. As regards money, a silver coin slipped into the pocket was a good-luck charm."

In nineteenth-century Cork it was common practice, as Bridey signified, to keep personal records in the Bible—births, marriages, deaths. Thatched roofs were common in Cork at that time. Galway was a port. There had been, in Bridey's time, a large rope company and a large tobacco company in Belfast. And her use of the words "banshee" and "tup" was correct.

The investigators state that there was a song—more than one —entitled "Sean" and pronounced Shawn (as Bridey indicated in this case). "The Londonderry Air" was very popular in Bridey's time. And Keats was born in 1795 and could have been read by Bridey, even though, as she complained, "He was a Britisher."

Her reference to monetary terms was accurate—pound, sixpence, tuppence, and the copper halfpenny.

A prominent Irish literary figure asserted that Bridey's account of the Cuchulain story was accurate in all details. (". . . When he was seven years old, he could slay big men. When he was seventeen, he could hold whole armies.")

Bridey provided several bits of evidence which did not seem particularly significant at the time but which later, owing to various peculiar twists, took on added weight. She had told us, for instance, that she had read a book entitled *The Green Bay*. I thought this of little consequence, because I presumed there would be several books similarly titled in twentieth-century America. To my surprise, however, I have been unable to find even one such title. (The New York Public Library listed *The Green Bay Tree* but not a single *The Green Bay*.) Yet the Irish investigators report that there was such a book—more than one—in nineteenth-century Ireland.

Another example is the matter of Carlingford and Lough Carlingford. Both of these can be found in almost any atlas. But Bridey added a fact that can't be found in any atlas. In telling us about these places, she had commented that the lough was there before the town had been established. "Lough was there first," she had said, "and then there was the place." The researchers in Ireland confirmed her knowledge. (We can't be sure, however, whether Bridey meant that the village had been established later or that she had approached the lough before the village while traveling from Cork.)

Then there is the matter of Mourne. The Mourne Mountains can be noted on almost any map of Ireland. But Bridey had indicated that there was a *place* called Mourne. Maps and atlases, however, disclose no such place. Yet we are now informed that there actually was such a geographical place.

As for the Blarney-stone matter, Bridey's account would have been correct for her day: ". . . you put your feet above your head . . . and then you get the tongue . . . the gift of the tongue." Curiously, the procedure has since been changed. An Irish authority wrote, "The individual was lowered by his legs over the parapet of the old castle tower. The procedure has now been changed, and what happens is that the person wishing to kiss the Blarney stone sits on the stonework inside the parapet where there is a hole in the ground."

When asked what kinds of crops her family had grown at Cork, Bridey had mentioned hay, flax, corn, and tobacco. While there is nothing notable about this, there is at least an interesting side light. An authority explains that only small quantities of tobacco would have been grown around Cork, and this fact would not likely have been generally known. (A reliable American source, for instance, reports that tobacco is not listed as one of the crops grown in Cork.)

In regard to Father John and the church, a solicitor of an Irish legal firm employed to check this matter reported, after several months, as follows: "I never received any acknowledgment of my letters to the parish priest of St. Theresa's Church."

Both the Belfast *News-Letter* and Queen's University were in existence in Bridey's time, and both are still there. But as this is written, there has not yet been a search to determine whether the Belfast *News-Letter* has any record of Brian—or whether the university has records of William McGlone, Fitzhugh, or Fitzmaurice.

There was more than one instance when experts and authorities disagreed with Bridey's statements, yet it turned out that Bridey had been correct. A case in point developed when Bridey was challenged as a result of her insistence that Brian had taught at Queen's University. Brian, she had contended, was Roman Catholic. Queen's University, though, was a Protestant institution. That a Catholic could have taught at this particular school, therefore, seemed inconceivable to at least one authority, who promptly registered his objection. But research disclosed that instructors and students were not barred on the basis of religion. The authority was wrong; Bridey was right.

Two Irish authorities maintained that, while Bridey's remarks about the Deirdre story were essentially accurate, the king involved in this tale was the King of Ulster, not Scotland. (Bridey had said, "She was . . . beautiful girl, and she was going to marry . . . this king . . . this King of Scotland . . . and she didn't love him . . . and this boy came and saved her.") It is true that Deirdre was to become the bride of the King of Ulster, who figures prominently in all versions of the story. It is also true that most accounts, including the two best-known works on the Deirdre legend (W. B. Yeats's *Deirdre* and J. M. Synge's *Sorrows of Deirdre*), contain no mention of the Scottish King. But another researcher found that there definitely were at least two other versions (one based on the Glenn Masain manuscript in the Advocates' Library in Edinburgh and the other on a translation by Theophilos O'Flanagan) which included the additional episode with the King of Scotland, who had heard a description of Deirdre's beauty and had then sought her as a wife for himself.

Objection was also made to Bridey's use of the word "slip." It was contended that this word was anachronistic, that if she had used "petticoat" it would have been more in keeping with the times. Further checking, however, proved that "slip" is an old and honored word and that one of its old-fashioned usages was as a name for "a child's pinafore or frock," undoubtedly the meaning in this case. (Refer to her description in the sixth tape—". . . they had wide sashes").

Bridey's reference to the uncle who married "the Orange" came in for criticism too. Several persons felt certain that she would have said "Orangeman" instead of "Orange." Here again, however, research supported Bridey. The term "Orange" applied to the ultra-Protestant party in Ireland, in reference to the secret society of Orangemen formed in 1795. And an individual member of the party, especially a female, could have been referred to as "an Orange."

Then there was the word "linen." After she had suddenly sneezed during the fourth session, Bridey had asked for "a linen." She was obviously referring to a handkerchief, but there is apparently no such usage in Ireland today. Once again, though, it was found that one of the meanings of the word "linen"—a meaning now *obsolete in the singular*—was something made of linen such as a linen garment or handkerchief.

A noteworthy fact developed from the very odd name of Brian's uncle, the uncle "that married the Orange." Bridey had said his name was Plazz. On this point an Irish investigator reported: "Plazz. This is genuine all right and throws a sense of authenticity about the whole thing. It is the very, very rare Christian name Blaize, called after the Irish Saint Blaize, patron of those afflicted with disease of the throat." This researcher made it clear that Plazz was the popularized, phonetic spelling of the Christian name Blaize.

I had been unable to find anyone who had even heard of such a name, so it is hard to understand how Ruth Simmons (who had been raised from infancy by a Norwegian uncle and a German-Scotch-Irish aunt) could have been familiar with it.

The Plazz incident is also representative of another type of authentication found throughout Bridey's testimony. When she was asked, for example, the name of Brian's uncle, she does not make a perfunctory, laconic reply—the kind of mechanical answer that would mark the testimony of one who is either making up or repeating a story. Instead, there is an obvious association of ideas as with one who is reflecting upon actual experiences and personal memories: "You mean his uncle that married the Orange?" she asks.

The same question also reminds her that Brian's father had been upset when the uncle had "married an Orange." And this, in turn, moves her to recall, "He wasn't upset when he married *me*." All this from merely asking the name of Brian's uncle. And the tapes are fraught with similar examples.

Undoubtedly additional evidence will continue to develop after this goes to print. Indeed, it may even be possible that some of the book's readers will be able to contribute pertinent information.

I think it only reasonable to expect that some of Bridey's memoirs are colored, that some are in error, and that even key dates might be in error. But this is not an area from which an airtight case should be expected. The whole issue, rather, is whether the principles involved here merit more intensive consideration.

The Bridey Murphy experiment, after all, was merely a personal exploration. I am hoping, however, that many more professional people—trained experimenters, doctors, psychologists—will launch their own research programs. Perhaps even one or more of the nation's leading foundations will become interested. Certainly the stakes involved are high enough.

As Pope said, the proper study of mankind is Man.

Mine has been the trail of a skeptic, a path first glimpsed when I looked away from business and the latest stock quotations long enough to learn that the wonders of hypnosis are realities, not nonsense. The trail wound through the psychic phenomena associated with telepathy and clairvoyance, then it crossed the work of Edgar Cayce, and finally veered smack into Bridey Murphy.

As already indicated, I have been hoping that academic circles would become interested in this work. But the edges of my optimism have already been chipped away. I have been talking to the psychology department of an eastern university, suggesting that they investigate these matters for themselves. But I can see that I'm not getting anywhere.

As Bridey Murphy might have expressed it, *"They won't listen."*

There are a few, however, who do somewhat more than listen. Recently, for instance, a doctor heard about my work and called on me. He reminded me that, even though the general public may not be familiar with the Bridey type of experiment, it represents nothing new, nothing really original.

He then proceeded to outline an idea for expanding the Bridey experiment—an idea so fascinating that I can hardly wait to set up the experiment.

It looks as though I'm about to take another step on the long bridge.

APPENDIX A

SAMPLE OUTLINE FOR USE OF HYPNOSIS IN THERAPY

The following outline sheet, lifted from my file concerning a stuttering case, indicates the extent of the groundwork involved in each session. This particular record includes a review of past sessions, a detailed outline for the next session (including seventeen separate points and numerous subheadings), and notes for future sessions.

CASE OF STUTTERER

Name: *For Session number____*

Date: *Scheduled date of session____*

A. *Review:*

At this point there have been two sessions. Each session has followed the same general pattern: pre-induction conversation; explanation of the nature of hypnosis; detailed discussion of subject's ailment; statement of what is expected from subject, pointing out the necessity for facing his problem and discussing it frankly; discussion of embarrassment it has caused him, etc. The subject has shown decided improvement after each session. The autosuggestion appears to be a very effective tool.

B. *Outline for Session No. 3:*

1. Any questions from subject?
2. Pre-induction conversation, including discussion of subject's progress and current problems.
3. Induction of trance:
   a) deep-breathing exercise
   b) candle-flame technique
   c) deepening of trance
4. Explanation of nervous tension and its relief.
5. Explanation of different manners by which nervous tension discharges itself.
6. Explanation that relaxation will end the nervous tension: first through hypnosis, then automatically through the action of the subconscious.

7. Discussion of the subconscious.
8. Repetition of the key sentence: "When I speak slowly, I speak perfectly."
9. Mental pictures during hypnosis: the imagining that he is making speeches before large groups, at the basketball dinner, at school assemblies.
10. Explanation of autosuggestion with direction of its utilization by the subject. Autosuggestion includes following:
    a) repetition of key sentence
    b) mental pictures
    Autosuggestion should be employed at following times:
    a) at night before falling asleep
    b) morning, upon first awakening
    c) during middle of day at fixed time
11. Urging interest in social activities, especially those involving girls.
12. Explanation that setbacks are only bumps on road to recovery; they are only temporary and do not alter fact that he is on road to total recovery.
13. The setting up in the subconscious of an automatic warning signal to speak slowly whenever he becomes excited. By setting up a subconscious signal he will, the moment he becomes excited, be automatically reminded that he is to speak slowly.
14. Speaking during trance:
    a) repetition of key sentence
    b) detailed discussion of his most exciting basketball game
15. Relaxation of facial and throat muscles.
16. Post-hypnotic suggestions:
    a) employment of autosuggestion three times daily
       1) repetition of key sentence
       2) mental pictures (specific)
    b) relaxation suggestions
17. Awakening:
    a) discussion
    b) set date of next session

C. *Future Sessions:*
    Future sessions will include following:
1. Summary and review of past sessions.
2. More detailed speaking during trance.

APPENDIX B

THE PROBLEM OF SYMPTOM REMOVAL

There has been much ado about the question of whether hypnotism treats only symptoms and not original motivations and basic organic causes. Several medical hypnotists, notably some well-known English specialists, have attacked this argument. They point out that when this therapeutic method is properly used the results are permanent and no new symptoms appear.

But even if we consider only symptom removal, should any apologies be necessary? Should a stutterer be left with his irksome speech difficulty on the theory that his problem really goes much deeper? Must a victim of hysterical paralysis be compelled to remain in that state, satisfied only with the argument that the symptom is really only the sign of a more deeply rooted personality conflict? Why argue? Why not just remove the painful symptom thus relieving the distress of the patient and rendering him, at the same time, fit for further therapy and progress?

Another way to regard this problem is to consider the plight of a man hanging from a window ledge. Upon encountering someone in this position, it would be preposterous to react by leaning out and quizzing the unfortunate fellow as to how he happens to be in such a situation—or to rush out for a psychoanalyst. No, first the poor man must be promptly pulled in.

APPENDIX C

WHY HYPNOSIS ISN'T MORE WIDELY USED
A History of Misunderstanding and Prejudice

The unfortunate fact about hypnotism is that the "dangers" have been dramatically overplayed, while the benefits have either been glossed over or entirely concealed. I have read scores of articles, the headlines of which glaringly proclaim the horrors of hypnotism. Boiled down, however, these commentaries usually constitute a simple statement: Hypnotism can effect amazing cures, but maybe it's dangerous!

But just what are these dangers? We have already seen that the subject, far from being a helpless automaton, can break the trance whenever the suggestions are sufficiently adverse to his fundamental principles. Obviously, then, he is not nearly so much at the mercy of the operator as a person under an anesthetic.

Nobody would consider doing away with the science of medicine simply because there are each year a number of unfortunate results engendered by inaccurate diagnoses or improper treatment. Nor would anyone advocate the prohibition of surgery owing to the few cases in which lack of knowledge or skill aggravated, rather than improved, the condition of the patient. Quite the contrary. Indeed, we find a full measure of literature describing the progress, contributions, and miracles of modern medicine and surgery, just as these fields so decidedly merit. This printed material does not dwell upon and exaggerate the dangers; instead, it justifiably points up the benefits.

Now hypnotism deserves the same break. It is time that the "scare articles" taper off and be replaced by clear-cut exposition of the truth. This wonderful science of the mind has been too long buried under superstition, misunderstanding, and neglect. Within the next few decades we may at last, there is good reason to believe, see hypnotism take its rightful place as one of the most important sciences.

At this stage, then, a logical question appears: If hypnotism is entirely safe in the right hands, and if it has such an extensive application, why is it not more widely used? Some of the answers have already suggested themselves. Now let's consider still other salient factors.

To get the proper perspective, let's survey a segment of the historical outline. The first thing that strikes us in the story of modern hypnotism is its cyclical nature; it has bobbed up and down like a yo-yo. There has been a high point of interest roughly every thirty years, followed by a decline. *Time* magazine (March 30, 1953), in its usual pithy style, takes a broader look at these peaks and valleys:

Hypnosis has been a hard-luck kid among medical techniques. A century ago it was just beginning to win acceptance as a pain killer when ether anaesthesia was discovered, and hypnosis was discarded. It was making a comeback sixty years ago when Freud hit upon the idea of psychoanalysis, and the experts again lost interest in hypnosis. Now, the third time around, it is once again winning the support of reputable men in both the physical and psychic areas of medicine.

During all these ups and downs of hypnosis bitter battles were incessantly being waged. Franz Anton Mesmer, the grandfather of modern hypnosis, published his discoveries regarding "animal magnetism"—

his name for what later was to be known as hypnosis—in 1779. As a result, he was ultimately forced out of Vienna and then out of Paris. John Elliotson, one of the most brilliant men in the history of medicine, was compelled to resign his position at London's University College Hospital because he would not give up his interest in mesmerism. *The Lancet,* a British medical publication, summed up the feeling of Elliotson's opposition in 1846 as follows:

"Does he himself [Elliotson] treat the harlotry, which he dares to call science, with any respect?"

A young Scottish surgeon practicing in India, James Esdaile, performed three hundred major and thousands of minor operations with patients under hypnosis. Yet he was criticized by the Calcutta Medical College; medical journals refused to print accounts of his findings, and the Medical Board never even so much as acknowledged his letter on the subject.

Lafontaine, a Swiss magnetizer (hypnotist) traveling in Italy, was ordered by King Ferdinand to leave Naples unless "he made no more blind people to see nor deaf ones to hear." But Pope Pius IX was more enlightened; he commented, "Well, Monsieur Lafontaine, let us hope that, for the good of humanity, magnetism may soon be generally employed."[1] (Hypnotism was then known as magnetism.)

James Braid, who coined the word "hypnotism," offered in 1842 to read a paper on the subject before the British Medical Association. His offer was rejected and his reports of cures termed ridiculous.

A French doctor, Liebault, who was obtaining excellent results with hypnosis, was attacked as a quack by Professor Bernheim. And when one of the latter's patients was quickly cured by Liebault, it was too much for the professor! Bernheim went to investigate Liebault with the intention of exposing him once and for all. Instead, he was so astounded by what he learned that he himself promptly undertook the study of hypnosis.

In 1886 Bernheim published a book, *Suggestive Therapeutics,* and hypnosis reached the zenith of its glory. But now the scene was set for a man in Vienna who was to send it skidding downward once again. The man was Sigmund Freud.

In order to study hypnotism Freud visited Bernheim and Liebault at Nancy, France. Freud learned, as have all hypnotists, that not every patient can be hypnotized. He was aware, however, that there was one thing every patient could do—talk about himself: He reasoned that, via this "talking out" process, satisfactory therapeutic results

[1] From *Hypnotism and the Power Within,* by Dr. S. J. Van Pelt.

could be obtained, given plenty of time, without hypnosis. And so psychoanalysis was born.

There has never yet been a full-scale truce in the dispute involving hypnosis, and the dissension continues even today. And out of this hodgepodge of misunderstanding, acrimony, fear, charges, and countercharges, there has emerged a genuine problem of semantics: Hypnosis has become a distasteful name. Perhaps, therefore, if hypnosis is to be fully accepted, it must make its debut under a new name.

The very word "hypnosis" is a signal for a train of prejudices in the public mind—misconceptions, obsolete traditional beliefs, propaganda. There are some subjects about which we can never think clearly because we are blinded by the negative connotations called forth by certain words. In this case the mind is immediately influenced by pictures of the hocus-pocus variety: Svengali-Trilby; the ridiculous antics of stage performers; witchcraft and sorcery.

With these delusions infecting the public mind, should a doctor be blamed if he shuns any association with this word? He runs the risk of arousing suspicion and damaging his own practice. And can the fault be attributed entirely to the public if this word is genuinely misunderstood? The real problem is semantic and psychological; the old worn-out word should go!

A word like "tranceology" (the science of the trance) would be somewhat more palatable. It goes down without regurgitating the old unsavory connotations.

So the name "hypnotism" itself embodies most of the objectionable elements. It is tied up with all the old taboos, a battle-scarred background, popular misconceptions, stage demonstrations, and with fear.

In this respect, the name is also related to objections put forth by some religious sects. Their opposition is understandable in view of the general impression that the hypnotist usurps the free will of the subject, that one mind completely dominates the mind of another. Far from depriving subjects of their free will, hypnosis can actually be instrumental in "giving back" a healthy power of will to those who have become so distressed, so burdened by worry, that they have lost the ability to exert their normal will.

Here again misconceptions need to be eradicated through re-education. And this new education would be much more easily ushered in behind a new name. Indeed, full enlightenment might even be impossible under the shade of the hoary scare word "hypnotism."

As far as doctors and psychologists are concerned, there are two other obstacles in the way of their professional use of hypnosis. One concerns the fact that their medical qualifications, however imposing, have little bearing on their ability to become proficient hypnotists.

The qualities essential to a skilled hypnotherapist are somewhat different from those demanded of a good doctor. In short, an excellent doctor might turn out to be a poor hypnotist. This is, to be sure, a field for specialization.

The other factor is the possibility of embarrassment. Doctors and psychologists are, after all, human beings; as such they can hardly relish the possibility of failing to make a favorable impression during the first meeting with the patient. They well know the impact of the doctor-patient relationship. Until an easy, sure-fire technique is developed, the best professional therapists will be stopped cold in some cases. Understandably, a dignified doctor cannot be expected to welcome the prospect of assuring his patient, while inducing a trance, that he cannot possibly open his eyes—and then suddenly find himself looking into the patient's wide-open eyes. This is a brand of embarrassment to which doctors and psychologists need not submit in their ordinary practice.

This objection, however, can be obviated to a considerable extent by avoiding all direct challenges and utilizing only positive, curative suggestions. Even so, a few patients will remain unimpressed by a light trance and may therefore lose interest. So, regardless of how this problem is approached, there is still a need for an unfailing, more effectual method of trance induction.

A further obstacle is exemplified by a personal experience. A man with a speech difficulty asked whether I would accept him as a subject. I explained that, in the first place, I was taking only those cases which were referred to me by doctors; and secondly, since I made no charges of any kind, I usually had more to do than I could manage. I suggested, however, that he see a medical hypnotist or psychologist, as he was soon to spend several months in a large city where professional therapists were available.

Almost a year later I encountered the same man, and I immediately observed that his old speech difficulty was still very much with him. "Did you ever see a medical hypnotist?" I asked.

"Well, no," he admitted. "I telephoned my doctor and asked him what about this hypnotism business, and he answered in no uncertain terms, 'Stay away from hypnotism. It's dangerous! Besides, I don't know anything about it!' "

Aside from the obvious fact that anyone with no knowledge has not the right to make the charge of "dangerous," it is clear that the semantic problem pops up even in the professional field. Some medical men, including those who have never even witnessed hypnosis, will unhesitatingly condemn it. And since the very first act of a layman, before submitting to hypnotherapy, often is to ask his doctor's advice on the matter, the upshot sometimes takes this pattern: *Both* the doctor and the patient erroneously regard hypnotism as "dangerous"; the patient never submits to hypnotherapy; the patient retains his affliction. Fortunately, though, most medical men now recognize the merits of hypnosis.

In summing up the current status of hypnosis, these points tell the story:

There are numerous complaints for which hypnosis is the ideal treatment; and in an even greater number of conditions it is a powerful adjunct to ordinary medical methods.

Already the list of what hypnosis has actually accomplished is imposing in length and equally impressive in content. It must be admitted that it was long ago forgotten that this science was supposed to be confined to functional disorders; time and again it has been applied in the field of organic disease with extraordinary results.

What may finally be achieved by hypnosis once science has turned its full attention to it can only be surmised. Even now there are indications of its potentials—such as the fish-scale disease (ichthyosis) cure, cases of organic changes, and the electrifying possibilities of age-regression work. But if the nervous system actually has the faculty for "listening" to direct suggestion, then where are the boundaries of this science?

Despite wondrous attainments, hypnosis is still forced to fight for existence.

Just as soon as a quick, universal method of inducing a trance of impressive depth is developed and the most antagonistic, unyielding subject can be rapidly and decisively hypnotized, then hypnosis will automatically become a therapeutic instrument of paramount importance.

APPENDIX D

HYPNOSIS IN MEDICINE

Although we can only guess what hypnotism may eventually accomplish after it is fully accepted and explored, we already have a lengthy list of achievements—and some spectacular hints as to what we may expect in the future. Such a hint was provided by the staid *British Medical Journal* in 1952. The article relates the almost fantastic episode of a British lad who had been born with ichthyosis. This is one of the most hideous diseases imaginable, a congenital affliction, often dubbed fish-scale disease, in which the skin forms a thick black casing over practically the entire body. The skin, furthermore, is covered with close-set black bumps between which is a scale as hard as a fingernail. When this scale is bent, it cracks and oozes a bloodstained serum. For this loathsome disease neither cause nor cure is known.

But this particular victim, even though his condition was so repulsive that his teacher and fellow students at school resented his presence, was more fortunate than others. An English hypnotherapist heard about the case and offered to try hypnosis. Understandably, other doctors were skeptical of what seemed to be a ridiculous gesture. Already the boy had undergone, to no avail, treatment in the best British hospitals. And even a trial operation for grafting new skin to the hands had only aggravated the matter. The grafted skin blackened, shrank, and brought more pain.

No wonder, then, that many scoffed at the young hypnotist who dared think that he could "talk out of existence" a serious congenital disease. Nevertheless, he started his cure, after taking only ten minutes to induce a trance, with five words: "The left arm will clear." He repeated the direct suggestion several times. Sure enough, to the amazement of everyone, within five days the coarse external layer turned soft and crumbly and fell off. Soon the skin underneath became pink and soft. The hypnotist shifted his suggestion to other parts of the body with similar results. Twelve doctors witnessed the hypnosis and the outcome.

There are many other clues, too, indicating that hypnosis, instead of dealing only with functional diseases to which it is ordinarily confined by standard textbooks, may actually cure certain organic conditions as well. Indeed, the boundary between organic and functional diseases is growing ever dimmer in the light of new knowledge. Gastric ulcer, for instance, becomes an organic lesion once the ulcer has formed in the stomach; yet it is generally admitted that this disease has frequently yielded to hypnosis.

Even without referring to sensational cases and the promise of still greater discoveries in the future, the array of ills which this science is successfully tackling every day is so imposing that one wonders why it is generally overlooked. A list of these would include psychoneuroses, alcoholism, bed-wetting, excessive smoking, insomnia, stammering and stuttering, homosexuality, stage fright, blushing, overweight, nail-biting, drug addiction, high blood pressure, asthma, migraine, rheumatoid arthritis, skin diseases, and many more.

The effectual use of hypnosis in dentistry is spreading rapidly, and there are constant gains, too, in obstetrics and surgery. Some psychiatrists are employing hypnosis to facilitate analysis and to accelerate psychotherapy. Keep in mind, moreover, that a brief psychotherapy means a less expensive one. It is interesting to note that in many prisons, where a fast, inexpensive method of psychotherapy is a necessity, a combination of narcosynthesis and hypnosis is frequently employed. Still, the unfortunate fact remains that the majority of practitioners, both in medicine and psychology, snub this mighty weapon.

True, at first glance it appears curious that one method of treatment can be of assistance in such a varied host of complaints. The real answer to this enigma will turn up only after the mystery of hypnosis has been finally solved. But this much we know now: Regardless of what may have caused many of these conditions, the nervous system has the power to alleviate the trouble or to banish it altogether. It is actually possible, under certain conditions, to "tell" the nervous system what to do; evidently it really has the power to "listen" to proper suggestions. This is one of the miracles of human nature. And we would be foolish indeed to ignore its reality.

While hypnotism is no cure-all, there are many complaints for which it is the ideal treatment and a still greater number of conditions for which it is a valuable adjunct to conventional medical methods.

APPENDIX E

HYPNOTIZABILITY

Practically all authorities agree that the higher the intelligence and the steadier the concentration, the better are a subject's chances of entering a trance. But a third factor, an unknown "X" factor, is the missing key to hypnotizability. Since the trance state is not yet understood, it follows that the capacity for entering a trance is not yet defined.

Many current studies are being made in order to determine the correlation between hypnotizability and mental and personality traits. Perhaps something may eventually come of these efforts.

Most authorities concur that almost 90 per cent of all people can be hypnotized. But my own experience places the effective figure closer to 50 per cent. The remainder fall into three groups: those who cannot be hypnotized; those who require too much time to hypnotize; and those who enter such a light or mild trance that they do not think it has occurred.

Leading texts also agree that one out of every four or five subjects can enter the deepest trance (somnambulism), but I find that fewer than one out of ten can achieve this depth. It may be that classic texts are entirely sound regardless of whether my own experiments show the same results. On the other hand, it is remotely possible that, on some points at least, each authority has accepted the findings of the last authority. If the latter is true, then we need an entirely new experimental investigation of hypnosis.

In regard to the matter of hypnotizability, there are several tests of susceptibility that are quick tip-offs as to what sort of hypnotic subject a person will make. These tests are usually referred to as susceptibility tests, and a favorite is the handclasp test. The subject is asked to clasp his hands together and place them, usually palms out, on top of his head. He is then told that he will notice that his hands will, as the hypnotist counts three, become more tightly locked together. As the hypnotist counts, he makes suggestions to this effect, and on the last count he insists that the hands are so tightly locked together that it will be very difficult for the subject to pull them apart. The response to this little test, which requires about sixty seconds, is ordinarily a direct indication of how good the subject will be. Other quick tests are concerned, in the same fashion, with locking the eyelids, hand levitation, and body swaying.

APPENDIX F

SOME NOTES ON AGE REGRESSION

As to the genuineness of hypnotic age regression, Dr. L. M. Wolberg has this to say:

> The consensus at the present time is that regression actually does produce early behavior in a way that obviates all possibility of simulation. This is the opinion of such authorities as Erickson, Estabrooks, Lindner, and Spiegel, Shor, and Fishman. My own studies have convinced me of this fact, although the regression is never stationary, constantly being altered by the intrusion of mental functioning at other levels.[1]

My own experience is in accord. But I believe that there may sometimes be elements of both fact and artifact during a regression experiment. This business of hypnosis is no cut-and-dried matter.

The literature on this topic is fraught with interesting examples. In one case a forty-five-year-old man was regressed to his third birthday, at which point he violently gasped, wheezed, coughed, and choked. It was obvious to the doctors who were present that the subject was undergoing an attack of asthma. An examining physician reported the presence of a high pulse and rales (a bubbling sound in the bronchi). Later the man's mother stated that he had had asthma during childhood and that his third birthday had been the occasion of a severe attack.[2]

Another case concerns a woman whose eyesight had been defective since childhood. She had worn glasses since the age of twelve. During a hypnotic regression, however, she complained that her glasses were uncomfortable. And when her glasses were removed, her vision improved as she was regressed to earlier and earlier levels.[2]

Dr. Robert M. True explored another idea. He asked a group of unhypnotized subjects whether they could remember the day of the week on which their last birthday and Christmas and other events had occurred. Almost none could answer. But the same persons, when hypnotically regressed, could name the day of the week of their tenth, seventh, and fourth birthdays. They could similarly designate Christmas and other events. The large group participating in this experiment gave 82.3 per cent correct answers.[3]

As to how far back through time a subject can be regressed, it is to be noted that very few researchers have concerned themselves with any sort of prenatal experiments. (There are exceptions; e.g., Dr. Sir Alexander Cannon.) Even so, the work in this field has been most interesting and would seem to call for deeper exploration. Dr. Wolberg writes, "To what earliest period a subject can be successfully regressed is difficult to say with certainty. On one occasion I attempted to regress a somnambulistic subject to the first year of life. The subject was unable to speak, and he exhibited definite sucking and grasping movements."[1] The type of regression referred to here, of course, was the total or true regression, not the recall type.

Drs. Hakebush, Blinkovski, and Foundillere believe it is possible to utilize regression to a neo-natal state.[4] Also, Dr. Nandor Fodor contends that prenatal events are recorded in our memory,[5] and Dr. W. Stekel[6] states that patients in analysis sometimes recall the experience of having been born.[7]

[1] *Medical Hypnosis* (Vol. I).
[2] *Experimental Hypnosis*, edited by Leslie Le Cron.
[3] *Science*, 1949, 110, 2866, 583.
[4] Trud. Inst. Psikhonev. Kiev, 2:236, 1930.
[5] *The Search for the Beloved*, by N. Fodor.
[6] *Conditions of Nervous Anxiety and Their Treatment*, by W. Stekel.
[7] The very fact that so many doctors and hypnotists report cases in which

APPENDIX G

POST-HYPNOTIC SUGGESTION

The post-hypnotic suggestion is an amazing bit of business. Commands that are in keeping with the individual's character will usually be carried out even though they are downright silly. On the other hand, unreasonable suggestions that run counter to the fundamental moral character will probably not be acted upon even though the subject has been in the deepest somnambulistic state.

Even after a light trance, simple post-hypnotic suggestions will ordinarily be effective despite the fact that the suggestion is clearly remembered by the subject. If the subject is told, let us say, that he will become aware, after awakening, that his wrist-watch band is irritating his wrist and that the itch will persist until he removes the watch and massages the wrist, he will usually follow through just as instructed. Although he distinctly recalls the suggestion and regards it as rather foolish, he will usually discover, much to his amazement, that his wrist really does itch; he is finally compelled to remove the band and rub his wrist.

The power of the post-hypnotic suggestion depends upon the depth of the trance, the nature of the suggestion itself, the manner in which it was phrased, the technique employed in its deliverance, and the personal reactions of the subject. Consequently, such a suggestion may remain in effect for only a few minutes or it may persist for a lifetime. The latter fact has obvious therapeutic importance.

Another interesting fact is that the subject can be directed to act upon the suggestion, not only immediately after awakening, but many years after awakening. There are countless cases on record in which the post-hypnotic act is to be executed after a long lapse of time, and in these cases the passage of time does not appear to diminish the force of the suggestion. One authority, for instance, reported the case of a person in whom a post-hypnotic suggestion was still potent after

---

their subjects were aware of scenes at a time so early that their infant eyes had not yet focused would tend to suggest that there might be a visual consciousness apart from physical vision.

twenty years had passed. Another subject, told that he would write a letter to his brother exactly one year from the date of the trance, did exactly that. A famous medical hypnotist recorded the following case:

> . . . A subject was told by myself that exactly two years and two days from the date of trance he would read one of Tennyson's poems. He complied with this suggestion on that date, having a week before developed a yearning to read poetry. Perusal of the bookshelves of a library caused him to finger through one of Tennyson's volumes so that he borrowed it. He then placed it on his own desk until the prescribed day when he suddenly found the opportunity to read the poem. He was positive that his interest in Tennyson was caused by a personal whim.[1]

Two extreme types of post-hypnotic suggestions that may be carried out by somnambulistic subjects are positive hallucinations and negative hallucinations. An example of the positive type, which refers to the subject's "seeing" a suggested object or scene which is actually not present, is the "television hallucination" which I effected with a very good subject. This person, capable of entering the somnambulistic trance quickly, was told that after she awakened the television set would be turned on and she would notice that Jack Benny would be clearly visible on the television screen. At that time we did not yet have television in our city; it was due in about one month, but her set had already been installed.

After the subject awakened I walked over and turned on the television set. The screen lighted up, but nothing, of course, appeared; all this time the subject was watching intently. Suddenly she looked over at her husband and exclaimed, "Why, there's Jack Benny on television!"

"Is that so?" asked the husband. "What's he doing?"

"Can't you see?" She was wondering at his blindness while she gestured toward the television set. "He's talking to Rochester!"

"Well, what is he saying?" asked the startled husband.

"I don't know; I can't hear any sounds." Then she turned to me and asked me whether I wouldn't please go to the TV set and bring in the sound too. I explained that it would be a mighty good trick if I could do it.

The negative hallucination, which is probably the most fantastic of all, occurs when the subject, as the result of a post-hypnotic suggestion, insists upon being blind to a particular person or object very much within the conscious observation of all other witnesses. Such an instance

[1] L. R. Wolberg, *Medical Hypnosis,* Volume I.

developed after I told a deep-trance subject that she would observe, upon awakening, that her husband was not wearing a tie. Soon after I wakened her she turned toward her husband, whose bright red tie was probably the most glaring thing in the whole room, and asked, "Darling, how did you get into the restaurant tonight without your tie?"

At this point the husband yanked out his tie so that it lay across the front of his suit coat. "You don't see my tie?" he asked.

"How can I see your tie if you don't wear one?" she said, somewhat piqued at what seemed to her a foolish answer.

Many other cases of post-hypnotic negative hallucinations are reported, but probably the most striking are those that concern the "disappearance" of a person in the room.

Let us assume, for instance, that there are several people in a room, including the hypnotist, the subject's wife, and the subject. The latter is told, during a somnambulistic trance, that his wife will be absent from the room after he awakens, that she had left the room while he was sleeping and will definitely not be present when he awakens. After the husband awakens he will look around the room and see everyone but his wife, even though she is still sitting in the same place. He will probably ask, "What happened to my wife?" It is explained that she has left the room and will return later. She can then walk around the room at will, but the husband will still fail to take notice of her. If she moves a table or drops a book, the husband will be alarmed at the curious behavior of the animated table or book. Furthermore, should she start smoking a cigarette, the husband may exclaim, "You may think I'm crazy, but I actually see a lighted cigarette moving through the air all by itself!"

An interesting incident, demonstrating the compulsive nature of the post-hypnotic suggestion, developed one night after an experiment. I told the subject, who was engaged in a dual hypnosis test, that he would ask, after he awakened, for a sheet of my stationery, as he would want to write a friend in California later that night, using my stationery. I repeated the suggestion and later awakened him.

As he was very much interested in the experiment in which he had just participated, he promptly joined the rest of us in examining the results of the test he had just taken while under hypnosis. But we hardly had a chance to get started on the scoring when he suddenly asked me for a sheet of stationery. "I want to write a letter to a friend in California later tonight," he explained, "and I'm not sure that I have stationery at home."

At this I smiled and pointed out that this had been a post-hypnotic suggestion; I now assured him that he could forget about it, because after all it had been designed only to help determine the depth of his trance.

"Let's get back to the results of the experiment," I urged, as we were all anxious to learn the outcome. He should have been particularly anxious to do so, because he had been the best subject and usually was eager to learn whether he was maintaining his high score. Nevertheless, he would not return to the score pads, nor would he permit me to do so. Instead, he pulled me aside, saying, "I want that piece of stationery."

So once again I explained, this time in considerably more detail, that I had inculcated this desire for stationery during the trance, that it was only a post-hypnotic suggestion, that he should now forget about it, as it would be pointless to carry it out. "Now let's get back to the tests. After all, these experiments are important."

As I turned again toward the tests, he grabbed my shoulder and said, "Now look, I'm not kidding. I want that piece of paper and I want it now!"

I finally realized that, test or no test, I had to get this lad his paper —and promptly, too. As soon as I gave him the sheet of stationery he folded it, put it in his pocket, and relaxed. Then he resumed his interest in the experiment.

Later that night he wrote to his friend in California!

The strength of a post-hypnotic suggestion can be increased by repetition during one session, and it can be further reinforced by additional sessions. The cumulative effects, therefore, can expand to overwhelming proportions, an excellent reason why hypnosis can be so powerful from the standpoint of therapy.

There are a few post-hypnotic suggestions that have become standard practice with most hypnotherapists. One is concerned with assuring the subject that all his functioning will be restored to normal after the trance period, that he will feel fine in every respect. Another suggestion is designed to increase the depth of the trance during subsequent sessions; and still another, to set up some signal in the subject's subconscious which will shorten the time required for inducing the next trance.

As an instance of the latter, the subject may be told that in the future he will enter the trance whenever the hypnotist counts to five and then snaps his fingers twice. This is often further abridged by omitting the counting; the hypnotist merely snaps his fingers and the subject passes at once into the trance state. This is a principle often used by stage performers, who may use as a signal anything from the ringing of a telephone to a picture of Joe Louis.

APPENDIX H

HYPNOTISM AND EXTRASENSORY PERCEPTION

There are so many instances of telepathy and clairvoyance which developed with subjects under hypnosis that some of the most famous cases might well be cited here. For instance, Dr. E. Azam, a French physician, found that one of his patients apparently could, when hypnotized, taste substances which Dr. Azam had put into his own mouth. Consequently Azam carried out a series of tests in which he tasted various substances without giving any clues whatsoever to his patient. The astonishing results convinced the doctor that there must have been some inexplicable transmission of sensory experience.

Two experimenters at Cambridge University, taking a considerable amount of precaution to prevent the transmission of cues by any sensory means, attempted the transfer of pain sensations from the hypnotist to the subject. The blindfolded subject was told that the hypnotist, standing behind his subject, would be pinched somewhere on his body. The subject would feel the pain, he was told, in the corresponding part of his anatomy. A striking degree of success was reported.

Several famous cases are concerned with an especially celebrated subject known as Léonie. A day after Léonie had been hypnotized by Dr. Paul Janet she suddenly screamed and rubbed her elbow. It was later shown that the doctor had accidentally burned his elbow at the same instant.

Léonie's uncanny responsiveness to those who had hypnotized her was further demonstrated by two French physicians, Gilbert and Pierre Janet, when they successfully hypnotized Léonie from a distance of one kilometer (about six tenths of a mile). The doctors attempted, at random times by the clock, to induce a trance in Léonie from this distance. No one in Léonie's household knew of the plan, but the housekeeper had been asked to record the times when she went to sleep. Janet reported in his autobiography that there were "sixteen times out of twenty when somnambulism exactly coincided with a mental suggestion made at a distance of one kilometer."

One of the most electrifying combinations of hypnotism and ESP is the phenomenon known as "traveling clairvoyance." This is another example of the ability of human perception to transcend time and space. In these cases the entranced subject gives detailed reports of scenes or occurrences at a distance, sometimes a very considerable one. The fabulous Léonie, for instance, was told (in Le Havre) to observe what Dr. Richet was doing at his laboratory in Paris. At this, Léonie became very excited and declared that Richet's laboratory was in flames. A later check confirmed that it had burned to the ground that day.

Two doctors from Sweden have added to the amazing reports of traveling clairvoyance. Years ago Dr. Alfred Backman sent a peasant-girl subject, while she was entranced, to various distant points unfamiliar to both the doctor and his subject. It was claimed, furthermore, that the subject made her "presence" felt by the persons whom she "visited."

More recently, Dr. John Bjorkhem of Stockholm, a minister-psychologist-physician, has made further contributions to the literature on traveling clairvoyance. This busy explorer of the psychic realm has worked with about three thousand subjects and has performed more than thirty thousand hypnotic experiments. The *Parapsychology Bulletin*[1] describes two of his experiences with traveling clairvoyance as follows:

> In one instance of this sort, Dr. Bjorkhem hypnotized the subject, Miss Klaar, and told her to go in her thoughts down from the second floor of the house in which the experiment was taking place onto the first floor and to enter the flat with the name WALGREN on the door. Miss Klaar appeared to act on the suggestion, and although she had never been in the Walgrens' apartment, she accurately described many of its contents. Among other things she told of the layout of several rooms, noted a mirror mounted in a door and gave its approximate measurements, correctly described the flowered plush covering on a sofa and identified the color of draperies, rug, and books, as well as naming and pointing out the position of half a dozen articles of furniture. When she said she saw a thick album in a dark leather cover on a certain table, Dr. Bjorkhem asked her to open it and look at the photographs.
>
> "Yes, I have done so," she said. "There is Mr. Walgren without a hat, the eldest daughter Rut is there too on a separate photo and both the right-hand side." The album was actually a family Bible with a photograph section, and the descriptions of the pictures Miss Klaar gave were right in all details.
>
> In at least one such case of "traveling clairvoyance" the apparition of the traveler actually appeared in the assigned place. While in Uppsala, Dr. Bjorkhem once had a Lapp girl brought to him for an experiment. After hypnotizing her he told her to visit her family home, which was several hundred miles away, and to tell what was

[1] Number 27, August, 1952.

going on there. She described a scene in the kitchen, told what her father and mother were doing, and mentioned an item in the paper which the father was reading. A few hours later the parents telephoned a friend of the girl in Uppsala to inquire whether anything was wrong with their daughter. They had seen her appear in the kitchen and thought it meant bad news.

At the end of these reports the *Parapsychology Bulletin* adds, "Material of the sort found in these cases is difficult to evaluate, and it was not intended that it should be cited as proof of ESP. . . . [But it is] an important part of our field of inquiry."

APPENDIX I

THE DUKE UNIVERSITY TESTS FOR TELEPATHY AND CLAIRVOYANCE

For those who are unfamiliar with the work of Dr. J. B. Rhine, this very brief discussion may be helpful. In order to facilitate the testing for both telepathy and clairvoyance, Dr. Rhine and Dr. Zener had early devised a deck of special cards. Each card was to bear one of five simple, easily distinguishable symbols: a cross, a circle, square, star, and three parallel wavy lines. The deck consisted of twenty-five cards; this meant that each symbol was included five times. This deck, generally known as the "ESP Cards," became quite famous; many people found it an interesting pastime to test their own extrasensory capacity.

Although the entire deck of cards is utilized actively when testing for clairvoyance (or a combination of clairvoyance and telepathy), the pure telepathy tests were concerned only with the symbols themselves. The sender would select *mentally* one of the symbols, and the receiver would then try to identify the symbol of which the sender was thinking. As soon as the receiver made his decision, he would mark it on a record sheet, and the sender would then be signaled for the next trial. At this point the sender would record on a separate record pad the image he had held in his mind, and he would then take up (mentally) another symbol. In other words, only *after* the sender received the next signal did he make a record of what he had been thinking; and of course at all times he was unaware of the symbol which the receiver had recorded.

Tests for clairvoyance took several forms; in one the deck of cards, after a thorough shuffling, was placed face down on a table. The subject was then asked to name the top card, and as soon as he named one of the symbols his call was recorded and the card removed. But it was not looked at. This procedure was repeated until the deck was finished. Then a new "run"—a series of twenty-five individual trials—would be made in similar fashion.

In this manner more than eighty-five thousand individual card-calling trials were amassed, and the scores showed conclusively that something more than chance had been in operation. In addition to the phenomenal general average, which left no doubt as to the significance of the results, there were, furthermore, spectacular individual performances. One man went through the deck of ESP Cards more than seven hundred times, and his score was so high that only an astronomical figure could express the odds against achieving such a score on the basis of chance alone. One subject scored fifteen successive hits, and another tallied twenty-five, a perfect score for one entire run.

Other investigators, too, were encountering perfect scores. One such case was that of Lillian, a nine-year-old girl who was tested by researcher Margaret Pegram. A prize of fifty cents had been offered for a perfect score of twenty-five, while candy would be given for other less perfect scores. Serious little Lillian, though, had her heart set on the half dollar, not the candy. She made it clear that she was determined to win the money. Then she said, "Don't say anything; I'm going to try something." Turning her back, she stood for a moment with her eyes closed. When she turned again, her lips were moving, and she continued to move her lips all through the test, as though she were speaking to herself. When she was asked what she had been saying, she answered, "I was wishing all the time that I could get twenty-five." And she did. This is one of many indications that the more emotional the background and the more keyed up the subject, the greater the possibility for a high score.

APPENDIX J

ESP IN RELATION TO SPACE

If ESP is purely physical—if the mind is strictly mechanistic—then the factor of distance (space) should have some measurable, lawful effect upon its occurrence. The next step, therefore, was to ascertain whether the mind truly transcended space—to determine, that is, whether distance has any systematic effect upon telepathic and clairvoyant perception. Long before the controlled laboratory experiments were inaugurated, the possibility that mind transcends space had at least been suggested by myriad spontaneous occurrences.

There had been, for instance, such cases as the one concerning Dr. Emanuel Swedenborg. This renowned Swedish scientist and philosopher while in Göteborg (in 1759) one day described a fire blazing in Stockholm, three hundred miles distant. Rendering a detailed account of the fire to city authorities and naming the owner of the burned house, he even stated the time when the fire was put out. The accuracy of his clairvoyant vision was confirmed several days later by royal messenger.

Another account, involving a span of about six thousand miles, was sent to me by an actress who had always been fascinated by her mother's extrasensory talents: "I remember very well that day that my mother and sister and myself sat at breakfast. Mother had had a particularly vivid dream the night before. In the dream she passed through a great deal of black space and found herself entering the parlor of her home in Verbacz, a small town formerly in Hungary and now in Yugoslavia. The parlor was filled with mourners sitting around a coffin, and my mother suddenly knew who was in the coffin, and crying, 'Mama, Mama!' rushed forward. The dream was so vivid that it still disturbed her as she told us about it, and before we left for school she had already sat down to write to her sister, Lisl, about it. It would take several weeks to get a reply to the letter, as there was no air mail to Europe at that time, and Pueblo, Colorado, is quite a long way from Verbacz. The weeks passed, and the answer came. On the date of my mother's dream my grandmother had died. She had been in perfect health, without a day's illness, had done the baking and a washing, and died quite suddenly. Due to the time difference, she had undoubtedly been laid out and the first mourners had arrived at the time my mother had the dream. Whether the dream was a dream or an actual passage through time and space, I don't know. I know my mother has the letter substantiating her unique dream, and quite possibly Aunt Lisl still has the post-marked letter from my mother. Perhaps my mother would correct several of these details, but this is substantially the story of what happened. I'm sure every family has its own stories of this nature, but I'm rather glad we have it documented at any rate."

An interesting dual case, which concerned one person at sea and another on land, was featured in *Coronet* magazine.[1] A British lieutenant aboard a submarine dreamed that he saw his sister sleeping at a desk in a munitions factory where she worked. And then he saw in his

[1] August, 1952.

dream that a fire was starting, so he tried desperately to awaken his sister. Suddenly there was a terrible explosion, and the lieutenant awakened abruptly from his nightmare. To his surprise, he found the watchkeeper and the others near asphyxiation from escaping gas. But he finally managed to rouse them in time to avoid disaster. It was ten o'clock in the morning.

When the lieutenant reached port, there was a letter from his sister —a letter which described a calamitous explosion, which took place the same day as the lieutenant's asphyxiation episode, in the factory where she worked. She wrote:

> I escaped without a scratch. I had dozed off at a desk in another building and was having a terrifying dream about you. I saw you and your crew lying motionless in your submarine.
>
> I tried to awaken you but I simply couldn't. The munitions explosion shattered my dream and woke me. Had I not fallen asleep where I was, I, too, would have been blown to pieces. The explosion occurred at 10 in the morning. . . .

As interesting as the many spontaneous cases may be, they are still not sufficient to decide an issue of such consequence. The question of whether ESP was independent of space had to be submitted to the laboratory. But here, too, it was found that distance did not limit the success of the ESP experiments in any measurable way. From North Carolina to Yugoslavia—in fact, one series of controlled experiments was actually conducted between Dr. Marchesi of Zagreb, Yugoslavia, and collaborators at Duke University in Durham, North Carolina—numerous researchers handed down the same verdict: Distance has shown no effect whatsoever upon ESP performance. And since no known physical energy remains unaffected by distance, it would seem to indicate that extrasensory perception must be non-physical.

APPENDIX K

PSYCHOKINESIS

So far, the scientific method has demonstrated that the mind can perceive the thoughts of another person and that it can also perceive objects or events without the use of the senses. The laboratory has further established that these facts, telepathy and clairvoyance, are capable of snubbing the physical properties of space and time— the mind can reach across space and forward into time. But there is still another facet to be explored: What about this business of "mind over matter"?

During a conversation many years ago with a corporation executive, after the topic had drifted from steel production to the lack of knowledge about human mental processes, I listened to a statement that startled me. "If we really knew how to utilize the power of the human mind," the tycoon stated as he pointed to an ash tray on his desk, "we could probably move that ash tray across the desk just by skillfully employing the force of the mind."

To me, this statement seemed wild enough in itself. But coming from a conservative corporation official, it was sheer heresy. He observed my puzzled glance, but he didn't back up. Instead, he reminded me that literature, from the most ancient writings to the magazine of last week, was studded with records of mind over matter.

On thinking it over, I had to admit that there is no scarcity of indications that the mind can influence matter. There are, for one thing, the countless religious miracles, and these are by no means confined to biblical references. And even when we turn our attention to fields other than the religious, the incidents keep right on piling up. There are many accounts of "suspended animation" which involve the defiance of physical laws while the subject either remained under water or was "buried alive" for incredibly extended periods of time . . . the charming away of warts and other growths without physical means from the skins of animals . . . the fantastic effects of voodooism, as related by anthropologists, including the levitation of objects, the hurling of stones by unseen hands, and magical rain-making.

A made-to-order thunderstorm is described by Geoffrey Gorer in his book, *Africa Dances:*

It was a particularly fine and cloudless afternoon when we visited the convent of the worshippers of Heviosso, the thunder fetish. After the usual sacrifice, three men went into a trance inside the hut, while we stood in what shade we could find in the courtyard. Suddenly against the blue sky there was a flash of lightning followed shortly by a loud peal of thunder, the flashes and thunder got more frequent and louder, till they seemed simultaneous and the thunder gave that peculiarly unpleasant crack which it does in the tropics when the storm is nearly directly overhead. Gradually the thunder and lightning got fainter and finally died in a rumble. It had been exactly like a quick tropical thunderstorm, except that there had been no rain and no clouds; the sun was shining all the time.

There are still more: The curious circumstances of hauntings; the stopping of clocks and the splitting of steel upon the death of a person;

the influence of direct hypnotic suggestion upon the pulse and blood pressure; the uncanny performance of excited gamblers who "will" their dice to run up an astonishing sequence of sevens.

This dice matter—the fact that many people feel certain that they can mentally influence dice—gave inspiration to the researchers of the Duke University parapsychology department: Why not expose the dice-throwing procedure to laboratory tests in order to determine whether psychokinesis is a reality—whether there really is scientific foundation for the principle of mind over matter. This would be an ideal method; it was interesting and challenging, easy to control, and easy to tabulate and appraise.

What a picture this must have been! Dignified Dr. Rhine leading his grave group of scientists while they converged, armed with statistics and scoring pads, on their latest object of research—the crap shooter!

But the parapsychology laboratory was hardly a gambling casino. The dice throwers found themselves subjected to a number of unusual restraints. The first innovation made it necessary to throw the dice from cups rather than by hand. Then the cups were fitted with roughened interiors, and special dice tables were built. Finally, decisively to confound any "gamblers" who might somehow be skillfully influencing the dice by other than purely mental means, completely mechanical methods of dice throwing were introduced, cameras were used to record the scores, and special precautions were taken against the possibility of defective dice.

But even under these extraordinary circumstances, a total of 21,600 dice readings (900 runs), so significant were the results that the odds against obtaining such a score by chance could be expressed only by a number of approximately twenty digits!

Try it yourself. Two sevens can be expected from pure chance, on the average, in a run of twelve throws. Just be certain to make a determined mental effort—"will" those sevens to turn up.

Oddly enough, very strong evidence in favor of psychokinesis (mind over matter) also turned up from a phase of the dice tests which had been altogether overlooked for several years. Not only at Duke, but with other investigators as well, it had been noticed that the dice thrower's ability to score fell off rather sharply from one run to the next. At first this was regarded as a mere nuisance, but it was later observed that these declines in scoring followed a definite pattern and far exceeded anything that could be expected from chance. The odds, in fact, were better than a million to one. The falling dice, in short, were worked on by something more than the machines which threw them. The indication here, then, was that the mind does indeed control a force which can act on matter.

Yet it remained to be shown whether the force which acted on the dice was physical energy emanating from the brain, or whether a nonphysical mental process was responsible for the effect. If it could be demonstrated that the scoring rate would not vary with the changes in physical conditions, it could be safely concluded that such energy would not fit the picture of anything we know as physical. And that is exactly what was proved next—mass, number, and form were not determining factors in the psychokinesis tests. As Dr. Rhine summarized: "There can scarcely be any doubt that PK [psychokinesis] is non-physical."

APPENDIX L

PARAPSYCHOLOGY: THE SIGNIFICANCE OF THIS NEW SCIENCE

Only faint traces of the paranormal powers of the mind have so far been demonstrated. But every new force, from steam to atomic power, in its beginning has been feeble and undependable. Each of these, in its time, must have induced speculation as to why serious men were "fooling around" with such toys. And much of the suspicion, oddly enough, has usually been generated within the ranks of the very profession that discovered the "toy."

Probably, however, the parapsychologists rally behind the knowledge that this force, of which they have already proved the reality, will in time revolutionize our universe to an extent beyond the wildest imagination.

We have already observed something of the "history of impossibility." Now let's glance over at the "history of acceptance of new evidence," touching on a few random examples. Keep in mind that we are dealing in these cases with evidence which had *already* been established, ideas which had *already* been demonstrated. Remember, too, that these were the judgments of *experts,* not ignorant amateurs. Take the words, for instance, of Professor Erasmus Wilson in 1878:

With regard to the electric light, much has been said for and against it, but I think I may say without fear of contradiction that when the Paris exhibition closes electric light will close with it and very little more will be heard of it.[1]

[1] "What's the World Coming to?"

Despite the thousands of successful applications of hypnosis and the evidence set forth by the most eminent and respected physicians, a British publication arrived at this verdict:

Mesmerism [hypnotism] is too gross a humbug to admit of any further serious notice. We regard its abettors as quacks and impostors. They ought to be hooted out of Professional Society.[2]

Need it be added that Semmelweis was driven out of Vienna, and out of his mind, by scientists who scorned his theory of bacteria—even after his ideas had saved hundreds of lives? The value of his work was really not recognized until twenty-five years after his death. And when Galileo's telescope revealed Jupiter's moons, his fellow astronomers refused to look through it; they knew that such bodies were not possible. The telescope, therefore, must be deceptive. So why look through it?

And do you suppose that the Wright brothers' first flights caused a sensation? Far from it! Most newspaper editors considered the reports of witnesses to be "impossible" and dismissed the matter without even printing the news. Several years passed before many realized that a young man named Orville and his brother Wilbur had begun to reshape our world on that December morning in 1903. The brothers were many years, in fact, trying to find a market for their new flying machine. In a letter to the inventors in 1907, the First Lord of the Admiralty wrote as follows:

The Board of Admiralty were of the opinion that they [airplanes] would not be of any practical use to the Naval Service.

There is good reason to believe that here again, in the cases of extrasensory perception and psychokinesis, we are witnesses at the birth of another scientific revolution, perhaps the most important of all. Indeed, this mere embryo could develop to mammoth proportions.

Already there are scattered examples at hand. A Dutchman named Peter Hurkos, for instance, has been successfully employed by several European police agencies, including Scotland Yard, to solve unfathomable crimes which had brought conventional methods of detection to an impasse. Hurkos is not a Dick Tracy. He is a clairvoyant who discovered his psychic gift after an injury when, as a painter, he fell from a scaffold. He has been responsible for the apprehension of thieves, pyromaniacs, and murderers; he has diagnosed disease and located missing people. After one demonstration, a leading police official ad-

[2] British Lancet.

mitted that ordinary criminologists were mere children compared with Hurkos.

Dr. B. J. F. Laubscher, a psychiatrist-anthropologist, describes in one of his books his experience with a native clairvoyant known as Solomon Daba, whom he had investigated over a long period of time. Having explained to Solomon Daba that none of the many claims made for his supernormal powers would be acceptable unless they could be verified, the doctor reports that the native agreed to any test which might be suggested. He was subjected, therefore, to a number of tests and, according to the doctor, acquitted himself remarkably well, displaying supernormal mental ability.

One occasion presented itself after Mr. Victor, a charge nurse at the doctor's hospital, had lost two cows. During one of Solomon Daba's visits to the hospital, the doctor, seizing upon the opportunity to test the native's psychic powers, told him only that Mr. Victor had lost some cows and asked him to describe the cows and to state their present location. He agreed to try; then he shut his eyes and sat still for a while. What followed is here quoted from Dr. Laubscher's book:[3]

. . . On opening his eyes he said, "I see the cows and I know where they are and how they have been stolen," and then proceeded as follows:

"There were two cows, both black and white, and the younger of the two was going to calve; in fact, she has calved, because there are three cattle now. The younger of the two cows has a peculiar mark on its left side, the hair has grown in the opposite direction in the form of a crown or whorl. There was a little white boy about six years old who was very fond of this cow. He always fed her with bits of grass and corn stalks. Late one evening the cows were drove away from the field by a native man who works in this hospital. He kept them in the house in the location that night and the following morning early he hired a native boy to drive these cows to a friend's place near Lady Frere (30 miles away). The boy left with the cows while it was still dark and drove them to the kraal near Lady Frere. He crossed the railway line this side of Essex and took a little-known track across the veld."

I, of course, could not verify his descriptions of the cows, having never seen them, but I doubted his statement about the little white boy since I was well aware Victor had no such child. As instructed, none of the members of the staff present said a word.

After Solomon Daba left, Mr. Victor corroborated his description of the cows to the minutest detail; even the doings of the little boy

[3] *Sex, Custom, and Psychopathology*, by B. J. F. Laubscher.

turned out to be correct. This was a neighbor's child. As the matter was already in the hands of the police, nothing more was done. The suspected man went off sick a few days ago and while at his home sent a native boy with a note to the ward. Mr. Victor, having in mind what Solomon Daba had told him, asked his native boy whether he drove some cows for "X" to Lady Frere some time ago. The boy, in my presence and that of other members of the staff and the police, admitted driving the cows and gave a description tallying in every detail with what Solomon Daba had said.

Consider for a moment the fantastic possibilities once clairvoyance, even if it is exhibited *reliably* by only one person, comes under the full scrutiny and control of science. Instead of "seeing" concealed cards at a distance, as in the Duke experiments, this power could then be focused upon more practical targets. Plans for warfare, secret weapons, criminal schemes, impending epidemics of disease, any nefarious design directed against mankind—all these could be exposed in the making. Each of us is tempted to exercise further his imagination to visualize all the problems that might be solved, all the mysteries that would be unveiled. Where would we stop?

When we ponder the application of psychokinesis (mind over matter), we find ourselves in more familiar territory. In the field of psychosomatic medicine, science some time ago conceded the influence of the mind upon the physical body. To be sure, we can hardly pick up a magazine without encountering some reference to the curative powers of the mind. "Heal yourself!" proclaim the articles. And a surprising number of stricken people apparently proceed to do exactly that. Almost every doctor is prepared to cite case histories of patients who have achieved near miracles through the application of will power. Hypnosis, too, continues to deliver dramatic evidence of the degree to which the mind dominates the body.

How much farther can the mind reach in this particular direction? Already we have observed that the mind doesn't seem to recognize the line at which it is supposed to stop healing and sometimes spills over into areas which have been professionally judged beyond its domain. If even now we are given cause to wonder, then where are the limits once the full weight of science has converged upon these phenomena?

Is it conceivable, then, that this mental force might eventually give us insight into those elusive diseases which have so far yielded hardly an inch to intensive physical investigations? Is it possible, in short, that the magic of mind will start the unraveling of such enigmas as cancer and coronary disease? Perhaps—just possibly—the mind, consciousness, extends even to the very cells of which the body is composed.

We have so little to lose and so much to gain by continuing to trace the reach of the mind. If it seems laughable to link the mind with the growth of malignant cells, or with the hardening of arterial walls, let your thoughts flash back to the lad who shed his fish-scale skin after a few words were whispered into his ear. Besides, this is no laughing matter. We must not be too proud to pursue any hopeful possibility. Millions of dollars and years of indefatigable research have availed relatively little; the puzzle remains as baffling as ever.

It is time to start thinking of "the mind" as something bigger than the area of the brain—something even more comprehensive, maybe, than the individual himself.

There are, furthermore, aspects other than health to which the mental horsepower might be harnessed. Floods of books, articles, lectures, and sermons attest to the general belief that our minds, following rather simple rules, can help us realize any rational desire. The idea common to almost all these plans, which usually point up the power of belief and imagination, is to utilize the force of the subconscious so that it will be automatically directing us, almost without conscious effort on our part, toward our chosen goals.

Heralding this general design, a Frenchman named Emile Coué once had the whole nation murmuring over and over again, "Every day in every way I'm getting better and better." Recognizing that the "twilight zone," through which we pass each night just before falling asleep and each morning as we awaken, finds us in a state very similar to hypnosis, Coué maintained that these periods were ideal for making suggestions to ourselves (autosuggestion). He insisted, and so do his many followers, that as a result of this hypnotic-like repetition the subconscious would start grinding away at the job of improving the individual, not only health-wise, but in other respects as well.

Since the time of Coué's simple system there have been numerous refinements, modifications, and extensions. But basic to all is the recognition of the power of the subconscious and the belief that the mind can influence health, external objects, and the minds of others.

One especially prominent man, whose accomplishments in several fields result in his being known as a genius, told me that he attributes his success to the persistent use of one of these subconscious systems. "The Chinese were right," he assured me, when they pointed out that one picture is worth more than ten thousand words.

"So I use pictures," he continued. "Mental pictures. Before I fall asleep at night, and as I awaken in the morning, and at any other time when I have a few moments, I concentrate on a mental image. What is most important, I believe, is that I center attention on my *final* goals, not all the problems and headaches in between. When I persist in

255

visualizing the ultimate outcome—'seeing' the results as I want them to come out—all the thorny details somehow seem to fall apart or to take care of themselves.

"Don't ask me how or why it works. It just does, that's all."

The formula of this tycoon is very much akin to the advice given by the magnetic Dr. Ervin Seale:

"What your attention dwells on grows. The idea here is to center your attention on the state you want. Don't play around with the things you don't want. If you consistently take your attention from your problem, it will die. For instance, if you would manifest health, you must go within and become conscious of health. You must exult and rejoice in the finished state even though all the outer facts contradict you. . . .

". . . Don't outline the solution to your problem. The spirit has its own mechanics. The mood knows the way. Leave the details to it."

This technique is not new. About twenty-five hundred years ago Confucius gave the same advice: "In giving heed to the beginning think of the end; the end will then be without distress."[4]

Of all the findings that have emerged from parapsychology research, perhaps the most significant is the fact that man is not, after all, merely a physical machine. For three centuries the scientists of human nature have regarded man as nothing more than a physical contraption. The new evidence to the contrary is a wonderful step toward learning what man really is, and the ultimate upshot is bound to result in better relations among men.

There is no telling how far the parapsychology research will lead us. The proof that there is something extraphysical, or spiritual, in human personality has momentous implications. Eventually the *laboratory* will answer even that all-time prize winner among questions: Does any part of a human being survive the death of the physical body? Already research in extrasensory perception has indicated, in its freedom from the effects of time and space, the plausibility of some sort of survival. And remember that this relatively new science has barely begun.

[4] *Shu Ching* 5, 17.

Printed in the United States
by Baker & Taylor Publisher Services